SIMON & SCHUSTER

New York   London   Toronto   Sydney   Tokyo   Singapore

YURI B. SHVETS

Washington Station

MY LIFE AS A KGB SPY IN AMERICA

Translated from the Russian
by Eugene Ostrovsky

SIMON & SCHUSTER
Rockefeller Center
1230 Avenue of the Americas
New York, New York 10020

Designed by Karolina Harris
Manufactured in the United States of America

10 9 8 7 6 5 4 3 2 1

Library of Congress Cataloging-in-Publication Data is available.

ISBN 0-671-88397-6

AUTHOR'S NOTE

SOON after I resigned from the KGB in September 1990, I started to work on a book based on my experiences as a spy. Since my former bosses at the KGB were watching me closely, I decided to write a novel to avoid prosecution for revealing state secrets. My novel, however, consisted largely of true facts about recent KGB efforts to recruit U.S. citizens.

When the book was finished, I started to look for potential publishers. I could not publish my novel in Russia; even though the Soviet Union had collapsed, the KGB remained as powerful as before. So in February 1993, I walked into the Moscow office of the *Washington Post* and gave the *Post* an interview. This interview helped me to find my literary agent in America, and in April 1993 I came to the United States to meet with publishers and negotiate a possible book contract.

Since my publisher was going to be based in the United States, I no longer had to disguise my book as a novel. And in fact, all the U.S. publishers I met with were interested in knowing about my actual KGB experiences in Washington and Moscow.

AUTHOR'S NOTE

I returned to Moscow to write my book. My former bosses at the Russian intelligence service were becoming increasingly alarmed, even though they believed I was still writing a novel. My application for a new foreign passport was denied, and I was told that I was under an eight-year ban against travel abroad.

In September 1993, I crossed the Russian border illegally and came with a draft version of my new book as an immigrant to the United States.

This book is a reconstruction of events that took place several years ago. I remember them as if they happened yesterday, for these events left deep furrows in my soul. Before I wrote this book I recorded many of these events in the KGB file on Socrates, my agent. While I was working on the book I did not have access to the KGB file anymore and could not check all the things I would have liked to check. The dialogue in the book is based on my recollection, and the text of written documents is also as I recall them. The actual dialogue and documents may have differed somewhat, but I am certain that my memory of the substance of these conversations and documents is accurate. For me, memories of the ugly past and my hope for a better future will die last.

Finally I want to thank Valentin Aksilenko, my former boss at the KGB Intelligence Service and one of the characters in this book. His participation made the project come true, and he still has his own story to tell.

PREFACE

FOR ten years of my life, I was an officer of the KGB intelligence service of the USSR. My primary mission was to try to recruit U.S. citizens to acquire secret information about U.S. domestic and foreign policy.

I no longer work for the KGB; indeed, the KGB no longer formally exists, and the country it served has also disappeared. But even before I resigned from the KGB I began to question what I was supposed to do. What does it mean to turn a foreign citizen into a KGB agent? To persuade a person to commit a crime—treason—against his country? And to use any means, including blackmail and even force, to accomplish this goal?

Often enough, those who commit treason are unpatriotic and psychologically unstable even before they are approached by foreign intelligence officers. But this is no justification for spying. Nor is the fact that countries permit one another to spy any justification of this practice. From time to time, agents are caught and jailed or even executed. In every case, some foreign government is an accessory to their crime. But while the agent suffers, the government seldom does, or it suffers only briefly.

Curiously, this kind of spying is called "human intelligence." But it seems inhuman to me.

The Cold War is over, but U.S. and Russian intelligence services still spy on each other. Why? What will Russian intelligence find in the United States that will alleviate Russia's all but intractable domestic problems? What does the CIA want from a country where now virtually everything is for sale?

I am not an expert on Western intelligence services, but I am sure that they have the same problems that the KGB had. Any bureaucracy is inherently flawed. The bureaucracy in an intelligence service is probably worse because it is surrounded by a thick wall of secrecy, and it rots behind this wall.

The KGB was caught by surprise as communism crumbled in Eastern Europe. The KGB brass actually accelerated the demise of the Soviet Union by their actions. The CIA didn't do any better if we can believe press reports, and they failed to detect such international episodes as the Iraqi buildup on the border with Kuwait. What were these intelligence officers doing to earn their keep?

Sometimes I think of the intelligence game as a hockey match where both teams are so busy chasing each other around the ice, checking, blocking, and fighting with each other, that they forget about the puck, forget about putting it into the net.

The fact is that the KGB and the CIA needed each other. The budget of each intelligence service was determined at least in part by how powerful the other spy service was believed to be.

It took me ten years to understand all this, ten years to realize I was working not for my country but for the personal ambitions of KGB bureaucrats. When I realized that, I resigned. But I learned some lessons, which I have put into this book. I learned, for instance, that anyone who offers his services to an intelligence service is doomed. He can be as smart as a hundred James Bonds, but his new employers can be counted on to lead him to perdition. Intelligence is an art, albeit of a demonic variety, while an intelligence service is a bureaucracy utterly incompatible with any kind of art.

I learned that spies provide only a small portion of the overall volume of information obtained by intelligence services, and their information is almost always suspect. On the other hand, when spies are exposed, it inflicts severe damage on international relations. Such damage could be tolerated during the Cold War, but today the cost of their failure dramatically exceeds their questionable effectiveness.

I also learned that permitting spy agencies to operate in one's country is like allowing drug dealers to flourish while condemning drug abuse.

I believe that it's high time to eradicate so-called human intelligence. This goal can be achieved if there is the political will to do so, and it would make everybody's life better except for the bureaucrats in intelligence services.

And the Lord spoke unto Moses, saying: Send thou
men, that they may spy out the land of Canaan. . . .

Numbers 13: 1–2

ONE evening in late April 1985, I arrived in Washington, D.C., with my wife and two sons as a correspondent of the Soviet news agency Tass. I was thirty-three, could speak English, French, and Spanish, and was somewhat ambitious, even though I had already realized that in my country ambition was a recipe for misery.

At that time very few people knew that, in fact, I was a KGB officer attached to the First Chief Directorate (external intelligence). My position as a journalist was a convenient cover.

The trees bedecked with electric lights at the hotel doors were touching; the silent car engines were surprising; the smell of trees in blossom was pleasantly dizzying. It was cherry blossom time in the U.S. capital. But alas, I had not come to have fun.

The primary mission entrusted to me and my colleagues at the Washington residency, as spelled out in the KGB chairman's orders and instructions, was to prevent a sudden U.S. nuclear missile attack against the USSR. No more, no less.

I had come prepared for the job. In the summer of 1980, I graduated from the Patrice Lumumba People's Friendship University. This university is generally believed in the West to be a training center for international terrorists. In fact, however, in my time it was one of the most liberal educational institutions in Moscow and the whole of the Soviet Union. True, the future terrorist Carlos, who was jokingly called "Vladimir Ilyich Lenin," was a Lumumba University alumnus, but he spent most of the time on secret trips abroad and was not a typical student.

Our student body consisted of young men and women from some ninety countries of the world. Talking to them, I learned far more about the wide world than could be gleaned from Soviet textbooks. Some of our professors had been partially trained abroad, including in the United States, and their experience also colored the atmosphere at the university. Ideas of freedom and democracy invisibly wafted through the classrooms.

I was neither a convinced communist nor a dissident. Far from worshiping the Soviet system, I regarded it as viable enough, based upon the fairly respectable national economic statistics. Of course, my closest schoolmates and I experienced some doubts as to the veracity of the official statistics, but our incredulity was due more to our innate skepticism than to actual knowledge. The facts describing the true condition of the Soviet economy were kept under lock and key and were available only to a handful of the highest officials. I suspect that even the general secretary of the Central Committee of the Soviet Communist Party—the leader of our country—had no inkling that the Soviet Union was mortally ill.

I had graduated with honors as an expert in international law. Life seemed wonderful and full of promise.

I was slated to join the intelligence service, the KGB, knowing that I would be deployed at the decisive sector of the front: against the powerful and inscrutable United States. Worthy opponents—the FBI and the CIA—were lying in wait. I was not afraid. On the contrary, I was eager to cross swords with the opposition, to test my mettle—and to gain an insight into the most profound secrets of world politics.

I was also deeply convinced that my country needed intelligence and that the Soviet intelligence service was staffed by spying virtuosi driven by a sense of civic duty. It was just about the gravest error of my life, for which I was eventually to pay dearly. But at that time I had no idea what the future had in store for me, and so I looked confidently ahead.

After graduating from the Lumumba University, I, like all spies, had to attend the Intelligence Academy. I spent the next two years in the Yurlovo facility, situated in a marvelous forest not far from Moscow. I was taught the secrets of the trade by the covert heroes of the Cold War, the people who had stolen the U.S. atomic secrets, who had worked with the Rosenbergs, Kim Philby, Guy Burgess, Donald Maclean. To the callow cadets they seemed majestic figures, beyond the reach of mere mortals, their lives an exalted sacrifice for the glory of our motherland. We dreamed of being their successors.

The training course began with a two-month stint in a Spetsnaz (Special Forces) unit, where any doubts we may have had about our future were dispelled; we were being readied for combat under special conditions. We parachuted from planes, mastered a variety of weapons, learned to plant mines, negotiated a napalm-drenched obstacle course, captured "prisoners" for interrogation, "blew up" bridges, and "destroyed" enemy supply lines.

A wiry paratrooper colonel taught us: "Your duty is to execute, at any cost, any task assigned by our motherland. You should not harbor any doubts as to the moral justification or political wisdom of such a task. The Soviet Union is the bulwark of progressive mankind. Everything coming from its leadership serves the cause of world progress."

"How about surviving along the way?" one of the cadets asked.

"That's your problem," said the colonel, adjusting the straps of his parachute. "If you have the will to survive, you'll survive. But as far as our motherland is concerned, the important thing is for you to accomplish your assigned task."

That was the first time I had heard such a shocking definition of my duty, but it failed to impress me as overly cynical. The idea of sacrifice for the sake of lofty ideals was popular in our crowd.

Before long, many of my schoolmates ended up in Spetsnaz units in Afghanistan. Some of them died, for instance, Volodya Fomin. He was literally beheaded by a burst of machine-gun fire in front of his six-year-old son right in the center of Kabul.

When the zinc coffin containing Volodya's body was brought back to Moscow, I was still mastering the secrets of the spy trade. A lot of the stuff we were taught came straight from the Cold War arsenal. Indeed, who would be crazy enough today to use a long-range radio station to maintain communication with our agents in the United States, or the microdot, a photograph of a document less than one millimeter in diameter? The KGB generals, like their army counterparts, were obviously busy preparing to fight past wars.

Time has erased much from my memory, but some episodes I will certainly remember to my dying day.

A huge map of the Soviet Union, ringed by the military bases belonging to the U.S. or their allies, hangs on the wall of a classroom next to numerous charts representing the American war-making capability. The figures are very impressive. The instructor comments on them, then says: "I hope no one doubts now that the United States is capable of wiping our country off the face of the earth."

"But does it have the desire and the will to do so?" I ask.

"This is exactly what you will have to find out when you are sent there," the instructor replies. "The American people will not start a war, but there are no guarantees that their government won't do it."

Ideological indoctrination at the Intelligence Academy was aimed at inculcating in us one basic idea: rather than controlling their government, the American people were being manipulated by their rulers, which is why U.S. behavior is so unpredictable.

To test the merits of this idea, one had to go to the United States and learn the ways of that country. Meanwhile, we had to take such statements on faith.

Around that time, news came of the defection of an operative from our Tokyo residency named Levchenko. Once, discussing things among friends, we touched upon that subject, and, naturally enough, to a man denounced the defector. Treachery was regarded by us as worse than death. All of a sudden, an instructor, a grizzled colonel, said: "Levchenko is not to blame. The system is."

We were flabbergasted. What had he said?

"Levchenko was a smart operative, but people like that are rejected by the system." The colonel smiled sadly. "And since he found himself unwanted by his own state, what options were left open to him?"

"What will happen to the state if it rejects smart people?" I muttered in confusion.

"The state is like a ship that picks up barnacles and sooner or later sinks," the colonel said. We were a bunch of innocent kittens in his eyes.

I was to recall the wisdom of the old-timer on many later occasions.

Once a group of cadets slated for posting in NATO countries were summoned by the academy commander, Colonel Malakhov, and asked a single question: "Let's assume that you have an opportunity to get hold of extremely important information about the main enemy, but to do it you have to kill a child. What will you do?"

Some of us, after some hesitation, expressed their readiness to do whatever is necessary. Others mumbled incoherently, afraid of saying either yes or no. Still others, myself included, tried to turn the whole affair into a joke. Malakhov listened intently to all the answers and let us go without a word.

To this day, I don't know the meaning of that exercise. Sadism? Senility? I have no idea. What kind of trait did they hope to develop by playing with us in this way? Interestingly, all the people in our group, irrespective of their responses to the chief's question, received the very assignments for which they had been earmarked all along.

There was among us a cadet who had four years of experience working in the personnel department of the intelligence service. He looked the picture of an inveterate intriguer, and claimed that he knew all the ropes in the external intelligence arm of the KGB. His nickname was "The Experienced One."

The Experienced One loved to talk, which was his Achilles' heel.

"Disregard everything they teach you here," he would pontificate to his close friends. "Nobody needs your undercover agents. An operative's career is shaped exclusively by his relationship with his superiors. You'd be better off thinking how to suck up to your boss."

We did not believe The Experienced One. He was even suspected of provoking us on orders of the personnel department in order to weed out the weak of spirit and impure of thought. Who could have believed that he was merely disclosing the truth?

I graduated from the Intelligence Academy with honors. The guest speaker at the graduation ceremony was Colonel Vitaly Yurchenko. At that time he headed the Internal Counterintelligence Department of the First Chief Directorate of the KGB—the group that policed the KGB personnel in the First Chief Directorate—and was widely regarded as one of the best informed and most influential members of the intelligence service. No one could have imagined that, just three years later, he would become a turncoat.

Yurchenko delivered a brilliant and inspired speech: "You are extremely fortunate to have been chosen to become the elite of Soviet society. You will learn the secrets that will make you omnipotent. Behind you stands a great power that will never let you down. Very soon you will have to do battle with strong adversaries. The most potent of them are the intelligence services of the United States. They always aim to succeed . . ."

"They are not alone in that regard," my friend Igor Kessov, sitting next to me, said portentously.

He was right, damn it. We felt like Roman centurions preparing for combat, ready to win or die trying.

After a month-long vacation, I found myself at the North American Department, the most important of the divisions within the First Chief Directorate. The First Chief Directorate was the rough equivalent of the American CIA. It was divided into several branches: political intelligence, external counterintelligence, technical and scientific, and so on. The most important of these was the political intelligence branch. That branch contained the various geographical departments, and of these, the most important by far was the North American Department. I was gripped by uncertainty bordering on timidity. After all, I had landed with the Holy of Holies.

At that time, the department was led by General Dmitri Yakushkin, a scion of nobility whose ancestry included a member of the Decembrist anti-monarchist plot. In 1982, he had returned home after an extremely successful seven-year stint as head of the Washington residency. It was widely believed that with Yakushkin at the helm, the KGB had managed to do the greatest damage to U.S. national security during the entire period since the end of World War II. Of course, that was the time of détente, and the

Americans had again let their guard down, as is their wont. But that was of minor importance. The primary reason for General Yakushkin's success was his ability to take risks and not to shirk responsibility.

Now he harbored plans of expanding the North American Department into a superdivision coordinating the recruitment effort targeting Americans on a worldwide scale. An ambitious man and a strong leader, he aspired to rise, with time, to the position of deputy to the head of the First Chief Directorate—at least. Naturally enough, he was heartily disliked by his peers.

Yakushkin had an imposing presence: a tall, distinguished, gray-haired man who looked like a genuine Russian aristocrat.

When I entered his office, Yakushkin came to his feet, walked out from behind his desk, and shook my hand.

"You have an unprecedented opportunity to distinguish yourself," he said gravely. "If there is still some room left for heroism, you can find it in my department. So everything depends upon your skill, and a little bit on luck. You will be working in the Washington Section. And here is your immediate superior." The general majestically gestured toward a middle-aged man sitting in an armchair: "Colonel Valentin Aksilenko. I strongly advise you to listen carefully to what he has to say; then you will have a good chance of becoming a recruiter."

I followed the colonel into the small anteroom of Yakushkin's office and was introduced to "Grandma Lida," secretary of the department. No one knew when she had joined the intelligence service, but it must have been in the very first years of Soviet rule. Grandma Lida was known for her uncanny clerical expertise in all secret matters, and for her stupendously bad temper.

Each residency staffer coming home on vacation made it a point to bring her a gift in the hope of gaining favor with her. She accepted the gifts, but no one ever succeeded in

winning her over. There was only one star in her firma-
ment: Yakushkin.

"Here is another future recruiter," the colonel said by
way of introduction to the redoubtable secretary.

"How do you know if he'll pan out?" she said peevishly.
"Go away, you are interfering in my work. Just you wait,"
she directed to me, "one of these days I'll check the way
you keep your files, and then you'll be in big, big trouble."

Thus dismissed, we entered Valentin's office. Nothing
there indicated its occupant's line of work. A clean desk
with two telephones, an unwieldy safe in the corner with a
tennis racket on top.

As expected, our conversation began with my life story. I
had had to tell it scores of times in my many previous
interviews. The colonel listened intently, then asked just
one question: "Were you a good student?"

"Straight As," I replied with considerable surprise.

No one had ever asked me that question, either when I
was interviewed for a job with the KGB or in the Intelligence Academy. I had had to answer all sorts of questions
about my relatives, possible contacts with foreigners, family relationships—in a word, they were digging diligently
through my dirty linen, but it never occurred to anyone to
find out if I had any brains.

I couldn't help liking the colonel.

"I was an honors graduate, too," he said, smiling, and I
liked him even more. I have always been fond of people who
strive to succeed at everything they do, whatever it is. Unfortunately, I have met a mere handful of such individuals.
The overwhelming majority of my acquaintances—but not
friends!—relied on luck or influence rather than their own
industry to advance in life. People in the mold of The Experienced One were typical of the Soviet system.

In this sense, Valentin Aksilenko was a rare exception.
He looked like anything but your typical spymaster. All
the intelligence agents I had hitherto encountered bore the

stamp of a special caste of glamorous heroes. He, on the other hand, was as down-to-earth as they come. Moreover, he seemed to be a shy person, quite the opposite of the way I thought a typical "knight of the cloak and dagger" should look.

"While in the Intelligence Academy, were you attracted by operative psychology?" the colonel asked.

"Sure," I lied.

Psychology, my ass! I was taught to beat surveillance, to load and unload drops, to make the prearranged clandestine exchanges that we called brush exchanges, to open letters surreptitiously. Psychology was on such a far back burner that nobody ever noticed it. Apparently the Cold War had left its stamp on the curriculum.

Once the intelligence service ran an experiment. They selected a group of the best operatives in the history of the KGB, fed their characteristics into the computer, and obtained a generalized description of the superspy. Surprisingly, however, that synthetic hero turned out to have no higher education and only a rudimentary command of a foreign language. Everyone was stumped; they even thought that the computer was playing tricks on them. Finally, the truth dawned on them.

The fact is that the intelligence service had scored its greatest successes in the 1930s, 1940s, and maybe the 1950s. In those days, the West crawled with admirers of socialist ideas, as well as people not averse to earning a buck with Moscow's help. Very often a successful recruitment job required just a few broken phrases in the local tongue, such as: "I have money. You have secrets. Let's swap."

In those days, it had never occurred to anyone to put the prospective agents—foreign citizens who knowingly cooperated with Soviet intelligence—on an analyst's couch. Cooperation with the KGB was regarded as a great honor. The operative was supposed to issue orders, the agent to show blind obedience. Much water has passed under the bridge since that epoch, the world has changed, but the intelligence service is still its old self.

"You will be well advised to pay special attention to psychology," Valentin said. "I think psychology is the most potent intelligence weapon today. There was a time when we recruited with ideology, but who believes in these ideals anymore? Then we switched to money, but the standard of living in the West has risen to such an extent that we can no longer afford to pay enough to attract good assets. So only psychology is left. That is, you must look for individuals with certain psychic deviations, primarily adventurers. Furthermore, you must find a way to communicate with such types if they are to agree to work for you. You can hardly succeed in this task without a knowledge of psychology. It looks as though the James Bond era is over for good. The technology of spying has lost much of its importance."

I listened to him, hardly believing my ears. I certainly liked Colonel Aksilenko. But alas, the whole intelligence service was much less to my liking.

Very soon and much to my surprise, I found out that what I had been taught at the Intelligence Academy bore very little relevance to the real world of intelligence. There I had been taught to serve my motherland and recruit agents; here in the intelligence service intrigue was king.

The personality of any Soviet bureaucratic organization was personified by its chief—much as the dog often resembles its beloved master. In this sense, Colonel-General Vladimir Kryuchkov, chief of the KGB's external intelligence arm, the First Chief Directorate, was a notable personality—the quintessence of the Soviet system.

When he became head of the First Chief Directorate in 1974, Kryuchkov brought his party skills to his new job. He had never been involved in intelligence and had little understanding of it. However, it was an article of faith in the Soviet Union that a communist leader could lead just about anything. Thus did a man whose experience consisted entirely of taking papers for signature now to one boss, now to another, become the country's premier spymaster.

At that time, the intelligence service was a very compact organization. Everyone knew everyone else, and everyone was busy. They might have been doing good things or bad, but nobody was idle. The service included fanatics and sincerely misguided persons, victims of a colossal fraud; there were even evil individuals. But one category was totally absent: amateurs. Each employee knew his trade and worked for the good of the state as he understood it.

That was not enough for Kryuchkov; he wanted size. With the approval of the then KGB boss, Yuri Andropov, he launched a campaign to globalize intelligence. Pretty soon, the huge headquarters building in Yasenevo, so recently half empty, came to resemble an ant heap. The service mushroomed, swelling the personnel rolls, giving birth to new divisions, and, most importantly, spawning new senior positions.

The intelligence service bred generals like rabbits, and each one of them had to justify his existence. How? By a superlative imitation of work.

There has never been a country where the gulf between the word and the deed has been as great as it was in the Brezhnevite Soviet Union. Bit by bit, the system had evolved into a theater of the absurd, where the deed was shorn of significance while the mendacious word was passed off as the ultimate truth. That characterized Kryuchkov's contribution to the KGB, as well.

Skillful fieldwork was no longer the criterion of success; artful imitation took its place. Mid-level officers, the backbone of the intelligence service, had a cynical joke: "The best operative is one who strives mightily to recruit an undercover agent, but can't do it because he is tailed around the clock."

Those who mastered the trick of imitation early could confidently count on a successful career. Others were doomed to a complete downfall or a dreary existence in secondary positions with the ever-ready dressing-down by the boss as the chief diversion. They were turned into scapegoats who had to bear the blame for the progressive impotence of the Soviet intelligence machinery.

Under Kryuchkov, "Lord Paperwork" became the principal substance of intelligence activities. The service annually churned out some three million documents, whose practical value had been tending toward zero. One office produced a question, another supplied the answer. A well-composed document became an end in itself, a sufficient reason for a reward or a promotion. That it had nothing to do with intelligence did not matter. One could become a general without ever setting eyes on a live agent. "The main advantage of the Soviet intelligence service resides in its newly acquired ability to exist without undercover agents," ran an old-timers' bitter joke as they watched the figure of the undercover agent recede into irrelevance in the Kryuchkov organization. More important business was pushed to the forefront. For instance, the party meeting.

Many other Intelligence Academy graduates realized soon after enrolling in the intelligence service that they had walked into a trap. They had consented to work in intelligence, having no idea of what it was like there. But when they found out, it was too late; the way out was blocked. Their only option was to perform their duties, trying against all odds to avoid breaking down. Few of them succeeded; the rest sooner or later succumbed to their fate and turned themselves into their superiors' playthings.

Of course, not all bosses were autocratic dilettantes, but their numbers grew under Kryuchkov. Old-school generals were aghast at the ever more brazen profanation of their trade and grumbled about it. They despised Kryuchkov for his incompetence. He reciprocated their feelings with tacit hatred, and gradually replaced them with his own men—that is to say, communist apparatchiks. The result was an increasing paralysis of leadership. The more the intelligence service expanded, the less effective it became. Its principal task officially consisted of recruiting undercover agents in the U.S., and it was in this area that its growing debility was particularly striking.

There is no denying that Kryuchkov's KGB did score some direct hits against the U.S. The Walker network, which sold U.S. Navy top secret codes to Moscow; National Security Agency ex-staffer Ronald Pelton and former CIA man Edward Howard, who agreed to work for the Soviets— all of them were indeed prime sources of great joy to the KGB and much grief to the U.S. The Kremlin agents, as sometimes depicted by the American media, seemed ubiquitous and devilishly cunning. But it took me only a year at the intelligence service to realize how far from the truth that flattering picture was.

Practically all Americans recruited by the KGB under Kryuchkov had decided to work for Moscow of their own accord and sought out Soviet intelligence operatives to volunteer their services. All of them, to a greater or lesser extent, exhibited certain mental anomalies that set them apart from what are generally perceived as normal persons. The KGB played a minor part in their recruitment: the American volunteers were not shown the door when they turned up at the Soviet Embassy—and that was the extent of the "recruitment" effort.

Yet no intelligence service can survive by passively waiting for volunteers; it must hunt its prey. But alas, throughout the entire period from 1974, when Kryuchkov was appointed head of the external intelligence service, to 1982, when I arrived at the North American Department, only one KGB operative had found and successfully recruited an undercover agent in the U.S.: Valentin Aksilenko. I decided to follow his example whatever the cost.

It seemed to me that having the American agent by and large set Valentin free, to the extent an intelligence officer can be independent. Valentin had no need to engage in make-believe and to try to convince his communist bosses that a bluff was, in fact, real work. He ran his agent and reported, for all practical purposes, only to General Yakushkin, one of the few old-timers who still managed to hold on to his position. One could only dream of such a privileged status.

Can this entire huge edifice run on paperwork alone? Of course, it can't, I reasoned to myself. Kryuchkov must have some successes to report to the Politburo. In fact, he needs at least several American agents to justify his own existence and build his bureaucratic empire on the information supplied by them. The only good bluff is one based on something real. And whoever provides this dose of "reality" becomes indispensable and acquires the greatest of all privileges: he can dispense with the need to pretend to be a moron all his life.

Needless to say, I realized how difficult a task I had set for myself. Indeed, what bait could I dangle in front of a normal, modern-day American to make the prospect of cooperation with the KGB enticing at a time when the communist state, as we now know, was going through its last agony? Most of my colleagues knew full well that they had as much chance of recruiting even one American as an airplane pilot had of flying to the moon. It would take an extraordinary stroke of luck to beat the overwhelming odds.

I knew that my goal was all but unreachable, but I just could not reconcile myself to such a sorry reality. I cherished a hope that by recruiting an agent I would be able to break into a small but coveted compartment ruled by national interests and common sense, where real pros held sway and there was no need to suck up to the boss.

I had three alternatives: to become an honest failure; to turn into a thriving hypocrite; or to recruit an agent. I chose the last.

Upon arrival in Washington, I immediately reported to the KGB station. The residency, as it was known, occupied a tiny space in the embassy building on Sakharov Plaza, slightly more than half a mile from the White House. In reality, there was no semblance of a plaza here. The Soviet Embassy had had a 16th Street address for ages. But after the authorities exiled Andrei Sakharov to Gorky, the Americans had decided to drive a painful thorn into the Kremlin's backside, and had renamed the territory around the embassy after the rebellious academician. The address in the telephone directories remained unchanged—1125 16th Street, N.W.—but a small plaque right at the entrance proclaiming "Sakharov Plaza" was a constant reminder to the Soviets of their nefarious deed.

Outwardly, Moscow's "spy nest" in the very heart of America bore little resemblance to the sinister image that name evoked for many Americans. Its total area did not exceed 80 square meters (roughly 860 square feet), where some thirty intelligence officers were cooped up.

As the years went by, the overall staff of the embassy grew by leaps and bounds, and so everyone—"clean" diplomats as well as spies—had to work in incredibly tight quarters. Thin partitions divided the residency into four extremely small rooms, tiny as birdcages, which accommodated its four sections: Political Intelligence, External Counterintelligence, Scientific and Technological Intelligence, and Technical Operations.

The resident—what the CIA calls the "chief of station"— his deputies in charge of political intelligence and counterintelligence, and the secretary of the station occupied private cubicles.

There was not a single window in the rooms, and the dim light given off by the neon bulbs and desk lamps somewhat inappropriately conveyed a feeling of intimacy.

To gain access into the residency, one had to dial the code on the digital lock at the entrance door, after leaving one's coat in a closetlike room in the corridor. The latter precaution had long been considered a very important security measure. Analysis of numerous defections of intelligence officers had indicated that some of them had smuggled in their pockets spy equipment (miniature cameras and tape recorders) furnished by the Western special services to obtain documentary proof of the KGB's spying activities. The finding resulted in an order: no access to the residency with your coat on. The leadership apparently assumed that the fewer pockets a Soviet intelligence agent had, the less chance there was that he would become a turncoat.

I entered the residency and saw a peculiar picture: intelligence and counterintelligence operatives crammed into their tiny compartments. Some of them were reading newspapers, others composing cables to Moscow, still others simply chewing the fat.

At that time the Washington residency was headed by General Stanislav Androsov, one of Kryuchkov's favorites. He had come to the intelligence service from the Ministry of Foreign Affairs, where he had been secretary of the Young Communists' Committee, and was immediately appointed to a senior position. A bureaucrat to the core, Androsov knew instinctively what qualities Kryuchkov valued in his subordinates, and skillfully played his hand. Not that it was all that difficult, considering that they were kindred spirits.

While stationed in Moscow, Androsov always stayed in his office till late at night and never allowed himself to go home before Kryuchkov did. To tell the truth, there was very little for him to do to merit such diligence. He just sat there.

But how could Kryuchkov know? Leaving late at night, when almost all the department heads had been long gone, the intelligence chief invariably saw the light in Androsov's window, and imagined that his industrious subordinate was busy concocting brilliant intelligence schemes somewhere in the Third World. Actually Androsov was merely reading his newspapers, even though he might just as well have done his reading in more comfortable surroundings at home.

Androsov came to the U.S. at a difficult time. President

Reagan had launched a massive rearmament program. The détente was over, relations between Washington and Moscow had sunk to a new low and now hovered at the danger point, beyond which began the realm of the unpredictable.

Androsov told Moscow that Americans were unrecruitable—the same message he had sent home about the Chinese in his previous posting in Beijing. But his words met with resistance. The rebuff came from Androsov's predecessor as Washington resident, the head of the North American Department, General Yakushkin.

This was the situation when I reported for my first day of work in the spring of 1985. Androsov gave me a fatherly welcome and then ordered me to stay away from the residency for three months to stump the FBI sleuths. I decided to use the unexpected hiatus to rent and furnish my apartment, buy a car—in short, to settle down, without which no intelligence activities were possible.

I rented an apartment in Alexandria, not far from Landmark Shopping Center. A wonderful place, cozy and quiet, though I was warned that the Soviet diplomat who had occupied that apartment before me had found a couple of bugs in it.

I had no doubt that the FBI would put me under surveillance, and was prepared to endure it. Of course, I wished I did not have to submit my personal life to constant scrutiny by strangers, but everything has its price, and living in a fishbowl seems to be the inevitable trade-off for the privilege of being a KGB intelligence officer.

As I went about my mundane tasks, I studied the lay of the land. After I had a good grasp of the city topography, I memorized several countersurveillance routes suitable for throwing off a tail, and decided that that was enough. Dead-drop operations—the means of communication between an intelligence officer and his agent—were not in the cards for the foreseeable future, and the routes I had selected for countersurveillance would be sufficient in an emergency.

In my first weeks in Washington I heard stories about residency operations of the recent past. One concerned Henry Kissinger, who in his memoir tells of his relationship with an ill-concealed KGB officer who flattered himself by thinking he was gaining Kissinger's confidence. Although Kissinger saw right through the Russian, the officer was reporting that thanks to his virtuoso performance, the development of "Lord" (Kissinger's code name—meant in the sense of a nobleman, not in a religious sense) was right on target.

When Kissinger became President Nixon's national security advisor, no sooner had he settled into his new office, a few yards from the Oval Office, than the First Chief Directorate headquarters in Moscow prepared a report for Brezhnev that the KGB had successfully penetrated the U.S. administration.

An old, experienced general took a long time reading and rereading the report. On the face of it, the report looked flawless. Lord supplied information; he even invited his KGB acquaintance to visit him at the White House, and seemingly agreed to go on seeing him . . . Could it be true that, at last, the penetration effort had succeeded? Could it be true that a source was planted at the very heart of the U.S. government? It certainly looked that way!

And yet, and yet . . . He couldn't put his finger on it, but the old general felt that something was amiss. He refused to countersign the report, opting to wait and see what would happen. What happened was exactly what could have been expected. Lord failed to provide any classified information; instead, he caused a lot of headaches to the Kremlin. The general thanked his lucky stars that he had had the good sense not to report the "successful penetration" upstairs.

I'll never forget the bravura performance of the deputy resident as he told that story.

"So what happened?" he would ask, assuming a mysterious air. "On the one hand, we have a source at the White House, in an extremely high position at that. Which means that the penetration succeeded, right? On the other hand, where is the information?" He would spread his arms in a theatrical gesture, his face a picture of childish amazement.

Of course, the operative who had maintained contact with Lord was punished and warned to keep his wild imagination in check in his future reports.

The residency penetrated Congress as well as the White House. In 1982—I was a rookie at the North American Department in Moscow at that time—I was reading an interesting file on a congressman. I opened it to the first page— and read compulsively to the very end. What a case! A residency officer whose cover job was that of the first secretary of the Soviet Embassy in Washington was developing a promising American legislator. It was a gem of an operation.

He would drop by the congressman's office on Capitol Hill, they would descend together to the cafeteria, buy a cup of coffee, and talk. The operative demonstrated phenomenal mastery as a conversationalist. With incredible skill and subtlety, he penetrated the most secret recesses of the legislator's soul, inexorably pulling him further and further into the trap from which there was no escape. The officer brought reams of information the congressman supplied at each meeting. Recruitment seemed a foregone conclusion.

Consumed by impatience, I skipped to the very end of the file where I expected to find a memo to the chief of the intelligence service on the recruitment of the representative. Instead, I found an envelope containing a clipping from the *Washington Post* with an interview with the "development subject." My God, what a disaster!

The congressman told the interviewer that he had alerted the FBI after the very first contact with the Soviet operative, and all subsequent development naturally proceeded under the watchful eye of American counterintelligence. But that was not the worst. The congressman noted with some surprise that the Soviet "diplomat" had asked almost no questions in their conversations. Instead, he talked nonstop, initiating his American contact into the subtleties of Soviet foreign policy.

At the end of the interview, the congressman remarked that he had learned a lot from the Soviet "diplomat." Someone had underscored that paragraph with a red marker.

General Yakushkin unceremoniously kicked the hapless operative out of the North American Department. But times changed, and now bluff was king in the intelligence service. Everyone—from the lowliest operative to the ranking general—knew what was going on but pretended to see nothing. Everyone had to report some successes, and half a loaf is better than no bread at all—or, in the lively metaphor of the KGB resident in Rome: where there are no birds, even an asshole sounds like a nightingale.

Under Kryuchkov, the intelligence service built a huge repository of interesting files, which read more like fiction than real-life accounts. Their protagonists were some of the better-known Americans careless enough to meet Soviet representatives on a regular basis. Officially, needless to say. But the Americans never suspected that the official nature of the meetings was no saving grace; the intelligence officer had little trouble creatively turning the meetings into clandestine contacts—on paper.

Once, a colleague of mine, whose pragmatism bordered on the cynical, came up with an ingenious idea.

"The most devilishly clever active measure that the KGB could carry out in the U.S. would be to go public with all of these fake cases. I would bet my bottom ruble that America would be hit with a gale-force political crisis. It would be so bad they would probably have to create a brand-new political elite from among those who had had the good fortune to steer clear of all Soviet representatives."

No question about it, the Americans seriously underestimated the flights of fancy of which the Soviet "knights of cloak and dagger" were capable.

I could have followed this well-trodden path. For instance, find a couple of Americans who would agree to see me at least once a month on condition that I pay for lunch, chat about the new Madonna CD, the last Washington Redskins game—anything at all except politics so as not to scare them away, God forbid—and then skillfully relate the contents of an article from the *Washington Post* in my report to Moscow, passing it off as confidential information obtained in the course of the last encounter.

After a while, my trusting American contacts would, unbeknownst to them, turn up as assets in our files under the code names of, say, "Tango and Cash." Meanwhile I would acquire a reputation as a solid operative while actually leading a pleasant existence in the "imperialist hell." After four or five years of this bliss, I would return to Moscow to receive a promotion, followed in due course by another tour of duty abroad, with the coveted colonel's stars, in all probability, looming on the horizon. In short, the beaten path promised an easy life, an enviable career, and material success.

The sober mind of a Soviet citizen was whispering to me conspiratorially that it was the only way to go for a normal, i.e., "successful" operative. But at that time I was just beginning to suspect that I did not belong in the class of "normal" officers of the Soviet intelligence service. The more I was told that Americans were generally unrecruitable, the stronger was my yearning to challenge the prevailing wisdom.

A spy can't help looking at the world around him through the prism of his trade, and the picture he sees is always distorted. He sees a lush park—and looks for a suitable place for a dead drop or a clandestine meeting. A passerby asks him a question—and he wonders if it is an FBI agent casting his net. He talks to someone—and his mind is racing: Does this man have access to classified information? If not, can he gain it? Are there any abnormalities in his psychological makeup? Does he have any serious problems? How to arrange a covert meeting with him?

I, too, looked at the world around me intently, hoping to find the slightest chink in the armor, the smallest crack in the security fence surrounding the places that intrigued me in the U.S. To enter through the front door was out of the question. I thought with longing of the time not so long ago when our operatives could walk anywhere, even in the Pentagon, as though it were their own apartment. Those were the days!

The exploits of one veteran were legendary in the North American Department. At the height of the détente during the 1970s, his favorite pastime was stealing documents from Pentagon desks. The method he used was simple but effective.

The operative would wander about the Pentagon corridors, poking his head in any room from which a group of staffers had just emerged. On occasion, the room would be empty; in those days the carefree denizens of the Pentagon did not even bother to lock the doors. Then he would instantly sweep the desks clean of all documents—sometimes there were important papers lying around—stuff them under his coat, and make a beeline for the nearest exit.

Once, when he was leaving the Pentagon with a bulky load of classified documents under his coat, the papers slipped out and fell to the ground. A sergeant standing guard nearby was dumbfounded. So was the operative, but he quickly regained his wits.

"Hey, give me a hand with these damn papers, will you," he growled to the guard. The thoroughly confused soldier helped him pick up the documents, and our hero spy walked away unmolested, carrying his booty with him.

But those days were long gone, and the stories of our operatives' visits to the Pentagon had acquired a fairy-tale quality.

According to Valentin Aksilenko's calculation, about two thousand contacts had to be sifted through in order to acquire an agent. But how was one supposed to make so many contacts with Reagan in the White House, at a time when adversarial relations between the governments were immediately parlayed into mistrust and hostility at the street level? I can't count the number of times I found myself in this quandary. You are talking to an American; everything is normal, he is affable and smiling. But as soon as you mention in passing that you are Soviet, the American's face changes and he vanishes, dissolves into thin air, leaving you staring, mouth agape, into the surrounding void. Believe me, it's not my idea of fun. Sometimes I felt like a pariah.

My room for maneuvering was further severely circumscribed by yet another important consideration. One rejected recruitment offer, just one, and I would immediately be kicked out of the country—if I was lucky. I did not even want to think what would happen if I was unlucky.

In the late 1970s, two of my colleagues at the New York residency, Enger and Chernyayev, did time in an American jail. About the same time, Konstantin Koryavin, an officer with the very same New York residency, was apprehended by the FBI in the act of unloading a dead drop (usually a transfer of documents, money, or equipment) set up for him by his asset, a U.S. citizen. It was late at night. He was blindfolded, thrown into a car, brought to an empty cemetery, and put on the edge of a freshly dug grave.

"Tell us the name of your contact and we'll let you go. Otherwise, we'll shoot you and bury you in this grave," an FBI agent told Koryavin. "None of your colleagues know your whereabouts or what's happened to you. You'll just vanish into thin air, that's all. You have exactly one minute to make up your mind."

Koryavin was staring in horror into the black maw of the grave. The FBI men stood behind his back, one of them loudly counting off the fleeting seconds. Finally, he said,

"Sixty." Koryavin heard the metallic click of the gun being cocked, followed by dead silence. He stood, frozen with fear, waiting for the dreaded instant when the promised bullet would pierce the back of his head.

The torture dragged on for several minutes. Then he heard the car doors slam shut and the engines roar back to life. The Soviet spy stood at the edge of the grave, transfixed with shock, not daring to turn around and look, long after the FBI crew had left. He couldn't believe he was spared.

Konstantin Koryavin only reported the harrowing adventure to his immediate superiors, but before long the whole North American Department was privy to the secret. Of course, there was little chance of verifying the story through "independent sources," but it was cold comfort. As a Tass reporter and so without diplomatic immunity I had one chance, two at best. The prospect of landing in an American jail or at the edge of a grave had little attraction to me. Even mere expulsion from the U.S. would spell the end of my field career. Expelled intelligence officers were regarded as burned, and hence of no value in the field.

It is widely assumed that spies usually acquire contacts at all sorts of social gatherings, such as parties, press conferences, and the like. Maybe it used to be that way long ago, but not in my time. It didn't take me long to realize that to look for would-be agents on the Washington cocktail circuit was a waste of time. Everybody seemed well aware of the KGB tactics, and I decided to follow a different route; in professional terminology, it is known as contactless evaluation of prospects.

One day in the summer of 1985, going through the stacks of newspaper clippings kept at the residency, I came across an interesting item: a bundle of copies of articles under the byline of Phyllis Barber, carefully collected by someone over several years from a number of U.S. and West European periodicals.

I have never been able to find the person who compiled that collection to tell him that I am in his debt, but he deserved my gratitude. Phyllis's articles were absolutely amazing. She gave a new definition to virulent anti-Americanism; she hated all things American with a passion, while exhibiting a profound and intimate knowledge of the ins and outs of U.S. domestic and foreign policies. That was exactly what I needed; I had found my "subject." All I had to do now was find a suitable pretext for introducing myself to her, but it was merely a matter of technique. A glimmer of hope flickered on the horizon.

Then out of the blue lightning struck. Colonel Vitaly Yurchenko, deputy chief of the North American Department, disappeared in Rome under mysterious circumstances. Sometime later, he turned up at a secret villa belonging to the CIA in Virginia and—horrors!—started to talk. His revelations, occasionally appearing in the U.S. press, boggled the mind. The network of American agents built by the KGB over many years collapsed like a house of cards.

Anti-Soviet sentiment in the U.S. reached its peak. The U.S.-Soviet summit in Geneva was approaching, but Yurchenko had thrown a monkey wrench into the preparations for it. The Soviet leaders were apprehensive, fearing that the U.S. would use the defector's information to put them at a disadvantage.

In this situation, Androsov steered the residency into near total passivity, while keeping himself busy reading American newspapers and magazines. He soon realized that his operatives were going crazy from idleness, and so he took steps to alleviate their boredom, ordering his subordinates to improve their discipline. The residency was struck by paralysis.

Was I destined to spend my career in intelligence so dismally? The situation seemed almost hopeless. Then came a lucky break.

One morning I drove to work, listening to the radio. From time to time, the disc jockey interrupted the light rock music to dial some random telephone number and ask whoever answered the phone about his or her attitude toward the traitors who had recently been exposed: the Walkers, Ronald Pelton, and others of their ilk. All the respondents expressed their outrage, and some even demanded the death penalty for the traitors. Suddenly one woman said: "Why do you depict those people as some kind of monsters? They merely did their business the way they saw fit, that's all."

The radio announcer nearly choked.

"Now, wait a minute, wait a minute," he rasped. "You mean to say you could do what they did?"

"I don't know," the woman said. "But I would certainly think about it."

Bingo! I realized that as far as my professional interests were concerned, the more hostile Soviet-American relations were, the better. At the very least, there would certainly be a dramatic drop-off in the number of dead-end contacts. Given the circumstances, a person who dares to establish contact with a Soviet representative must be psychologically ready for it. It was time to introduce myself to Phyllis Barber. I had an excellent pretext: Mikhail Gorbachev was planning to visit Paris, and Phyllis was writing stories for a French weekly.

2

THAT night, I spent about an hour in the Tass Washington office on the tenth floor of the National Press Building calling journalists representing the French media, asking them for opinions about the prospects of Soviet-French relations. Frankly, I could not have cared less about the subject, but it was a ploy that is known in professional terminology as setting up a legend for subsequent operations.

Having done enough for my legend, I watched the CBS Evening News, and left the office feeling like a man after a job well done. The task of creating a cover had been accomplished. Ahead lay the routine work of an intelligence operative.

Like other correspondents at the Tass bureau, I kept my car in an underground garage on G Street, a hundred yards from the National Press Building. For fourteen days in a row, an FBI watch car, a silver-gray Chevy Impala, had relentlessly pursued me; the tail would appear when I got into my car in the morning and follow me all day long, wherever

I went. It seemed quite natural to me that a large CIA network should be at work in Moscow, and that an FBI car should follow me in Washington. I saw nothing wrong with the competition of the intelligence services, as long as it stayed within the bounds of propriety.

So far they had been following my car rather than me. When I visited somewhere or went into a store, the watchers stayed in their car, patiently waiting for me to come out. This is a standard procedure at the early stages of a counterintelligence operation, when the watchers study the places the spy visits. At the next phase, the FBI was logically supposed to start ferreting out my contacts; then, the agents would have to tag along, not merely in a car, but on foot, too. In the meantime, I enjoyed considerable freedom of action.

That night, the FBI Impala was stationed about fifty yards from the entrance to the garage, and I walked straight toward it. When the driver saw me coming, he immediately bent down. The other agent in the front seat tarried, but his partner's heavy hand immediately came down on his head and shoved it under the dashboard, out of my view.

The demonstrative surveillance was still on. So much the better, I thought, entering Hecht's department store, which occupies a whole block of G Street from 13th to 12th Streets.

What I did next flew in the face of all the precepts of intelligence. According to the doctrine taught at the Intelligence Academy, demonstrative surveillance is designed to exert psychological pressure on its subject. It can be accompanied by all sorts of provocations of varying degrees of severity. In situations of this kind, the prudent thing to do, according to the counsel of experienced spies, is not to tempt fate but to hide in an office, apartment, or anywhere else—and pronto.

But as far as I was concerned, that theory was so much bunk. From my viewpoint the important thing was that my FBI guardians knew that I was aware of them and in all probability were confident that, under the circumstances and without the traditional route test to shake them off my tail, I would never do anything rash.

I bought myself a necktie and went upstairs to the lingerie department. Not that I was keen on lingerie; what I needed was the pay phone tucked in a discreet corner that could not be seen from a distance. The spy term for such a locality is a "dead zone." The whole day had been but a prelude to the coming telephone call. I dialed the number, dropped a quarter in the slot, and, somewhat anxiously, waited.

"Hello," said a male voice.

"Bonjour, monsieur," I said. "Puis-je parler avec Madame Barber. Je suis un journaliste soviétique."

"Bien sur," the man replied. "Do you speak English?"

"Sure."

"Then wait a second."

My heart quickened its pace. The forthcoming few minutes would be crucial. The first talk to a contact is always the most important one. A few seconds later I heard a soft female voice with a slight foreign accent.

Again, I was talking bull: that I was given an assignment to write a large piece on the relationship in the USSR-U.S.-France triangle; that my career depended on that article; that I would love to hear Phyllis's informed opinion; and that, in exchange, I would be willing to advise her on any aspect of Soviet-American relations in which she might be interested.

I lost count of the number of times I had to spin this kind of yarn, my "legend." To me, it sounded so stupid that I sometimes wished the earth could swallow me. Thank God, Americans treated the press seriously.

"When do you need the answer?" Phyllis asked.

"Yesterday," I lied.

"Pity. I'd like to think it over a bit. But since you are in such a hurry, here goes."

She began talking about the new trends in the foreign

policy of the USSR; about the dynamism of the new Soviet leader; about the traditional Western suspicions of the Kremlin's intentions. I was listening—not to the words, but to the music in her voice. Yes, at that moment the receiver seemed to be playing magical music into my ear.

For one thing, she had not told me to go jump in the lake. Second, there was hope for a continuation of the contact. Third, I had only been on the phone a couple of minutes. Even if I had been tailed to the lingerie department, there was simply not enough time for the FBI to find out to whom I was talking.

I thanked her profusely, promised to take her to lunch for her invaluable contribution, hung up the receiver, and in excellent spirits walked to the garage.

I tuned in my favorite radio station, and vigorously stepped on the gas. I sped down an empty 14th Street, turned onto Shirley Highway, and headed home.

The warm lights of the city at night sped past the car window. The Americans were resting after a tough day. The air was pleasant and fresh. The ubiquitous Impala was right behind me, as periodic looks in the rear-view mirror confirmed.

My God, just think of the gulf separating us, I thought of the agents on my tail. But what's to be done when no one wants to surrender?

I had nothing against Americans. As a matter of fact, I liked them a lot. Unlike other Soviet citizens on their first visit to the U.S., I was not stupefied at the sight of American supermarkets, cars, or even the luxuries occasionally displayed for public viewing. I came to America psychologically steeled for the onslaught of its material abundance. But what really impressed me was the Americans' affability, their readiness to help, their willingness to forgive and forget. Moreover, those traits were not feigned or fanned by propaganda; they seemed to come naturally.

I was also deeply impressed by American patriotism, coming from the wellsprings of the soul, not imposed from above. The powers that be did not try to force the citizenry to love their country and treat the national symbols with respect. I was profoundly moved to see the national flag displayed at many American homes—a custom unimaginable in the Soviet Union.

"Daddy, why do Americans love their country so much?" my four-year-old son asked me one day.

"Because they have built this country for themselves," I replied, much surprised that even a small child could discern American patriotism.

"Who are we building the Soviet Union for?"

I wished I knew.

The FBI Impala saw my Chevy to the very door of my home.

The next day, after some hesitation, I decided to report my new contact, and set out for the residency. I had to obtain permission for a clandestine meeting with Phyllis.

As I approached the Soviet Embassy, I saw the wife of Soviet dissident Anatoly Shcharansky sitting on the sidewalk opposite the building. He had been sentenced to ten years in jail on a charge trumped up by the KGB of passing secret information to the CIA, and she had been on a hunger strike for several days, trying to force the Soviet authorities to set him free. On one occasion, the resident, enraged by Mrs. Shcharansky's perseverance, had promised a promotion to any subordinate of his who could figure out how to remove her from the vicinity of the embassy. But no one in the residency showed excessive zeal in the matter. Indeed, what could they have come up with?

Idiots, I thought irately. They should have let Shcharansky go long ago, putting an end to all the fuss surrounding his name. Why do they always create problems that we have to overcome—and then boast of our "successes" doing it?

After dawdling a few minutes outside the resident's office, I finally screwed up enough courage, softly knocked on the door, and entered. Androsov agreed without much enthusiasm to hear me out.

I related my telephone conversation with Phyllis Barber and noted the salient points. As a journalist she could be expected to have access to valuable information about U.S. policies in Western Europe. Besides, it was unlikely that the FBI had had time to trace my call, opening up the prospect of developing my contact with her on a clandestine basis.

I was in pursuit of the acme of intelligence achievement, an undercover agent. An undercover agent is a foreigner consciously cooperating with Soviet intelligence and willingly performing its assignments. Working with an undercover agent involves, among other things, a purely technical difficulty: right from the start, all contacts have to be covert. A single overt encounter of an operative with a prospect is the death knell to all dreams of recruiting him. The higher-ups would never approve him as an agent for fear that the encounter might have been spotted by the opposition's counterintelligence.

As for Phyllis, I thought that my contact with her had been sufficiently discreet—an extremely important consideration for me because a failure would cost me at least my career.

I concluded my presentation and I glanced at the resident expectantly. Androsov was looking at a point somewhere above my head, a subtle, ironic smile playing on his lips. His transparent eyes were expressionless. He seemed to be thinking of other, loftier things. But that was not the case.

"Do you have any idea how complicated the present situation in the U.S. is?" he started slowly.

"Yes, I do," I replied.

"And . . . ?"

"And what?"

"What do you mean, 'And what?'" the resident asked in astonishment, the smile slowly vanishing from his face. "The country is in the grip of anti-Soviet fever. Soviet representatives are being castigated all over the place. And yet, in spite of the circumstances, you dare raise the possibility of developing contacts with a foreigner—and covert contacts at that!"

"Do you mean to say that Moscow has relieved us of the duty to look for promising recruitment targets?" I asked in amazement.

"No, it has not. But you must be realistic. Or maybe you want us all to be kicked out of this country?"

The resident was clearly disgusted with me. My question went right to the core of the discrepancy between word and deed. The intelligence brass was unanimous in its loud demands for a strenuous recruitment effort, but as soon as some real action was required, they would invariably find a thousand excuses for nipping it in the bud.

"I just didn't see my primary task as clinging to my chair here as long as possible without even trying to score," I said bluntly, and saw immediately that I had just made a serious error.

Androsov stiffened, and when he spoke, his voice had a hard edge to it: "All of us want to obtain results, but there is a definite difference between reasonable risk-taking and rashness. From where I sit, you are lacking in operative experience. Why didn't you prepare for this dangerous operation in the prescribed manner? Why didn't you report your plan to me in good time? Why, contrary to instructions, did you fail to check out the countersurveillance route for a few hours? How do you know that the American special services were not eavesdropping on your telephone call? What guarantee is there that the subsequent development of Phyllis Barber will not proceed under their control, with all that that implies?"

"I don't know that, but in our business you never know for sure," I said, understanding full well that I was inviting trouble. "If you wait only for the sure thing, then what's the point of keeping our mammoth residency?"

"You will lie on the bottom like a submarine and stay there for two months—and that's an order," the resident said very softly. "No cables to Moscow regarding that telephone call to Phyllis Barber. You really have the nerve to think you are the smartest guy around. We've had a collection of her articles for several years, but no one has even thought of establishing contact with her. Do you know why?"

I screwed my face into a grimace of quizzical naïveté.

"Very simple. Because it is clear as day that a journalist of her caliber will never agree to cooperate with us," Androsov said confidently. "It takes some experience to understand things of that nature. You ought to come to the residency more often, peruse the press, draft proposals on the most promising operations against the U.S. We must prepare ourselves for the coming battles."

"Yes, sir," I said and retreated from the battlefield.

"Well, how did it go, Comrade Lewis?" a colleague asked me with a smile, nodding toward the office I had just left.

On Androsov's orders, only code names were to be used within the confines of the residency. He was terrified by the harrowing prospect that, in spite of all our elaborate precautions, the Americans with their unbelievable technology would somehow contrive to bug the residency. That's how we got Comrade Devil, Comrade Dart, and a bunch of other comrades with wondrous names. The colleague who had just spoken to me was Comrade Bright. I was Comrade Lewis, just by chance.

"It's hopeless," I held up my hands in surrender. "He is still convinced that prior to an operation one has to ride in a car for several hours in order to check out a tail. And that, even after the defection of Yurchenko, who has certainly told the FBI about our standard operating procedures. Isn't it clear that the best way to operate now is to violate those procedures? Otherwise, the Americans would be able to foresee our actions several moves in advance."

"You think too much, Captain," Comrade Devil said with a laugh. "Why don't you take to heart our Golden Rule: if you are the boss, I am the fool; if I am the boss, you are the fool."

"And then this strange requirement that we report to the residency on a daily basis, whether for a purpose or not," I went on, warming to my subject. "If I were an FBI agent, it would take me three months, tops, to figure out which of the Soviet journalists is KGB. Indeed, can you imagine a clean journalist running to the embassy day in, day out? Once a month to attend a party meeting is reasonable, but that should be it. In the beginning, I spent all my time at the Tass bureau, establishing my cover, but now I am at the embassy nearly every night. What business would a journalist have to run here every night?

"We ought to prepare ourselves for the coming battles," I mocked the resident. "What a strategic coup! A lion getting ready to pounce. But let me assure you he will die of old age before getting around to pouncing."

"Here is my advice: take a sedative and a laxative at the same time," Comrade Dart said. "A great combination to soothe the jagged nerve ends. Tomorrow is a weekend, a good time to let your hair down. You journalists are free, you lucky bastards. But what about us diplomats, seeing that an anti-alcoholism campaign is in full swing? We have to live in the embassy compound, under close supervision: the resident, the party committee. Furthermore, we have to ride the chairs in the residency from nine to five every day. And mind you, we must appear here on a daily basis, not to report our successes; the boss just wants to make sure that his subordinates have not yet defected to the Americans. In the present circumstances, I think he would prefer it if we just moved in here."

It became clear that my ordeal would meet with less sympathy here than I had thought, and so I headed for the Tass bureau.

* * *

A dreary, monotonous routine set in. Every morning I performed the official duties of a Tass correspondent: going to briefings, attending press conferences, writing copy for the Tass wire and memos for Soviet officials. This occupied much of my time but brought no fulfillment. A particularly galling part of the job was preparation of material for the Soviet press, an exercise in propaganda rather than journalism.

After lunch, I had to report to the residency, an even more onerous and useless duty than my cover job. Leaving the Tass bureau, I often noticed the wide-eyed stares of my clean colleagues, who had evidently figured out my true occupation. They obviously thought that, as soon as the door shut behind my back, I stepped into a mysterious world of romantic adventure. If only they knew how mundane and dull that world really was.

Take, for instance, the process of manufacturing certain kinds of informational messages that the Washington residency sent to the KGB center in Moscow. Pride of place clearly belonged to the "responses" to Mikhail Gorbachev's peace initiatives. The embassy usually learned of such initiatives via Tass before they were ever made known to the Americans, but that little detail in no way prevented the residency from immediately informing Moscow of the enthusiastic response of American public opinion. According to the rules, the response to any of the general secretary's numerous initiatives was to arrive the very next day and be overwhelmingly favorable. Who cared that very few people in America had any idea of yet another peace overture, and that those who did generally paid little attention to them? The cables sent by the residency painted an altogether different picture: all Americans of goodwill gratefully hail the peace-loving policies of the Soviet Union, which are rejected only by a handful of reactionary politicians and Wall Street plutocrats.

Everybody realized that such a farce only served to mislead Gorbachev, but kept their mouths shut and went on about their duties. I watched those merry games, but not once took part in composing a response to Gorbachev's initiatives that at that time aimed solely at a propaganda effect. I bided my time, waiting for a convenient occasion to meet Phyllis.

Early one morning, I came to the residency to find only the night watch officer, Comrade Dart (known among his friends simply as Tolian). He was in inordinately high spirits and immediately told me the reason: Yurchenko was back! The circumstances of his return to the fold seemed simply unreal. The previous day, which was a Sunday, Yurchenko had dined with a CIA officer at a Georgetown restaurant. On the pretext of going to the men's room, Yurchenko called the Soviet Embassy, declared that he was no traitor, and asked that the gate of the Soviet residential compound be left open for a couple of hours. Then he returned to the table, talked some more to his companion, again went "to the bathroom," and half an hour later turned up at the Soviet compound.

The return of the prodigal colonel convinced the residency operatives that he had indeed been abducted by the CIA in Rome several months ago, just as Yurchenko claimed. There has never been a single case of voluntary redefection in the history of the Soviet intelligence service. (There have been cases when they were brought back dead, but that's not exactly voluntary, is it?) Only an honest person could accomplish such an act, and the residency was beside itself with joy.

Chairman of the First Chief Directorate Kryuchkov sent a congratulatory cable, extolling Yurchenko's valor and applauding the residency's major success. In fact, the residency had had absolutely nothing to do with it. But Androsov saw no need to delve into such nuances. He was so overjoyed that he even offered Yurchenko a glass of wine when Yurchenko walked in, but the latter turned it down, "fearing the unpredictable effect of the drugs that the CIA has pumped into my body."

To exploit the propaganda success for all it was worth, a press conference was called in the Soviet compound, and the deputy resident permitted the operatives to invite their "prospective" contacts. I saw my chance. Androsov was completely absorbed in the fuss and bustle around Yurchenko, so I approached his deputy.

I had no trouble foreseeing his immediate reaction to my suggestion that Phyllis be invited to the press conference.

"How old is she?"

"I have no idea," I replied honestly.

"Is she pretty?"

"Haven't laid eyes on her yet."

"What do you need all the aggravation for?" the deputy resident asked me sympathetically. "Don't you know that all attempts to recruit women usually end up between the sheets, with all that that implies for the operative? Are you that keen on going home?"

I looked at the deputy resident with interest. He did not give the impression of being a ladies' man. Nor had he ever run female agents, as far as I knew. How come he is so certain about the inevitability of the amorous outcome? I thought in puzzlement.

The deputy resident read my mind and began reminiscing.

"At one time, an experienced intelligence operative, Vasily, worked in a European country. He made the acquaintance of a secretary from a NATO agency, and pretty soon started an affair with her. She fell madly in love with him, and once, in the throes of passion, asked her lover if she could be of any use to him. 'You know,' Vasily answered, 'my boss is killing me with demands for deep analytical material.' 'That's all? Don't worry, I'll bring some from my boss's safe,' the secretary exclaimed. True to her word, she began supplying him with extremely important documents. Vasily was awarded a medal and promoted ahead of schedule. He felt on top of the world. But sooner or later, any tour of duty comes to an end and one has to go back to Moscow. Upon returning home, Vasily failed to report his intimate relationship with the secretary. Of course, had he done so right from the start, he would have been put on the first plane bound for Moscow. That's why smart people keep their own counsel. Anyway, another operative, much older and far less virile than his predecessor, was sent as Vasily's replacement. He went to see the lady, she gave him the once-over and, without trying to hide her disappointment, asked: 'Couldn't your people come up with someone younger?' Thus the affair came to light. Vasily was stripped of his awards and packed off to the boondocks. And that was the end of it. So, in the final analysis, one is better off dealing with men."

"How do you propose to save our long-suffering operatives from the gays?" I asked.

"Cut it out, will you?" the deputy resident moaned.

"I hereby solemnly promise not to succumb to her charms as long as I am alive," I said very seriously, looking for all the world the epitome of an indomitable communist.

"Well, that's different," he finally surrendered. "All right, go ahead. But remember, if anything happens, it's not only your head, but mine, too."

I left the residency in high spirits and went to the garage on G Street where I kept my car. There, in a beautiful dead zone, was a pay phone I had spotted a couple of months back. I had ample reason to hope that the FBI would not eavesdrop on my call to Phyllis. They couldn't tap all the pay phones within my reach, could they?

Even though I had permission from the deputy resident, I had no intention of inviting Phyllis to the Soviet compound. That would definitely expose our connection. I had to arrange a meeting somewhere in the city.

"Where and when?" she replied laconically to my suggestion that we meet at dinner to discuss the Yurchenko story.

"How about tomorrow, seven P.M., at Le Jardin?" I suggested. "That's right by Dupont Circle."

"Excellent," said Phyllis. "See you tomorrow."

The next day I left home at 9:00 A.M. and got into my car. According to procedure, I was to run a three-hour route test. This was a laborious exercise intended to reveal and, if necessary, shake the tail prior to the meeting. Nearby I again saw the familiar Impala with a man behind the wheel whom I had seen many times before. I presumed that he was the one who was in charge of my case at the FBI.

The test seemed to me a hopeless loss of time, and I cursed bitterly the stupid procedure, the people who had devised it, and the bosses who insisted that it be followed to the letter. But I had little choice in the matter. *Faute de mieux, le roi couche avec sa femme* (If all other options are foreclosed, the king sleeps with his wife), said my inner self, and I turned the ignition key.

The test route started on Beauregard Street. The Impala followed about forty yards back. At the approach to Little River Turnpike, I noticed some major traffic congestion at the intersection and stepped on the gas. Breaking all rules of civility, my Chevy was winding its way among the cars in front of me. Some drivers expressed their displeasure by honking. The Impala fell back somewhat, a minor traffic jam formed between my car and the tail. At that moment, the traffic light changed to green, and the cars started moving. I managed to shoot across the intersection, running a red light and leaving the watcher behind. My car was bringing up the rear, with a lot of empty space behind. It looked as though I had lucked out and thrown off the tail.

If conditions had been different, I would never have done what I did. I knew full well that Soviet surveillance officers were punished severely for losing a subject, and I presumed that in similar cases FBI agents were not rewarded either. So in the absence of operational need, I usually slowed down to allow the tail to catch up with me. There was no point in playing Superman for no good reason, and spoiling relations with the competition in the bargain. But this time the situation was different; it was no longer a routine standoff, but active competition.

I turned into Shirley Highway, put the pedal to the floor, and looked into the rear-view mirror. The coast was clear. I had left the FBI Impala boxed in by other cars on all sides. Even if its driver had decided to run the red light, he would have been in no position to do so. I calculated that the tail was stuck for another two or three minutes, during which time I had to lose him once and for all.

I blended into the traffic flowing south, toward Richmond. Another two turns, and a quarter of an hour later I drove into the giant, citylike Springfield Plaza shopping mall. It had nearly a dozen entrances. I parked my car at the third one, and got out. The tail was still nowhere in sight. As I was walking toward the entrance, out of the corner of my eye I saw a parked Impala and my "godfather" emerging from it. A satisfied smile played on his lips.

I was not in the least discouraged; it was to be expected. A homing device, I thought. They have planted a homing device in my car. Well, what can I say? The boys certainly know their business. Formerly, I had merely assumed it, but now it was a certainty. How many times, running route tests in the remotest corners of Alexandria, I would see no cars on the road for an hour or two—and then out of nowhere my tail would suddenly appear.

I further assumed that my Chevy was fitted with a passive transmitter that remained mute at all times except when the car drove over an actuator embedded in the roadway. It was to be expected that the FBI installed such actuators at all key intersections within the radius of twenty-five miles of Washington where Soviet nationals were allowed to move about. This arrangement would allow the counterintelligence agents to monitor the movements of residency officers without leaving headquarters. In my mind I could vividly see a huge electronic board at FBI head-quarters with a colored light representing my car crawling across it. But now was no time for digressions. I had to beat a retreat, orderly if possible.

I cursed the stupid instructions yet again, went to the sporting goods section, and bought a fishing license, which was the only thing I could think to do to disguise my route test. As luck would have it, the Springfield Plaza mall was the closest place to my home where such licenses could be purchased. Then I got into my car and without further adventures drove to the Tass bureau.

Well, as Frank Sinatra used to sing, "I Did It My Way," I thought, picking up the *Washington Post* and going to the corner of the room where I was least visible to my co-workers. I looked at my watch: 11:25 A.M. There was still a lot of time until my meeting with Phyllis for me to collect my thoughts.

Seemingly engrossed in reading, I was actually devising various ways of throwing off the tail and planning the forth-coming conversation with Phyllis. According to instructions, at the first meeting the operative is expected to collect the maximum amount of personal data about the subject—background information, in operational terminology. This included the subject's age and place of birth, information about his or her relatives, friends, etc. All such data must be collected only during the first meeting; to do it subsequently is inappropriate.

Then I had to assess Phyllis's "intelligence potential," i.e., find out whether or not she had access to desired information. Finally, we had to set up our communication channels for the future, which was the most difficult part. Subsequently (provided, of course, there would be a "sub-sequently"), Phyllis was not to call me either at home or at the office, nor send me anything through the mail. Other-wise, the whole setup would have to be called off on the assumption that in all likelihood the asset would be com-promised.

If I try to do all these things, there will be no end to our meeting, I thought, and decided to play it by ear. As usual, I had to develop three alternative conversation plans to cover any contingency as events unfolded.

That day, time crept like a tortoise. I could hardly wait until my shift was over. On the stroke of 6:00 P.M., I left the Tass bureau unobtrusively. My first order of business was going to the bathroom, taking a small flask from my pocket, and thoroughly wiping my hands with rubbing alcohol.

At one time, the American press devoted a lot of ink to stories about a special compound that the KGB allegedly applied to the interior and steering wheel of any car belonging to U.S. Embassy personnel in Moscow. It was asserted that exposure to that compound turned a person into a "homing device" of sorts, whereby the places he visited and the people with whom he entered into physical contact (through a handshake for instance) could be identified. I had no idea whether the counterintelligence arm of the KGB had such a compound at its disposal, but there was always the possibility that the FBI did.

Having "purified" myself, I took the elevator to the lobby of the National Press Building with its numerous stores, and crossed to the other half of the building occupied by the Marriott Hotel. The Tass people never used that exit, and chances were the FBI did not monitor it on a permanent basis.

On Pennsylvania Avenue, I flagged a taxi (waving off the first cab that answered my call and taking the next one), and a quarter of an hour later disembarked at Dupont Circle, a short distance from the Le Jardin French restaurant. I walked the rest of the way and arrived at my destination ten minutes before the appointed hour, a sufficient amount of time to get my bearings and assess the situation on the ground.

The restaurant was quite cozy. The smallish room was illuminated by the rays of the soft autumn sun coming through the glass roof. Palm trees and lush tropical plants grew in the winter garden. Soft music was playing. Waiters moved about rapidly and noiselessly. A veritable idyll.

There were few patrons in evidence. I sat down at the bar, ordered orange juice, and, leisurely looking around, inspected the surroundings. Everything seemed to be proper. Then I proceeded to inspect the people entering the restaurant. Is there a tail or not? The persistent question was pounding in my temples. The clothes and manners of the patrons were of little concern to me; I watched their eyes. I knew from my studies at the Intelligence Academy that it was the eyes that always gave away the watchers.

It was already 7:14, but Phyllis was nowhere in sight. If the FBI had eavesdropped on the Tass office on a permanent basis, they must already have noticed my absence. The Chevy was still sitting in the garage, but the subject had vanished. Today my godfather is sure to get into hot water, I thought. It doesn't bode well. The FBI will definitely realize that I was off to some operation, so they are certain to clap a much closer surveillance on me from now on. And Phyllis is not coming. All that trouble for nothing?

Finally! It couldn't be anybody else. An elegant, middle-aged woman with auburn hair entered the restaurant and stopped in the doorway, looking around with her slightly slanting blue eyes.

"I bet you are Phyllis Barber," I said.

"And you are the Soviet correspondent," she replied in a businesslike manner.

"You mean you could read it in my face?" I smiled, right off the bat trying to steer the conversation into an informal channel.

"Exactly. Your eyes look into the future with utmost confidence," Phyllis said as if she were on *Crossfire*.

Boy, I thought, escorting my companion to our table. In keeping with the teachings of the Intelligence Academy, our table was in the farthest corner of the room. I took the seat facing the entrance so as to be able to monitor the people coming and going. The French menu was frightening in its exquisite murkiness, so I courteously allowed Phyllis to order for both of us. Besides, I did not want the waiter to know I was a Russian, and draw unnecessary attention to myself.

Our seafood was served, and I prepared to activate one of the conversation plans. There was no point to this meeting unless I was able to make Phyllis talk about herself. But her very first question took me aback.

"Tell me, have you ever noticed that you are followed?" she asked in a tone of voice that was almost stern.

My mind was racing. Is she a plant? Are they checking me out? I thought, trying to squeeze a semblance of a smile on my face. No, I don't think so. Doesn't look like it. Well, I've got to take the plunge.

I dug deep into my memory and came up with one of the lessons learned at the Intelligence Academy. In the life of any intelligence operative there comes a time when he has to step over the line that sets him apart from a clean journalist or diplomat, taught the old recruitment master. You can only rely on intuition to know if the moment is right. You yourself will have to decide whether or not you trust your interlocutor. No amount of background checking will do it for you.

My intuition told me now that I had to take the risk.

"A former *Washington Post* correspondent in Moscow wrote that, in preparing for meetings with his Soviet contacts, he always checked whether he was followed or not," I replied. "Do you think that Soviet journalists in the U.S. behave differently? Of course, I also run such checks. Otherwise I would have no sources of information, which would be absolutely disastrous for a journalist. So, don't worry, today I am clean as a whistle."

Judging by Phyllis's reaction, she was entirely satisfied by my answer. She began questioning me about Yurchenko's press conference. Our conversation turned into an interrogation of sorts, with Phyllis playing the part of interrogator. Her questions were raining down on me—precise, to the point, stinging. But they were not the typical questions of a Western journalist. Judging by their thrust, she was on a fishing expedition, looking for a chance to deliver yet another blow to the Reagan administration. Once I came to that conclusion, I threw my initial caution to the winds and proceeded to play up to her as best I could.

"Looks like I have enough stuff to write a good Yurchenko article," Phyllis said finally, her curiosity satisfied. "Do you like it here?"

"It depends," I replied evasively.

"I hate this administration," she went on, looking firmly into my eyes. "They imagine they have a license to do as they please."

"How do you stand up to them?" I asked innocently.

"It takes force and determination. These are the only things they respect."

My inner self whistled in amazement. I had never heard such pronouncements in America. The gambler in me woke up and began stirring in my bloodstream.

"Is there a politician who commands your respect?" I asked.

"Of course, there is," she replied with some surprise. "His name is Qaddafi."

"I beg your pardon?"

"You heard me right," Phyllis smiled. "Libyan leader Colonel Qaddafi."

If lightning had struck our table at that moment, I couldn't have been more stunned. Cool it, don't let it go to your head, my inner self cautioned.

Seafood had never seemed so delectable as that night. The conversation flowed fast and furious, like a mountain stream. Phyllis poured out such an avalanche of information I had difficulty digesting it all. I figured that the next day I would have to compose at least two—no, maybe even three cables to Moscow. Phyllis turned out to be a rabid anti-Semite as well as an enemy of American conservatives. Her credo seemed to follow a very simple formula: whatever is bad for the U.S. and Israel must be good. The doctrine of the Soviet intelligence service taught that such beliefs constituted solid grounds for recruitment on an ideological basis. Unless, of course, she was playing me for a sucker.

The smooth flow of my thoughts was interrupted by Phyllis's sudden suggestion:

"Would you mind seeing me home? We'll have a cup of coffee, talk some more . . ."

"Do you think your husband will approve?" I said, and belatedly sensed how stupid it sounded.

"Don't worry," she said confidently. "He will be glad to get to know you."

Things were taking a serious turn. I had to make a decision on the spot, and there was practically no time to think.

I do need the resident's permission for a meeting of this kind, particularly under such circumstances, I thought desperately, and Androsov's stern features floated up in my mind's eye. He is going to eat me alive. Still, I have to jump. There might never be another chance like this.

"Sure, let's go," I said. "Only please call the waiter. I don't want him to know that I am a foreigner."

Unlike Moscow, it takes merely a minute to get a cab in Washington.

"Bethesda," Phyllis told the driver and gave him the address. She turned out to be an experienced hand at covert matters and kept silent throughout the whole ride. Which was a welcome respite.

I hooded my eyes and assumed the air of a man enjoying momentary relaxation. In fact, however, my mind was feverishly churning. Having made the decision to go for broke, I still had to contend with the possibility of a provocation or a plant. I had to be constantly on the alert, ready to cut my losses and bail out at a moment's notice. Absent Androsov's permission, the responsibility was all mine. I understood full well that if anything happened, my field career would crash once and for all. Androsov would never pass up the chance to punish me with the utmost severity as an example to others lest they also dare play spy on their own. If I were the American government, I would award Androsov the Congressional Medal of Honor, I thought acidly. He has done more harm to Soviet intelligence than all the Western special services put together.

About twenty minutes later, we arrived at Phyllis's house, a small, two-story structure in Bethesda, Maryland.

The cab disappeared around the corner, its tires rustling on the fine gravel. I lingered uncertainly, glad that it was too dark for Phyllis to see the expression on my face. She went up the steps and knocked. The door opened immediately; a tall, bespectacled man dressed in exotic white clothes that looked like the Greek national garb stood in the doorway. He must have been waiting for us.

"Martin Snow," he introduced himself, motioning me into the house with a polite gesture. "Make yourself comfortable. What will you drink? I can offer you genuine Greek brandy, Metaxa."

"Thanks, but no thanks," I said. "I still have some work to do tonight."

"Coffee then," Phyllis said and went into the kitchen.

Martin followed her and I heard them conferring in whispers. I sat down in an armchair and looked around the house. A small foyer, a fireplace, the furniture is quite modest, my brain was registering the surroundings automatically. Looks like they don't have any money to burn. A large glass door opens onto a lawn. If push comes to shove, I could use it to get out into the street. The most important thing in such a case is to raise as much ruckus as possible. Special services hate noise. A large bookcase contained several volumes of Dostoyevsky and Chekhov in Russian. Lots of food for thought here, no question about it!

Martin poured coffee and began talking. His speech, initially soft and smooth, was growing in intensity, his pitch now soaring like a bird into the sky, now dropping like a stone. Each polished phrase was punctuated by sharp gestures. He sounded like a lecturer speaking before a select audience being initiated into the secrets of high politics.

"Mikhail Gorbachev runs the risk of making the biggest blunder in the history of Soviet foreign policy. He seems to agree with the Americans as to the need for predictability in bilateral relations. Unless it is a subtle ruse on his part, the Soviet Union is in for a very rude awakening. Predictability is a boon to the stronger party, and the United States, much to my regret, is the stronger party. You must have an ace in the hole. You will be respected only if the White House has a constant headache, trying to fathom what's up the sleeve of the Soviets."

He seems to dissociate himself from the Americans, I thought.

"Gorbachev's closest advisers are of a somewhat different opinion," I replied, sipping my coffee.

"Small wonder," Martin exclaimed. "Just look at them. Academician Arbatov? Ambassador Dobrynin? Why, they tell Gorbachev what Henry Kissinger prompts them to tell. It's a disaster. You don't need mutual trust. What you need is an exquisitely refined technique combining power methods and compromises offered for a price you will name. And don't behave like a credulous whore; don't you believe that if you give yourself to America, you will get handsomely paid. As soon as the Soviet Union ceases to be a bogeyman, the West will lose interest in it. So if you have to make concessions, demand to be paid in advance."

"Will America be willing to pay in advance?" I asked with interest.

"She won't have any other alternative," Martin assured me. "It's axiomatic: the worse the state of Soviet-American relations, the weaker is the administration's hand in domestic politics. That, and not Mr. Arbatov's touted trust, is your trump card."

"But where can we find better advisers?" I asked, wondering, Is it possible that he will respond: "I am prepared to become such an adviser"? Naah. Miracles don't happen.

"You'll find them if you look hard enough," Martin said ambiguously. "Go to Vitaly Yurchenko for help. As a matter of fact, if his adventures were planned by the KGB, congratulations: a devilishly clever operation. Phyllis is going to write a heck of an article about it."

"Aren't you afraid that some Americans may take offense at such an article?" I asked with an air of innocence.

"To hell with them!" Martin said decisively. "They think they can do anything they please. But they are sadly mistaken."

"You think so?" I smiled.

"Absolutely," Martin declared with authority. "The U.S. is a Roman Empire on the verge of collapse. It is a well-known fact that the rot sets in at the peak of glory and prosperity, then shades imperceptibly into all-out decay."

"Frankly, I don't see any signs of all-out decay," I went on, cautiously provoking Martin in the certainty that that was the best way of cracking open his inner world, so mysterious and surprising.

"You must be new to this country," he said condescendingly.

"Yes, I've been here just a few months," I said.

"That explains it."

Martin jumped up and, gesticulating violently, began initiating me into the secrets of a Washington political insider. He poured out names, positions, quotations, gossip, and rumor. Listening to him, I felt now in the State Department, now in Assistant Secretary of Defense Richard Perle's presence, now in Senator Jesse Helms's office, now in President Reagan's bedroom. The roller-coaster trip took my breath away. Martin seemed to know and detest everybody and everything in this country.

There are many ways of studying the person with whom one is talking. It is best, of course, if he talks about himself, but at the initial stage people rarely do that. Fortunately, though, Martin opened up instantly. He took great pleasure in characterizing—by and large, mordantly—some of the best-known politicians on the Washington scene. Pretty soon it became clear to me that, like his spouse, he was a dyed-in-the-wool, rabid Republican-hater, with particular animus toward the Reagan administration's Richard Perle, and some of the people in his circle.

Best of all, I didn't have to lift a finger to get information of such inestimable value. All I had to do was listen and show maximum eagerness. I also came to an important conclusion: Martin was sure that his pronouncements were the ultimate truth. There was no use in arguing with him. He had to believe that I was a kindred spirit.

Listen carefully and memorize, my inner self told me. Martin clearly is dying for an admiring audience. But, considering his views, there is little chance he will find it in America. So you'll become his audience, and he will be in your debt.

That finding was the centerpiece of my subsequent strategy to cultivate Martin as a prospective asset. I became his soul mate.

But was Martin sincere? Or maybe it was a case of make-believe? To answer that question, I had a well-honed technique. Listening to a person talk, I usually look thoughtfully "beyond the far horizon" as if weighing his words, living through what he is saying. And then, a sharp, fast look straight into his eyes, like the click of a camera. The resultant "snapshot" impression can disclose a lot about the interlocutor's true feelings. Using this method, I had more than once caught people lying.

Martin seemed to be sincere. My "snapshots" invariably registered his eyes burning with excitement, like those of a gambler or a fanatic. I felt that he derived genuine pleasure from listening to himself.

On that occasion, I was ready to listen to him all night long. But a persistent question was buzzing in my head: how would I explain my disappearance to the FBI guys and reassure them as to the innocent nature of my doings during my long absence? I still had time to cook up something. I looked at the clock and rose to my feet: it was time to go.

"Do you want me to give you a ride as far as Wisconsin Avenue?" Martin asked, obviously eager to continue his monologue in the car.

It was very kind of him to offer. A few minutes later, we reached our destination.

"I hope you will agree to help me out from time to time, if I need advice on strategic matters?" I asked with a smile on my face and a prayer in my heart.

"Of course I will," Martin said magnanimously.

"I'll be calling you from a pay phone. The Tass telephones are certainly tapped, and I would hate to put you in an embarrassing position."

"Much obliged for your concern," he said with the air of a man who has been around the block a few times.

In a few minutes, I was sitting in a cab bound for the National Press Building. I told the cabbie to stop at the Treasury Building, paid up, hurriedly crossed 15th Street, and entered the Washington Hotel. There was a pretty good bar on the first floor, and a few late customers still lingered inside.

I ordered a double gin martini, drained it, and came out into the corridor where I had spotted a bank of pay phones. I dialed the Tass number and asked to speak to Oleg Polyakovsky. I knew he had planned to burn the midnight oil at the office, working on a major article. He was my closest friend among the correspondents. Unlike many other clean journalists, Polyakovsky did not think that as a spy I was paid better than he was, and consequently he was not in the least jealous—a very rare and valuable trait in the Soviet colony.

"Oleg, could you give me a lift home tonight?" I asked, slurring my words.

"Sure, why? Anything happened?" I could clearly hear curiosity in his voice.

"The usual thing," I lied. "I went to Chinatown for dinner, drank a couple of Chinese beers. Great stuff. Drank some more. Went to another Chinese restaurant. Ate a lobster. Had a martini. Well, one thing led to another, you know how it is. I can barely stand on my feet. Can't drive in this condition, now can I?"

"Of course not." Polyakovsky laughed. "Where shall I pick you up?"

"I'm pretty close. At the bar of the Washington Hotel, across the street from our office. When can I expect you?"

"In about twenty minutes," he replied. "I'm putting the finishing touches on an article about the State Department briefing. As soon as I'm done, I'll come over."

While waiting for Polyakovsky, I ordered another martini and took a table in the corner to think about the day.

I had met an obviously unconventional couple, which was very good; conventional people are generally of no use for intelligence purposes. I wished that I had learned more about them. Well, there is always a next time. The amount of information I had collected was staggering anyway.

Martin and Phyllis's anti-Reaganism was so rabid as to border on the absurd. On the other hand, they seemed to be extremely well informed—Martin in particular. Considering that our network of agents in the U.S. had been all but destroyed, that couple could become a solid source. Indeed, it would be quite a feat if, with the network in ruins and the brass panic-stricken, I were to bag two new recruits, a well-known journalist and her husband. That would be some coup!

But how should I go about recruiting them? What would I bait my hook with? It appeared that I had to target Martin first. I had no idea about his background at this point, but he was clearly the leader of the duo. He behaved like a man whose feelings had been badly hurt by someone—so much so that he had ended up hating the whole of America. So who could that offending party be? Quite possibly, big politics was involved. Judging by Martin's pronouncements, politics was his life. In which case the blame for Martin's bruised ego could probably be laid at the door of a highly placed official or a group.

A picture began taking shape. Deeply wounded feelings are regarded as a good basis for recruitment. Unless, of course, he was playing a game . . . No, it just didn't look like he was playing a part . . . If Martin was indeed acting, the stage has lost a giant of an actor. He gets almost literally drunk on his own rhetoric. No one can pretend that artfully. Besides, Phyllis has an unbroken record of anti-American writings going back many years. Is it all a setup, an elaborate trap to ensnare a Soviet spy if an opportunity presents itself sometime in the future? Nonsense! Both of them surely looked like the real thing. Besides, they were not the ones who had initiated the contact, I was.

But what if the FBI gets wind of our connection? Well, I've done all I could, but there is no certainty. Nor can there be, ever.

So, here is what I'll do. My call to Polyakovsky will give the FBI a reasonably plausible explanation for my disappearance from the office: a drinking binge. Such things happen. I hope they will withdraw surveillance from me till my next meeting with Phyllis and Martin. On my part, I'll try to be on my best behavior.

It is very likely that Martin needs me for some purpose. Clearly, he asked Phyllis to bring me home. There is a good chance he will open up pretty soon; a little prodding should do the trick. I have two or three meetings to do the job, but not more. If the FBI spots our meetings, the frequent contacts will attract attention, which will amount to failure. We'll see what it will come to. As Martin said, "If you look for good advisers hard enough, you'll find them." Maybe that is the opener that will pry open this particular can.

I think I gave him a very transparent hint that he shouldn't call me. Let's see how Martin will behave, whether or not he will call—it will show much about his intentions.

My reflections were interrupted by the arrival of Oleg Polyakovsky, smiling like a full moon, his eyeglasses merrily reflecting the lights of the candles on the tables.

Vitaly Yurchenko was packed off to Moscow, and the hullabaloo at the residency died down somewhat. It was time for me to report on my meeting with Phyllis and Martin. Androsov's reaction to my news would be predictable, so I decided to go through his deputy.

He listened to my story with rapt attention, and when I was done gave a big sigh of relief.

"You are one lucky bastard, let me tell you. Somebody up there must be looking after you. Some of your predecessors got themselves into a terrible mess in similar circumstances . . ."

His predilection to reminiscences was common knowledge and I braced myself.

"Once, our operative in New York likewise decided to see his female contact home after a dinner engagement," the deputy resident began with a sly smile. "While they lingered at the door, saying goodbye, her husband looked out the window, saw them and called the police. The cops here are very fast on their feet, as you've probably noticed, and our Casanova escaped just in the nick of time."

Playing up to my superior, I engineered an expression of utter amazement. Gratified by my response, he went on: "Another time, the contact's husband simply rushed into the street and punched out our guy. The next day he turned up to report to the resident sporting a black eye and a fractured jaw."

"Seems you are right, I certainly was lucky," I said and

cautiously touched my jaw as if surprised to find that, for some unfathomable reason, it was still intact.

"Stop clowning." The deputy resident frowned. "How old is Phyllis?"

"About fifty."

"Pretty?"

"Definitely not to my taste."

He looked at me suspiciously, but all he saw was the thoroughly innocent gaze of a professional spy.

"All right," he growled. "Sit here and stay out of sight. I'll deal with the resident myself. It certainly seems to be serious business."

He was absent for about half an hour. When he returned, mischievous lights were flickering in his eyes.

"Well?" My impatience got the better of me.

"Okay," he said smugly. "You can draft a cable to Moscow."

"How did you manage to win him over?"

"Young man, you still have a lot to learn." The deputy resident sighed with feigned sorrow. "You probably thought that as soon as you reeled in a promising contact your superiors, beside themselves with joy, would slobber all over you and start racking their brains about how to recruit the contact, right? Wrong! The contact *per se* is irrelevant; what is important is whether or not he jibes with the specific interests of a specific boss."

"And in this case . . . ?"

"In this case, he does. It looks like your new acquaintances are no fly-by-nighters who might spell trouble."

"You know them?" I asked in surprise.

"I've heard a lot about them," the deputy resident said weightily. "The counselor of our embassy, Alexander Zotov, maintained contact with them. He is now ambassador to Syria. So as you see, they are high-level people. Understand?"

I nodded, just in case.

"But if this couple have long been known to the residency, why hasn't anyone tried to recruit them?" I asked.

"Nobody likes to waste time." The deputy resident chuckled. "There is practically no chance they will agree to cooperate with us. I've told you, these are high-level people. There is no way they'll play ball with us, and that's precisely what reassures the resident. You'll be lucky if they agree to meet with you once in a while. But that's fine; it'll give us something to report to Moscow."

Those were not the words I wanted to hear. Still, I was happy; at least I had permission to work with Martin and Phyllis. Whether or not they would agree to cooperate with the KGB depended entirely on me.

About a week later, Moscow responded to my cable in a top secret message coded to Resident Androsov.

Top secret

Washington, D.C.

To: Comrade Krotov

Martin Snow (hereinafter "Socrates") is known to us. He was raised on the East Coast of the United States and graduated from Harvard in the mid- to late 1960's where he stayed on as an instructor for a while. A Ph.D., he is a leading management expert.

In the Carter administration, Socrates was a White House advisor. Subsequently, he worked for a while as a UN consultant, at times advising various Asian governments.

While a member of the Carter administration, he maintained occasional contact with several Soviet diplomats who characterize Socrates as an informed and energetic person and an unorthodox thinker.

Socrates' wife, Phyllis Barber (hereinafter "Sputnitsa" [Russian for "female companion"]), is well known for her radicalism and anti-American views. She is a stringer for a number of U.S. and Western European periodicals.

70

We see merit in Comrade Lewis' pursuing further contacts with Socrates and Sputnitsa. At this stage, our primary objective is to find out what caused them to agree to contacts with a Soviet journalist.

You are hereby instructed to maintain maximum caution while dealing with Socrates and Sputnitsa and to keep us fully informed about all subsequent developments in the case.

For your information, Sputnitsa's article about the Yurchenko affair was published in an influential journal of opinion. Our active measures service rates it as one of the most useful pieces on the subject to appear in the Western media.

Moscow
Comrade Vasily

That same day, the deputy resident and I were summoned by Androsov.

"Your new contacts have elicited a certain amount of interest on the part of Moscow," Androsov said dryly, with a ghost of a smile on his colorless lips. "We'll go on working with them, but very gingerly. The most important thing is to find out what makes them tick. As far as I know, you have not been able to determine their motivation thus far. Well, it's all right, operative experience is accumulated over time . . . Unfortunately I'm too busy to take charge of the case personally, so you will be calling the shots," said the chief, switching his gaze to his deputy. "If I were you, I would concentrate on pumping Socrates about Pakistan, Sri Lanka, and Bangladesh. I think it will be quite useful. As for Sputnitsa, exercise maximum caution. She is too formidable a journalist to be trifled with."

"What a brilliant scheme!" the deputy resident exclaimed when we left Androsov's office. "What a fabulous intelligence operative is contained in his body! Just think about what he's just said. He has washed his hands of all responsibility for the Socrates and Sputnitsa case. He has also warned us to be cautious and suggested that we concentrate on Bangladesh, Sri Lanka, and Pakistan—in short, anything but the U.S. From now on, if anything happens, the only guilty parties will be I and you—or rather, you and I. Frankly, under such conditions I don't see much percentage in taking up this case."

"Sometimes," I exploded, "I get the impression that our main enemy is not the American special services, but this communist worthy, this precious chief of ours."

"Listen, I've been planning to talk to you for some time." The deputy resident pulled me into his tiny office and shut the door tightly. "You should watch your mouth. God forbid, someone will rat to the resident, and you'll be done for. As a matter of fact he has already told me you are too independent and he doesn't like it one bit. Don't you know the score?"

I knew the score, it's just that I couldn't help myself. Sometimes, emotions boil over without asking permission; nothing can stop them, even the self-preservation instinct. No spy can live indefinitely with his true feelings bottled up tightly inside him. Sooner or later, he experiences an irresistible impulse to let it all out—if only to keep his sanity.

"Lately," I said, "I've had this persistent feeling that the main threat to our country does not come from external forces, be it America, NATO, China, or whatever; our main enemy is us. Do you remember Nikolai Gogol's dictum that Russia's two biggest problems are idiots and bad roads? Looks like the former problem has been going from bad to worse lately."

Judging by the expression on the deputy resident's face, he wished he had not started the conversation. He made a wry grimace and asked me sternly, as if pouring cold water on an overheated furnace: "Aren't you afraid to tell me all these things?"

"Not at all," I replied. "I know you are a decent person."

Just as I had expected, the deputy resident was disarmed.

My characterization of him as a decent person deeply moved him, even though "decency" was not the most popular word with the intelligence crowd.

"Thanks for placing your trust in me," he muttered in embarrassment. "Still, you are an intelligence officer and must control your emotions."

Each idea must ripen. It takes time. I had to pause in my designs for Socrates and Sputnitsa so as to lull the FBI into a false sense of security and not to frighten the prospects by being overly obtrusive.

For the next three weeks, I behaved as an exemplary newsman: working exclusively in my cover job; no countersurveillance maneuvers; no search for covert rendezvous venues, dead drops, or other spying razzle-dazzle. I even had to write an analytical report to Tass on the U.S. Strategic Defense Initiative.

In my report, I tried to prove that the "Star Wars" program was a strategic bluff aimed at intimidating the Soviet leadership, getting the USSR involved in a new, prohibitively expensive round of the arms race, and, in the final analysis, breaking the back of its economy. And the more ferociously the Soviet propaganda machine cried from the rooftops about the sinister threat of SDI to the whole world, the more incentive the Reagan administration would have to carry on.

I did not base that conclusion on stolen Pentagon papers, but rather on some articles in the American press. And that was its fatal weakness. The Soviet leaders were accustomed to trusting only classified documents kept under lock and key. I spent a long time racking my brains about how to convince our officials that I was right. Finally, help arrived from an unexpected quarter: Congressman Bob Dornan, an unabashed fan of the Star Wars program.

Once I had gone to Georgetown University to attend a crossfire-style debate starring Richard Perle and a Washington religious leader. The cleric had done a brilliant demolition job on SDI, and I could see Perle squirming.

Then Bob Dornan came to the rescue. He said something to this effect: "Ladies and gentlemen, SDI may not exist yet, but it is already working. Just read the Soviet papers. The Russians are frantic; they are afraid of SDI. Which means that it has already achieved its objective. Hence, it would be folly to cut SDI spending; on the contrary, it should be increased."

That was exactly the missing link I needed. Representative Dornan had brilliantly illustrated the main idea of my report. Of course, I had to lie and say that his speech had come at a closed hearing in Congress, but what could I do if Soviet officials believed only what was kept secret from them?

I concluded my report by suggesting that the Soviet press should refrain from attacking SDI and henceforth just ignore it. I was pretty certain that once that happened, Star Wars would go into a tailspin.

To my surprise, my report created something of a stir among the Tass insiders. As for the residency, all my previous attempts to write a cable on the subject had met with the resident's lack of appreciation—to put it mildly. Chief of the KGB Intelligence Service Kryuchkov had given an order to wage an all-out campaign against the SDI, and Resident Androsov was zealously doing his master's bidding. A curious situation arose: rather than giving Moscow facts, the residency was feeding it what Moscow wanted to hear.

And here is what Moscow wanted to hear. With Kryuchkov at the helm, the intelligence service developed a new program called "Sudden Nuclear Missile Attack Against the USSR" (VRYAN—Vnezapnoye Raketnoye Yadernoye Napadeniye, literally: Surprise Nuclear Missile Attack) and assigned it utmost priority. The aging Politburo, in the throes of progressive senility, lived in constant fear of the "growing aggressiveness of American imperialism."

In keeping with that program, the Washington residency was ordered to be on constant lookout for any signs of VRYAN and immediately report the same to Moscow, which prepared a daily operational briefing book for the supreme leadership of the country.

In practical terms, the anti-VRYAN vigilance took the following form. At nightfall, KGB operatives would spread out to make the rounds of the relevant government agencies, take stock of the number of windows lit after formal close of business, count the cars on the parking lots nearby, and examine the contents of local newspapers, looking for signs of a secret draft or a secret scheme to replenish the strategic materials and food stocks.

Those activities took prodigious amounts of time and energy with negligible effect. And here President Reagan comes with the SDI! As far as the leaders of the KGB intelligence service were concerned, this program jibed beautifully with the VRYAN concept, and could not have come at a more opportune time. There was no longer any need to peek into windows, count cars, and cut facts out of whole cloth.

While pondering the SDI issue, I did not neglect less weighty business. Never in my life had I lunched with so many numbingly boring individuals, but I needed them as a smokescreen for my contact with Socrates and Sputnitsa. During the weekends, I took my family shopping, as befitted an exemplary Soviet citizen. Then I would steam crabs and watch TV.

On the eleventh day, the Impala vanished.

Its disappearance could imply one of two things: either the FBI had decided that I constituted no threat to the U.S. national security and was not worth watching any longer, or, on the contrary, the sleuths had gotten suspicious and switched from overt to covert surveillance. The FBI could assign to me hundreds of watchers, scores of cars or even helicopters, if they wanted. There was no way humanly possible to identify and throw off such an armada. In practice, as often as not the problem has to be solved by relying on intuition alone. Outwardly, there were no signs of surveillance, but in reality—who knows? Appearances are deceptive.

While I was preparing for the next rendezvous with Socrates and Sputnitsa, they left on Christmas vacation, and sometime later I was astonished to learn that I was being recalled home for a vacation.

"Of course, winter is not the best vacation time in Moscow," the resident said with a silky smile. "But we cannot allow all our officers to go on vacation in summer, now can we? Some people will just have to reconcile themselves to R&R under less auspicious conditions."

"It means my son will miss more than a month of school," I mumbled in annoyance.

"Well, he'll just have to make it up," Androsov said with a grimace that immediately made me feel guilty for bothering the great man with such trifling matters.

The trip from Washington to Moscow at that time was particularly long and onerous. After a Soviet fighter had shot down the South Korean KAL 007 airliner over Sakhalin, the United States had banned all Aeroflot flights to the U.S., and Soviet travelers had to fly to Montreal via an American or Canadian carrier to board a Moscow-bound Aeroflot IL-62. For the passengers, it was tiresome; for the Soviet government, expensive. Aeroflot tickets were bought for rubles, but dollars had to be expended on the first leg of the journey. Under the rules, the government covered that expense. The sum was not extravagant, but still we were talking about precious hard currency.

But I was lucky—and so was my government. A Soviet airliner flew into Washington by special permission to pick up former Soviet Ambassador to the U.S. Anatoly Dobrynin. Sometime previously, he had been appointed to the exalted position of secretary of the Communist Party Central Committee to supervise the Kremlin's entire foreign policy domain, and the Soviet colony was swept by a rumor that Comrade Dobrynin would allow all his compatriots going home on vacation to come along.

"You are in luck," the Tass bureau chief's wife told me. "People at the embassy are making up a list of those who will take the special flight. So hurry up."

One of my characteristic features is profound skepticism as regards the potential for altruistic outbursts on the part of Soviet officials. That time, too, I muttered something about my doubts as to the feasibility of such a plan.

"Are you kidding?" the Tass bureau chief's wife exclaimed. "I can't imagine that Dobrynin would leave his compatriots stranded. After all, he is a Soviet ambassador!"

In spite of her advanced age, that nice woman had managed to preserve her belief in the basic goodness of man. As expected, she was once again cruelly disappointed. A couple of days before his departure, Comrade Dobrynin, without going into detail, informed his compatriots that he would not be able to let them accompany him.

The Tass bureau chief's wife was shaken to the core when I told her about it. But the next day, she approached me, with guilt unaccountably written all over her, and said in her gentle voice: "I've thought long and hard about the reason for Dobrynin's conduct and come up with just one credible explanation: he is afraid of a terrorist attack on his plane and is leery of putting other people in harm's way. After all, there are many children among those who planned to fly on board his plane."

I nodded agreement, because I did not want to disappoint the kindly old woman by telling her about the real motivation of the outgoing Soviet ambassador. It was already widely known in the residency that Dobrynin's plane would be chock-full of his personal belongings, the fruits of many years' labors in the U.S. Still, there were some vacancies left on the plane, but Comrade Dobrynin was in no mood to invite unnecessary witnesses to his material well-being.

The Soviet colony was quietly indignant. But I didn't care. I was mentally preparing for the coming debriefing with the chief of the North American Department.

3

A DEBRIEFING by General Yakushkin, chief of the North American Department of the KGB intelligence service, which invariably marked the onset of a residency operative's Moscow vacation, was the toughest imaginable ordeal for the overwhelming majority of intelligence officers. The redoubtable general was extremely demanding and never pulled his punches. Yakushkin's angry tirade was often capped with his favorite punch line, "You do not deserve your epaulets," whereupon the victim, pale and glassy-eyed, would stagger out of the office and go off to a well-earned vacation. Some of the more stout-hearted cynically joked about the debriefing session: "Ten minutes of shame—but the tour of duty still goes on."

By and large, Yakushkin had every reason to be angry. Very few of the residency officers lived up to his expectations. But he did not or would not understand that his demands ran exactly counter to the policy pursued by Resident Androsov. In Kryuchkov's intelligence service, writing skills—filing good reports—were valued more highly than the ability to recruit agents.

With some trepidation, I opened one door, then the other, and found myself in the chief's office. Yakushkin, his face impassive, was pacing back and forth along a traditionally red, narrow runner that looked very much like a landing strip. It was the only route suited for the general's indoor walking exercise, because on either side of the runner the cracked hardwood floor responded to the slightest touch with an ear-splitting creak.

The chief shook my hand warmly and with a nod bade me to take the armchair, whereupon he resumed his exercise, so that I had to twist my head from side to side in order to face the boss at all times.

"Well, the first year of your posting is almost up," the general said in an offhand manner. "Describe to me your feelings. Was everything the way you had expected, or were there any surprises?"

"I have mixed feelings. As for surprises, unfortunately there were too many of them," I said, trying unsuccessfully to catch the general's eye.

"What was it that surprised you most of all?"

"The gulf between what I had been exhorted to do here and the resident's policies."

"I see." Yakushkin frowned. "Unfortunately, it has been increasingly difficult to fight this trend. Last week, I attended a strategy meeting at the African Department called to discuss how to get their residencies more closely involved in the anti-American effort. As usual, there were torrents of eloquence, then all of a sudden one resident piped up, 'Yakushkin has three residencies in the U.S. Let them deal with Americans, our hands are full as it is.' He was roundly booed—not because the others thought that he said a foolish thing, but because he had carelessly expressed in public the viewpoint shared by most of our residents. They're scared to death of the Americans!"

The head of the department had never been that frank with me. Careful, my inner voice warned me.

"Recently, I heard an interesting story," Yakushkin went on. "After the treason by our operative Bogaty in Morocco, the local resident forbade outright all contacts with Americans. And if any of the young officers had the temerity to make the acquaintance of a U.S. Embassy staffer and report it, he was immediately marked as a CIA recruitment target to be shipped home under some suitable pretext at the earliest opportunity. It's easier to spy against the Central African Empire than against the U.S., no question about it. Although even there spying is not without some occupational hazards; one always runs the risk of being roasted and eaten by the locals. Still, the way some of our residents see it, it's less of a hazard than going toe-to-toe with Americans."

I watched the general in amazement. He was angry, but also perplexed and listless—qualities he had never exhibited before. He intercepted my look and collected himself as if waking up from a nightmare.

"What are your plans for Socrates and Sputnitsa?"

So the introduction is over, I thought and prepared for a long and substantive discussion.

"I've just had one meeting with them, so far-reaching conclusions would be premature," I observed cautiously. "But they seem to be excellent recruitment material."

"I don't know," Yakushkin said thoughtfully. "Socrates is a pretty big fish. He is described as an extremely intelligent and very complex man. I'm afraid he will be difficult to deal with."

"Why?"

"He is rather strange."

"We should welcome unorthodox behavior," I observed. "Ordinary people, unfortunately, are of severely limited utility as far as we are concerned."

"Impeccable logic." The general gave me a tired smile.

"Let's hope he'll play ball with you. I wish you had worked some more at the center; what you need is more experience. But who knows, maybe you are the better for it . . . A few years' experience here is likely to turn an operative into an outright cynic."

I was growing increasingly puzzled. I looked at the general and listened to him—and couldn't believe the evidence of my eyes and ears. Where was the resolute, tough, and supremely self-assured boss I had known and respected? He seemed to be mechanically going through the motions of doing his duty while his mind was wandering elsewhere.

"Well, have a good vacation. I wish you the best of luck. You don't look like a man who needs much prodding."

Yakushkin listlessly waved goodbye and sat down heavily behind his desk. I was dumbfounded. Never in my wildest dreams could I have imagined this kind of debriefing.

Usually, operatives are glad to be ignored by their superiors. I too should have been glad to have avoided the traditional tongue-lashing. Oddly, instead of jubilation I had a premonition of danger.

As I emerged from the office, Grandma Lida eyed me suspiciously. She was still the queen of Yakushkin's waiting room.

"What? No bloodletting?" she asked, and I could clearly hear notes of bewilderment and even some regret in her voice.

"I'll be right back. I brought American cigarettes for your husband," I said hurriedly.

My words had a magic effect: the frozen soul of the "devil in a skirt" suddenly thawed out and her face broke into an unexpectedly tender smile. Just two years before, she had finally managed to catch herself a husband, and she had lived ever since in constant fear that her spouse would realize what a bad mistake he had made. So the short-cut—indeed, the only way—to our secretary's heart ran through an intersection piled with gifts for her dearly beloved.

"The general seems kind of funny," I remarked, embold-
ened by Grandma Lida's positive reaction.

"He is about to be pensioned off." She frowned.

"Pension him off? What has he done?"

"None of your business," she said gruffly.

"And where is Valentin Aksilenko, the chief of our Washington Section?" I asked, ignoring Grandma Lida's habitual
rudeness.

"He is no longer with us."

"No longer with us?"

"Have you forgotten your Russian in Washington?"
snarled the secretary. She reverted to type and was again her
usual, somewhat acerbic self. "I've told you clearly, he
doesn't work here anymore."

"Where can I find him?"

"I don't know. Get out of here, I've got work to do. If you
want to find out all the latest gossip, go to the canteen."

I walked through the North American Department,
which consisted of four major sections: Washington, New
York, San Francisco, and Canada. They supervised and controlled the operations of the corresponding KGB residencies. I tried one door of the Washington section, but it was
closed; so was the other one. It was lunchtime, and everybody was off to indulge in gluttony. I had little choice but to
follow Grandma Lida's advice.

The canteen was the center of social life, frequented on a
regular basis mostly by younger officers. Here they drank
coffee, smoked, discussed the latest events, and gossiped.
Two or three pretty secretaries from the auxiliary divisions
of the intelligence service were always on hand. They flirted
with the "knights of the cloak and dagger," but in general,
beautiful women were few and far between in the intelligence service, because the personnel department was leery
of hiring pretty faces for fear of stirring up the young officers' natural instincts.

There was no tea in the canteen that day, and I had to make do with a badly watered-down Pepsi; catering personnel at the intelligence service engaged in thievery as brazenly as their counterparts in any other agency.

I found a vacant table and proceeded to ponder the dreary situation, slowly sipping my drink. The departures of General Yakushkin and Colonel Aksilenko boded ill for the North American Department. Among my many superiors, they were the only true pros. As long as they were aboard, I could still hope to fend off Androsov; but with them gone, I was a lone traveler aimlessly wandering in the desert without a compass or a map. All hope of recruiting an agent turned into an impossible dream, and employment with the intelligence service seemed to be a senseless pastime. It is only in fiction that a lone man can take on the whole world. In the Soviet intelligence service, you could go out and fight only if the center backed you up. But with Yakushkin and Aksilenko gone, nobody in the North American Department cared one bit about the recruitment of agents in Washington.

"Hi, old man, haven't seen you for ages."

I started, and immediately found myself in the bear hug of Peter, an old friend with whom I went back all the way to college. Peter was a man of enormous stature and an unbounded optimism. His gregariousness was nothing short of miraculous. After graduating from the Intelligence Academy, he had landed at the Internal Counterintelligence Department of the First Chief Directorate. And though political intelligence officers gave as much berth as they could to the representatives of that infamous division, I was still very fond of Peter. He was still the same fellow.

"Well, how are you doing in Washington? Have you managed to penetrate the Pentagon or the CIA?" he asked with a wide grin.

"Only as far as the parking lot," I replied equally facetiously.

"You'd better hurry up. Time is short."

"I figure we still have two or three years to go," I said.

"Who knows?" Peter remarked in an uncharacteristically serious tone of voice.

"What's this—another joke?" I pricked up my ears.

"Unfortunately, I don't feel like joking anymore. Looks like our field operations are over."

"Listen, Peter, my head is swimming as it is. What are you talking about?"

"All right," he agreed. "But on one condition: what I am going to tell you will stay between you and me. Nobody at the residency—or the North American Department for that matter—is in the know."

"About what?"

"Colonel Yurchenko, Yakushkin's ex-deputy, has broken down and confessed," he whispered and looked cautiously around him.

"Confessed to what?"

"That he came to the U.S. Embassy in Rome of his own accord and volunteered his services to the CIA," Peter rapped out, looking at me enigmatically.

"Oh, no, anything but this," I all but howled. "How do you know it's true?"

"Yurchenko himself told us," Peter assured me. "When he returned to Moscow, our guys began interrogating him, and he spilled his guts in short order. As a matter of fact there was no point for him to try to hide anything; the case against him was too strong."

"Incredible! How could a man in his position take such a step?"

"In cases of this nature the giants of world literature counsel: 'cherchez la femme,'—'look for the woman,' and they are absolutely right, you know," Peter answered with the air of a connoisseur. "For many years, Yurchenko had carried on a torrid affair with the wife of a highly placed Soviet diplomat. Conventional divorce was out of the question; it would inevitably have ruined Yurchenko's career, and his lady was used to affluence. So one day she goes with her husband to his next posting, which happens to be Canada. Yurchenko rolls the dice and defects to the Americans. He tells them everything he knows and gets his reward, a cool million bucks and a decent pension. The CIA people take him to Canada, arrange for him to meet his beloved. 'I have one million dollars,' Yurchenko says. 'Let's go to America together and live happily ever after.' And then the unexpected happens: the lady flies into a panic and says no. Yurchenko is devastated. He realizes that he has nothing to lose, gives his CIA minders the slip, and voluntarily returns to his homeland."

"To say I am surprised would be an understatement; I am stunned," I observed. "What had he hoped for? One would think he should have had no illusions about the kind of reception that would be awaiting him."

"Hold on to your hat." Peter smiled. "What I am going to tell you will blow you away. Either Yurchenko is smart as the devil himself, or he is the luckiest bastard alive, but the fact is that he is in no danger. Moreover, he will be an intelligence officer until retirement. True, he will have no duties, but an office, a clean desk, and a regular paycheck will be his for the taking. Come to think of it, it does seem to be an act of sophisticated sadism to grant him his life and let him face his conscience."

I couldn't refrain from a small dose of sarcasm.

"Please spare me the term 'sophisticated.' I am no longer a callow rookie, and I've long since lost all belief in our superiors' finesse. I'm quite sure that Kryuchkov had a very down-to-earth reason for such an extraordinary decision."

"I can't fool you spies, now can I?" Peter said with a grin. "You are right, of course. Kryuchkov ordered us to keep Yurchenko's case under wraps, bury his confession as a supreme secret, and officially confirm the story of his abduction by the CIA."

Peter gulped some Pepsi from my glass, lit a cigarette, and dashingly exhaled three impeccable smoke rings.

"The recent spate of defections of our intelligence officers has impaled Kryuchkov on the horns of a very tough dilemma: how to explain to the Politburo this phenomenon and not lose his head. He was able to ascribe the defections of junior officers to negligence on the part of the personnel department; the explanation was accepted. Then came the defections of the heavy hitters: Colonel Gordievsky and Colonel Piguzov, no less! Kryuchkov reported that they had cracked under constant stress—and again was able to get away with it. And then, the crowning indignity—Yurchenko defects—and not merely defects, but, much worse, comes back and confesses his sins. Yurchenko, who used to be Kryuchkov's fair-haired boy and one of the best informed men in the entire intelligence service . . . !"

"Wait a second," I interrupted Peter's tirade, feeling giddy. "What does Colonel Piguzov have to do with it?"

"Where have you been, on the moon? Piguzov has been exposed as a veteran CIA agent!"

I stared at Peter in stunned silence.

"Boy, you should have heard the uproar," he went on. "The head of the Communist Party organization of our Intelligence Academy—a CIA agent of ten years' standing! Piguzov was recruited sometime in 1974 when he was posted in Indonesia. And ever since then, he has regularly passed on to the CIA residency in Moscow the lists of our prospective officers. A bizarre situation arose: an intelligence cadet would still be learning his trade under a code name to maintain absolute secrecy from his colleagues— and Langley already knew his real name, detailed psychological profile, and the place of his future posting abroad. He had blown the covers of several generations of intelligence officers. And you, like an idiot, diligently worked on your cover at the residency, didn't you?"

"Yeah, but fortunately not for long." I chuckled. "So what comes next?"

"God knows. Looks like Yurchenko is the straw that will break the camel's back. If the Kremlin learns of his confession, Kryuchkov will be finished. For this reason, the true story of Yurchenko's defection is the biggest skeleton in our chief's closet. And now you are one of a handful of those in the know."

"Why did you tell me?"

"Listen, old man, I've come to the First Chief Directorate to do intelligence work, not to cover Kryuchkov's ass." Peter's face turned red with fury. It was clearly a cry from the heart, not a pose. "You must understand," he continued in a hot whisper. "Yurchenko delivered to the Americans our entire Italian network. Prior to defection, he conducted a conference at the Rome residency on how to run local agents, and found out their identities."

"What about the American network?" I asked innocently.

Peter gave me a suspicious look.

"Haven't they told you?"

"Spare my nervous system, will you?" I muttered glumly.

"You won't need it anymore," he averred with conviction. "Last week, Motorin, your former colleague at the Washington residency, was arrested."

I felt the world crashing around my ears. Major Motorin had worked four years at the Washington residency and returned to Moscow several months ago. He had a reputation as a smart operative, and the news of his arrest left me dumbstruck.

"I don't know all the details yet," Peter continued. "Other people have been put on his case, but it looks like he was a mother lode for the FBI. To make a long story short, my friend, the American special services have documented proof that you are a spy. From now on, you and your colleagues at the residency are hostages staying in Washington by the Americans' sufferance and likely to be kicked out anytime they feel like it."

"And when might that be?" I asked.

"Pretty soon, I think," Peter replied after a pause. "You see, the coverage of the Yurchenko affair by the American media has aroused grave doubts about his sincerity in the intelligence service and the Kremlin. Under the circumstances, I think Kryuchkov might pick a fight with the FBI and CIA, maybe even try to provoke them, with the upshot that all of you guys will be given the boot."

"Why would he do that?" I asked in surprise.

"Such a move could muddy the situation to such an extent that no one would be able to tell who is to blame for the destruction of our networks in the U.S.," Peter answered with a sly smile. "Chances are they'll find a scapegoat, Yurchenko's affair will be swept under the rug, and Kryuchkov will keep his job. It's quite likely that Motorin will be made that scapegoat—after all, he is a major, not a colonel. On the other hand, it would be better for Kryuchkov to make believe that the whole disaster resulted from some operational blunder rather than large-scale treachery on the part of our officers. In the latter case, he would be to blame; in the former, a fall guy would be found in the mid-level echelon. But this is all secondary now. If you have a prospect under development, you'd be well advised to step up your effort drastically. Leaving the stage, try to slam the door as hard as you can. Make some noise."

That night, I decided to find Valentin Aksilenko. I had to talk to him to determine, one more time, what to do about my future. He was just about the only person in the intelligence service whom I trusted implicitly. We set the rendezvous at the popular beerhall Rakushka, near the Southwestern Metro station.

On my way to the bar, I was gazing out the window of the trolley-bus curious to see if the Moscow cityscape had changed while I was away, and if it had, whether it was for the better. Alas, the city where I had spent the happiest years of my life, the years filled with strenuous studies, hard work, friendship, and dreams of the future, was a dismal sight. While I was away in America, Moscow had developed clear symptoms of decay. The streets were strewn with piles of trash; everything was dirty. The lines at the stores were even longer; the faces of the Muscovites even more sullen and stolid. The latter impression was the most devastating. While in America, I had eagerly read everything American newspapers wrote about perestroika and pinned much hope on it. But now it occurred to me that it was likely to turn out to be yet another beautiful fairy tale having nothing to do with bitter reality.

Fortunately, Rakushka was open, and with a sigh of relief I walked inside. While in college, I had spent a lot of time with my friends in that establishment. It was the in place to celebrate the successful completion of finals; to engage in noisy debates; to dream the impossible dreams. In those days, the beer had been fresh and the shrimp known for their impressive size.

It had been about six years since I had last been to Rakushka, and it did not take me long to wish I had chosen some other place for the rendezvous with Valentin. The beerhall was a dingy den, the air reeked of stale beer; the bathroom was the nearest thing to purgatory; the shrimp looked like insects. Two tipsy women in the corner were carrying on a noisy row. Shady characters milled about, filling me with a dark foreboding.

Valentin was waiting for me. He sat at a dirty table set with beer mugs and plates with meager appetizers, seemingly oblivious to his surroundings.

"Why don't we go to some other place?" I suggested.

"What's the point? Nowadays, it's like this everywhere," he said. "Sit down. Glad to see you. Let's have a drink."

He poured beer into mugs and we drank.

"An interesting quirk of fate, isn't it?" Valentin said as if apologizing to me. "You see, I am off operative status; kicked out into the reserves."

"Who came up with such a wild idea?" I asked.

"The circumstances are so complicated . . . I've divorced my wife."

"Well, it's a crummy procedure, to be sure," I agreed. "But a lot of our colleagues have gone through it, and they are still working."

"With me, it was much more complicated than that." He chortled mirthlessly. "They've thrown the book at me: a severe party reprimand for insincerity."

"Insincerity? What insincerity?"

"I failed to report the pending divorce, which was interpreted as an attempt to conceal the imminent breakup of my family."

"Are they crazy?" I sniffed scornfully.

"I am more concerned about another trend in our service that has acquired a lot of momentum in recent years. I mean the triumph of flagrant incompetence. In the beginning, I thought that the pros were themselves to blame for their dwindling numbers: they get carried away, burn out, and retire from the scene, while the dilettantes twiddle their thumbs and fill vacancies as they come along. But now I am increasingly convinced that in fact the situation is far more complex and alarming."

I refilled our mugs and Valentin continued.

"Just look at the list of an intelligence officer's punishable crimes: divorce, drinking, lechery, rowdyism—anything but poor performance. It is treated as a minor infraction at best, almost never as an offense deserving of severe punishment. Why? Because the system needs stability and serenity; whereas a pro stirs the pot, disturbing the blissful peace and quiet, injecting risk and unpredictability. Professionalism is a free creative endeavor, an art form inherently dangerous to the system."

I nodded my head as he continued.

"Let me share with you one story that Anatoly Dobrynin, our former ambassador in Washington, told a narrow circle of friends. Once, in the late 1970s, he came home on vacation and, as custom dictated, was summoned to the Politburo for debriefing. He took a long time describing the fine points of U.S. foreign and domestic policies. When he was done, Mikhail Suslov, then the number two man in the country after Brezhnev, asks him: 'Tell us, Comrade Dobrynin, what is the numerical strength of the U.S. Democratic Party?' The ambassador says mildly: 'Comrade Suslov, as distinct from the Communist Party of the Soviet Union, the U.S. Democratic Party has no permanent membership rolls, party cards, or monthly dues. Whoever votes Democratic is a Democrat.' Suslov gives him a suspicious look and asks another question: 'How long have you served as our ambassador to America?' 'Since 1962,' Dobrynin replies. 'You haven't done a very good job if in all that time you haven't been able to find out how many members the Democratic Party has on its rolls,' Suslov continued. Dobrynin, of course, was paralyzed with horror and in his mind's eye saw his posting sailing away. But Suslov suddenly relented and said, 'All right. This time we are going to send you back to America. But the next time you come home you'd better have an exact figure to put on the numerical strength of the U.S. Democratic Party.' "

It had been a long time since I laughed so heartily—I almost choked on a shrimp.

"It's not as funny as it may seem at first," Valentin observed. "The fact is that our paranoid leaders are used to reading and believing only classified documents. So Dobrynin had to plead for help to the resident, Yakushkin. The latter obliged. For several months, the encoded cables coming from the residency contained subtle hints to the effect that, according to the trusted agents, not a single person in America knew the exact number of members of the Democratic Party.

"Here's another example. Once Kryuchkov came to America, on an official visit, naturally. So here he is flying to San Francisco, and next to him on the plane sits a young American girl. He talks to her on a variety of topics, and on returning home calls the head of the North American Department into his presence. 'I wonder what your people are doing in America,' he says. 'I went there just once and still all but recruited an American.' He meant his fellow traveler, of course. Okay, it's a clear case of a dilettante's vanity, I can understand that. But the problem is that Kryuchkov had promised to give her a doll as a gift, but, needless to say, forgot to take her full name or address. All he knew was the girl's first name and her native city, San Francisco. And so on orders of that poor excuse for a boss, all our American residencies were kept busy for several months looking for the girl in order to present to her the great recruiter's gift. You can't imagine the amount of effort it took. And, of course, no regular work was done during the search."

"In a nutshell, we serve idiots," I summed up sadly.

"Let's hope Gorbachev will pan out," Valentin said evasively. "He is a subtle politician, but he needs time to get rid of the idiots without undue noise. The most important thing now is to replace the apparatchiks with real pros. That should be our goal."

I was listening to Valentin and thinking about the plight of a recruiter in Kryuchkov's intelligence service. Recruitment is almost like first love—a fateful, tragic love, whose price is sometimes paid in freedom, if not life itself. Danger, fear, the sense of uniqueness bind the agent and his control so strongly that in many cases they develop an addiction to each other. The enormous psychological stress requires an outlet, and the control is the best analyst for the agent—provided the former knows his business, of course. When the recruiter's tour of duty is up, in many cases an agent will refuse to cooperate with the successor control; he becomes capricious, uncontrollable. Then the original recruiter has to step in. He must be available at all times, always in top shape, always ready to take over the contact he has developed.

As long as an agent is at work, the recruiter is theoretically irreplaceable. In practice, however, there were no really irreplaceable people in the Soviet Union. As the in-house joke went: "The Soviet system is mighty by virtue of the fact that it needs no one." Still, a recruiter did have a reasonable guarantee of dignified existence—as long as his agent was at work.

Valentin was a recruiter, and his dismissal from the North American Department was an ominous sign. We drank another beer and he told me the story of one of his best recruits.

4

ONE rainy morning in the late fall of 1979 Valentin came to the embassy wondering how to kill all the time on his hands. He opened the *Washington Post*—no special events were planned for the day. He was about to throw the paper aside when a small ad caught his eye: the Committee in Solidarity with the People of El Salvador had announced that a number of its members would conduct a twenty-four-hour hunger strike at St. Matthew's Cathedral to protest U.S. policy toward El Salvador.

Why not go and have a look? Valentin thought. He had spent three years in Cuba, and since then had felt that Hispanics deserved the closest of attention.

On the stroke of noon, the embassy emptied out—it was lunchtime. Valentin got into his car and started on his usual route home. Having made sure that he was not being followed, he turned in the direction of St. Matthew's Cathedral. He had no specific plans or hopes or premonitions; he was dropping by just in case.

It was cold and drizzly. Strong gusts of wind swept yellow fallen leaves along the pavement. The area near the cathedral was nearly empty, except for fewer than a dozen immobile bodies on the sidewalk to the left of the entrance.

These must be the hunger strikers, Valentin thought and came closer.

The demonstrators lay right on the ground, covered with dark shrouds, so that only their faces were visible—vacant, frozen masks with half-closed eyes. If not for their steady breathing, they could easily have been passed off as corpses. All except one: black as coals; burning with an intense fire; beaming curiosity, irony, and intelligence, those eyes were boring into Valentin like two drills.

It would be difficult to imagine a more ridiculous scene: a well-fed Soviet diplomat under an umbrella, in an expensive suit and a silk tie, and prostrate at his feet a group of Third World fighters for peace and justice, exposed to the biting wind and cold rain.

Valentin dawdled, unsure what to do next.

"Hey, come on in," he heard a male voice.

He turned around and saw a young Hispanic standing in the cathedral doorway. Valentin followed him into a room, where pamphlets on the hunger strike and the demonstrator's personal effects were strewn on a small table.

"We are protesting the imperialist policies of the U.S. toward El Salvador," said the man. "Would you like to make a donation to our just cause?"

"Of course, it goes without saying," Valentin said hastily, pulling a ten-dollar bill from his pocket.

"Hey, thanks." The strike organizer smiled widely.

"Where is your office?" Valentin asked. "I've known about your committee for some time but never got around to paying you a visit."

"It's tough," sighed the Hispanic. "We can't find permanent accommodations. At the moment the committee is crammed into the home of one of our members. As a matter of fact, there he is." He pointed to one of the participants of the hunger strike who was entering with his companions. It was the young man whose gaze had struck Valentin with its intensity.

"Hey, amigo, come on over," the Hispanic called out to him. "I'd like you to meet a friend."

The owner of the extraordinary eyes, whom I'll call Bill, turned out to be a man of very small stature—the top of his head barely reached to Valentin's shoulder. Skinny and frail, he looked more like a teenager than an adult. And yet it was clear that he was about forty, around Valentin's age. His was the classic face of a Latin American Indian. Long, jet-black hair framed an emaciated face with high cheekbones and thin, yellowish skin, against which grew a goatee so thin that all the hairs comprising it could be counted. He was smiling a sincere smile, looking at Valentin with genuine interest.

"So you are the one to have given shelter to the Committee in Solidarity with the People of El Salvador? Glad to meet you," Valentin said. "I am a Soviet diplomat, and I've long wanted to get to know your organization. Could I get your address?"

"Sure, we'll be glad to see you," Bill said with some surprise as if he found it hard to believe that a Soviet diplomat could really be interested in their puny committee. "I live in Northeast, between 14th and 15th Streets."

He took Valentin's proffered card and wrote his address on the back.

"Are you going to be home tomorrow?" Valentin asked.

"Yes, in the afternoon," Bill said. It was clear that he did not believe Valentin was serious.

But Valentin was serious. The next day, after a customary countersurveillance maneuver, he went to visit his new acquaintance. The resident had no idea what he was up to. Had Valentin reported the forthcoming rendezvous, he would have been given explicit instructions, and from then on would have thought not so much about recruitment as about how to comply with orders or bypass them with impunity.

Bill was genuinely surprised to see the Soviet diplomat. When he opened the door and saw his guest, he was struck dumb with surprise.

Good, Valentin thought. Clearly, he has not expected me to come, which means that he is not a plant. No one could fake surprise so artfully.

Bill gave him a smile, as wide and sincere as on the previous day.

"Come in please," he said, ushering Valentin inside the house.

"Well, I'll be . . . It's a veritable palace," the KGB colonel said with surprise, looking around him. "Two floors, so much space. How high is your rent?"

Bill's abode in no way resembled a palace. It was indeed spacious, but looked old and musty, probably like most of the houses in the neighborhood.

"I own it," Bill said without much pride. "My ex-wife and I bought it for just twenty grand. So now, after the divorce, I have to pay her half back. For me, ten thousand is a lot of money, but I'll manage somehow. I'm a carpenter by trade and I'm renovating the house bit by bit. In a few years, it'll be as good as new, and I'll be able to sell it for a hundred fifty or maybe even two hundred grand."

Bill led his guest to an untidy, sparsely furnished family room that looked like a conference room immediately following a noisy debate.

"How long have you been in this country?" Valentin asked.

"A long time," Bill said. "I came here from Peru in search of adventure and found plenty of it. The adventure started as far back as in Lima, at the U.S. Embassy. When I requested a visa, the consul asked me whether I had any money to live on in America. 'I have $10,000 in savings,' I tell him. He smiles suspiciously: 'Show me.' 'All right,' I say. 'I'll be back in half an hour.' I go to a friend, a booking agent of a major airline. 'Could you give me $10,000 in cash? I'll bring the money back in an hour.' He was a nice guy, gave me the money without any fuss. I go back to the embassy, the consul looks respectfully at the thick wad, and without further ado stamps a visa in my passport."

"Did you have any problems with American Immigration?" Valentin asked.

"No, everything went so fast and smoothly that pretty soon I was drafted by the U.S. Army."

"Where did you serve?"

"In West Germany." Bill gave Valentin a sly smile. "In a psychological warfare unit."

"A noncitizen assigned to such a unit? I can't believe it!" Valentin said incredulously.

"I passed the IQ test with a very high score, two hundred points, so they sent me to conduct psychological warfare. Well, to say it was war would be an exaggeration. I merely listened to East European broadcasts and developed recommendations as to the ways we could influence public opinion in those countries. Of course, nobody paid the slightest attention to my suggestions—I was just a small-fry. But my superiors treated me well. So much so that when my tour of duty was up, I was offered a chance to reenlist, but I turned it down."

"What happened to you after you got out of the service?" Valentin inquired.

"At first I tried to study," Bill replied, obviously flattered that a diplomat representing a great power would pay attention to him. "I enrolled in college under the G.I. Bill, but found college life too stultifying. Then I decided to find a job. I have a good trade, carpentry, but I am too weak physically to work in a group. So I started taking custom orders. Several embassies in Washington, including the Chinese, offered me temporary jobs."

"Is their offer off the table?" Valentin reacted immediately.

While Bill was telling his life story, the colonel was furiously thinking how he could be utilized for intelligence purposes. As soon as Bill mentioned the Chinese Embassy, it occurred to him at once to use this fellow in order to plant a bug there.

"I hope not," Bill replied. "The Chinese liked the way I filled their order and told me that if they had any other assignment of a like nature, it would be mine."

Not bad for starters, Valentin thought. Now it's time to find out his attitude toward America.

According to the standard questionnaire filled out by the intelligence service for each target of recruitment development, the three crucial points were the subject's attitude to the policies of the Soviet Union, the United States, and Communist China. The answers to those questions were supposed to be a foolproof indication as to whether or not the subject would agree to cooperate with the KGB on an ideological basis.

"So you've come to terms with China. But what kind of relations do you maintain with the U.S.?" Valentin asked with a smile.

Bill's eyes flashed craftily, his grin spread even wider.

"America reminds me of a teenager who grows too fast and is given to stupid bragging of his prowess," he answered. "Sometimes I feel that Americans are lacking in historical perspective. They are extremely dynamic, they always run forward without knowing the ultimate destination. I have a feeling the act of moving itself is more important to them than the destination. I would call this quality an aspirin mentality."

"A curious thought," Valentin remarked. "Could you clarify it a bit?"

"Sure," said Bill, who clearly liked the attention. "What do you do when you are tired or when you have a headache?"

"I take a rest," Valentin said, puzzled.

"Exactly! So do I, and so do others—all except the Americans. They take a huge dose of aspirin and keep running. They have no time to wait until their headache is gone. They want to be cured of it once and for all."

He is a born philosopher, Valentin thought with something very close to admiration. One could argue with Bill about the merits of his theoretical precepts, but they were undeniably interesting. A mediocre person rarely if ever rises to such abstractions. The man had turned out to be an extraordinary personality, definitely worth developing.

"This aspirin mentality crops up in foreign policy as well, particularly in crisis situations," Bill went on. "Where others would wait till the dust settles and the problem takes care of itself, Americans immediately grab a club and start pounding right and left. Thank God for the Soviet Union, which deters America to a certain extent—even though you are not always up to the task," he added suddenly, giving Valentin a playful wink.

"Just give us a little time, and we'll catch up with America in terms of development," Valentin said. Being a Soviet official he was bound to react in exactly the way he did, even though as a private person he scarcely believed it.

Bill made a visible effort to restrain himself from laughing.

"It'll never happen," he exclaimed. "Neither the Soviet Union nor any other country will ever catch up with America. Believe me, I've been to Europe and know what I'm talking about. But it's good that the Soviet Union exists at all, that there is a country capable of standing up to and deterring America. Just imagine the kind of damage a teenager can do if he feels that he is the biggest kid on the block?"

The more Valentin listened to his new acquaintance, the more he liked the conversation. He had to collect as much information about Bill as he could so as to gain an insight into the man, find a clue to the secret of his personality, and decide whether it was possible and desirable to try to recruit him and, if so, in what way.

Bill pointedly looked at his watch. Valentin could take a hint.

"Are you expecting someone?" he asked.

"Yes, I am," Bill replied.

"It's been very nice talking to you." Valentin rose from his chair and began rummaging in his pocket. "I am extremely intrigued by your ideas and would like to continue our conversation. Could we meet again?"

"Sure, why not?" said Bill.

"Let's have dinner tomorrow." Valentin pulled out the card of a small Chinese restaurant and handed it to Bill. "It's not far from your place, on Georgia Avenue. How about eight P.M.?"

"Great," Bill said. "It just so happens that tomorrow night I'm free."

"See you tomorrow," Valentin said on his way out.

They were sitting in the Chinese restaurant, sipping beer. Bill was exceedingly modest in his tastes. Valentin was paying and, as Russian custom dictated, assiduously tried to ply his guest with food and drink. Initially Bill did not want to order anything, then he succumbed, but confined himself to a simple and inexpensive dish, eating without any visible interest. It seemed as though the material pleasures did not even adorn his life, much less serve as its core. Clearly, something else was more important to Bill, and Valentin was eager to find out what it was.

"What do you do in your spare time?" he asked. Finding a clue to a person through his or her hobby was a standard intelligence technique.

"Oh, my hobby is 'garbology,' " Bill said with his perpetual grin.

"Garbology? What's that?"

"I clean offices after hours. They are littered with huge numbers of discarded pamphlets and documents. Sometimes I bring them home, read them, and can't believe my eyes. Their contents are so different from the kind of stuff the newspapers feed to their readers."

"Where are those offices located?" Valentin asked, and felt his heart miss a beat in anticipation.

"Crystal City," Bill said, looking intently at the Soviet diplomat. Valentin did his best to keep his face expressionless.

It was well known to the residency that Crystal City, a fast-growing Washington suburb, was chock-full of all sorts of organizations directly involved in the national security area. There was not a single officer at the residency who did not rack his brains devising ways of penetrating Crystal City. And here was a living and breathing man enjoying unimpeded, nightly access to offices in that coveted place! Of course, he had no security clearance. He was merely a janitor. But didn't Resident Yakushkin tell his "cut-throats": "Just find me a reliable agent, and we'll find a place for him."

An intelligence service does not need to recruit an agent who is already employed by the targeted agencies. An agent can be recruited and then planted where needed. The trade name for such an agent is a prospect.

Acquisition of a network of prospects usually takes a lot of time; it is sometimes tedious and not always successful. But the method is not without its advantages: a person not employed by a sensitive agency is rarely watched by counterintelligence, and hence is easier to recruit and train. And once a prospect is infiltrated into the desired agency, he is a sure bet to be a great success. After all, he has already been trained; no rendezvous are required; communication is done by way of dead drops or brush-by transfers. How do you catch such an agent red-handed? It is not accidental that some of the greatest KGB successes have been achieved through prospects. Kim Philby alone was worth his weight in gold.

"Interesting," Valentin said noncommittally.

"Of course it is," laughed Bill.

What a nightmare, Valentin thought. Who is recruiting whom?

"There is so much interesting stuff in those papers—better than any books or newspapers," Bill continued.

"In what subject areas?" Valentin could no longer contain himself.

"Military technology, espionage, foreign affairs. But what is really intriguing is that everything is different from the way it is written up in the papers."

"Could I borrow some documents for a look?" Valentin asked cautiously.

"Sure, be my guest! I have a couple of boxes full of that stuff. The rest I've already thrown away."

"You mean you carry those papers home by the boxful?" Valentin asked, his throat going dry with excitement.

"What's wrong with that?" Bill made a great show of innocence. "They're discarded papers, aren't they? Nobody needs them anyway!"

Maybe it is indeed useless pulp, Valentin thought doubtfully. Well, we'll see. Anyway I have to see how far he is prepared to go. If all goes well, we can always plant him where we need him.

"Let's meet tomorrow at noon," Valentin suggested. "Can you bring one of those boxes?"

"No problem," said Bill. "Where are we going to meet?"

"Let me pay for the meal, and I'll show you," Valentin said.

They went out of the restaurant and found themselves next to a hardware store. Valentin planned a brush-by transfer on the store's parking lot.

"Here is what we'll do," he told Bill. "Tomorrow, on the stroke of noon, I'll park over there." He pointed to a slot at the far end of the lot that he had noted earlier to be vacant most of the time. "You'll park your car next to mine. I'll open my trunk, and you will place the box in it, whereupon we'll drive off in different directions. Okay?"

"Fine," Bill said.

"If for some reason or other tomorrow's rendezvous has to be scrubbed, let's meet at the same time the day after tomorrow," Valentin added. "There is no point calling each other on the phone. You've probably guessed that Soviet diplomats are under particularly strict surveillance."

"Of course," Bill said as if he had a very clear idea of Valentin's true identity and the nature of his business. He still had that quiet, kindly smile on his face.

"I've long dreamed of setting up a center to analyze all those papers in Peru," he said in a suddenly serious voice. "For America, they are pulp, while for my country there is a lot of useful stuff in them."

What if he is crazy? Valentin thought with alarm, shivering with cold.

"Listen, Bill, there is one question about your country I've wanted to ask for a long time," he said. "Everybody in the world is intrigued by the mysterious giant figures laid out on the ground in Peru in ancient times. Many people believe that they were created by aliens from space. What do you think, is it true?"

"Baloney," Bill said. "You can lay out such figures by managing construction from a great height. My ancestors made large balloons by sewing together animal skins, filled them with hot air, went aloft, and managed the construction of roads in the shape of giant animals. As for aliens from space, it's all hogwash."

He seems to be a pragmatist through and through, Valentin thought. A schizophrenic would be sure to support the aliens version or some other esoteric explanation. Hot-air balloons are too down-to-earth for a lunatic. Looks like he is absolutely sane. But I still can't understand who is recruiting whom. There is no escaping the impression that he is trying to drag me into this business. Is it possible that he is a plant after all?

Thus did Valentin come to the most important and complicated question of the recruitment business: who is it you are dealing with, a potential agent or a representative of the

U.S. special services who pretends to be your ally while in fact busily setting a trap from which you will be unlikely to escape unscathed?

How many high-flying intelligence operatives have been shot down by plants!

As long as an intelligence officer confines himself to official contacts, he can live in relative peace. But no sooner does he step over the line separating a clean diplomat, journalist, or businessman from a spy than he is immediately confronted by the specter of a plant.

Over the centuries of secret wars, thousands of spymasters have been racking their brains devising ways of exposing plants. Yet to this day, no one has come up with a surefire technique. And, oh! what confidence these spies need! After all, their fate is at stake.

At the Intelligence Academy, I once heard a lecture on the subject that lasted a few hours. Having listed several hundred telltale signs of a plant and scores of ways of exposing one, the lecturer noted that all such methods were only effective under favorable circumstances.

"So is there a reliable method of exposing a plant?" one of the cadets asked in disappointment.

"This is precisely what happens where the true diagnosis is only established upon postmortem." The professor chuckled. "In your case, the postmortem is when you are burned."

"Suppose I am not burned and the agent works faithfully for many years?"

"Then all through those years you will be consumed by doubt as to whether or not he is a plant," the professor said with a disarming smile.

Valentin was in no mood for smiling, however. In America the opposition was the giant FBI, and he had to decide right off the bat whether it was worthwhile trying to recruit Bill. In making that decision he had to rely on his own intuition, and nothing else.

That day, Valentin had a hunch that Bill was no plant.

But an operative's intuitive feeling is not a valid argument as far as the resident is concerned. Therefore, after pondering the issue for a short while, Valentin decided to defer his report yet again. The next day was to clarify a lot of things. If his intuition failed him and Bill did turn out to be a plant, then the FBI would be able to catch Valentin red-handed after his new acquaintance placed a paper-filled box in the trunk of his car. Just one classified document in the bunch would be sufficient pretext for a major scandal and an equally noisy expulsion of the Soviet spy. But if, on the other hand, Bill proved to be legitimate and his material interesting, no one would reproach Valentin for having failed to report the forthcoming rendezvous.

That night he tossed and turned for a long time before falling asleep.

The next day, at 11:55 A.M., Valentin parked his car in the agreed-upon slot. He had a good look around, walking about the lot. All the nearby cars were reassuringly empty. Looks like there will be no stakeout today, he thought. He opened his trunk and got back into the car. He had a minute and a half to wait.

Bill was a miracle-maker. He parked his car in the slot next to Valentin's on the stroke of noon. It never happens this way in real life, only in the movies, the colonel thought. Bill briskly jumped out of his car, took out a small cardboard box, looked alertly around, and put the box into the trunk of Valentin's car.

"Meet you in two weeks' time, same restaurant," Valentin told him through the partially open window, and stepped on the gas.

He drove into the Soviet residential compound on Wisconsin Avenue and parked his car in the underground garage, away from prying eyes. It was time to inspect his catch.

It was a veritable cornucopia—from economic reports on

various countries and analyses of regional development to charts and diagrams of indeterminate utility. Only one category of documents was lacking—those marked "classified." No problem, Valentin thought. If this guy is not a plant, we can always infiltrate him into a more suitable place. Looks like garbology is a heck of a hobby.

General Yakushkin, the chief of the Washington residency at that time, was less sanguine, however.

"What is the world coming to? Have we been reduced to rummaging in garbage dumps?" he grumbled in a good-natured manner, looking through the papers obtained by Valentin.

Yakushkin could afford the mild irony. The residency was doing its job; the agents were delivering; the resident knew his position was solid and hoped for new successes.

"Why don't we try to work with him?" Valentin suggested without much optimism. "Who knows, maybe he will pan out?"

"Okay," Yakushkin agreed. "Just keep me informed."

Valentin arrived at his next rendezvous with Bill well prepared.

"I talked to some people at the embassy, and they have agreed to set up a center to process your papers in the Soviet Union. Peru will also stand to benefit," he said.

"Great," Bill said jubilantly. "You know, I've been really depressed that such a huge amount of information goes to waste."

"That's settled," Valentin assured him. "But now we must decide what kind of information we need. The stuff you brought me the last time is good, but I think that other offices will have even better material. Could you get a job with another organization?"

"Piece of cake," Bill replied. "As luck would have it, I've just been offered a new job in Rosslyn, corner of Arlington Boulevard and Moore Street. It is said to house the offices of a few major Pentagon contractors."

"Will you be required to clean the whole building?"

"Yes."

"What's the exact address?"

A few days later, Valentin dropped by the building Bill had told him about and found the directory in the lobby. It listed, among other tenants, Boeing and Ketron. He realized that Bill was on the right track.

"Okay, go ahead," he told him at the next rendezvous. "Looks like it's exactly what we need. We'd like you to pay special attention to Boeing."

The garbage can turned out to have a pot of gold on the bottom. Bill began delivering material on military and strategic issues that would have been designated top priority by any intelligence service. The next problem was to establish a reliable and stable channel of communication with the agent, and Valentin was doing his best.

The countersurveillance routine preceding a rendezvous with an agent usually started at the embassy door. The best time to leave was high noon when a noisy multitude of Soviet diplomats went home for lunch. Valentin tried to lose himself in the crowd.

He would get into his Chevrolet Malibu and set out toward Hyattsville, Maryland. The drive took about forty minutes, a sufficient amount of time for a preliminary check. If nothing suspicious was in evidence, he would make a turn, take the main countersurveillance route, and it would be off to the races.

Valentin would roam about the city till 5:00 P.M., passing one after another of a variety of preselected control points. At each point, he would drive into a dead-end street, get out of the car, get back in, and continue his trip. An outside observer, watching from the sidelines, could hardly be expected to discern an ulterior purpose in all those wanderings. But for a pro the maneuvers clearly signaled a countersurveillance routine. Countersurveillance was standard operating procedure anywhere, though it was particularly sophisticated in Washington; the FBI was too formidable an enemy to permit oneself to relax.

At 5:00 P.M., Valentin would arrive at the parking lot of a major mall, where the residency's operative driver would be waiting in his car.

The residency watched that car at all times. Never, under any circumstances, was it to be left unattended, lest the FBI should grasp at the opportunity to plant a direction finder in it. Each time it was slated to be driven to an important rendezvous, the operative car would be totally dismantled to its smallest components, inspected, sounded, and sniffed to make sure that it was clean, and then reassembled. That titanic work was done overnight in the underground garage of the Soviet residential compound, away from prying eyes and ears. In a word, that car was guarded much as a pathologically jealous husband guards his promiscuous wife, never letting her out of his sight. And it was worth it. When it came to communication with the agents, that car was the last bastion beyond which began a dead zone marked "failure."

That was the case before the treachery of the double agent Motorin. He loved to use the operative car and naturally told the FBI about its purpose. Fortunately for Valentin, when he was running Bill, Motorin had yet to be posted to Washington. Who knows what the turn of events might have been had Motorin arrived in the U.S. capital a little earlier? But in those days, in the early 1980s, everything depended on Valentin's operative skill and the agent's resourcefulness. Up to that point, there had not been a single case of defection in the annals of the North American Department.

So Valentin would get into the operative car, and the decisive phase of the countersurveillance procedure would be under way. But now it was Sasha, the driver, who sat behind the steering wheel.

Sasha did not speak English; he was indifferent to U.S.

foreign policy and probably did not know the name of the previous U.S. president. But he was a genius at the countersurveillance game.

All his adult life Sasha had worked in Moscow, in the surveillance service, and honed his skills to an incredible degree. The countersurveillance routine was his *pièce de résistance*. He yearned for a bout with the FBI, supremely confident of his victory.

The car was flying as though on wings. The driver and the passengers kept silent—just in case. In spite of all the precautions, neither Valentin nor Sasha was sure that the FBI had not managed somehow to plant a bug in their car. Sasha was watching in all directions simultaneously. His phenomenal memory grasped and held fast the license plate numbers and makes of all cars that could conceivably be suspected, by the way they were driven, of being FBI. He had no problem recalling, for instance, that the Chrysler tailgating his car for the last ten minutes had stopped next to him two hours previously at the red light in Tysons Corner. And he had seen that Chevy twice over the last few hours.

The last leg of Sasha's route was a real show-stopper. He would enter some wooded area, turn off the headlights, and drive at breakneck speed on narrow, unlit roads. It was as dark as a tomb, the wind was howling wildly, tree branches were lashing the car. God knows how Sasha saw his way in that utter darkness.

Yet Valentin, sitting next to the driver, felt confident and serene. If only the bosses of Kryuchkov's intelligence service knew their business as well as Sasha, the organization would be invincible.

Around 8:30 P.M., the time came for a procedure known in the trade as "the operative bailing out of the car." The maneuver that bore such a frightening name was performed as follows: Sasha would stop the car at a red light, Valentin would open the door and silently vanish into the gathering darkness. The traffic light changed to green, Sasha roared away, and Valentin had thirty minutes to negotiate the home stretch on foot.

Usually it ran through a small, deserted park devoid of paved roads. Even in case a tail, by some miracle, was still following Valentin, he would have to crawl behind his prey along deserted trails. Mission impossible! This is not the movies; it's real life.

Bill would be waiting in his GM van at the other end of the park. They had three hours at their disposal. They would settle comfortably in the van, look through the fresh "catch," and select the most interesting papers. Valentin would listen to the agent's tales of his life, trying to determine whether he had been sent by the FBI, and discuss the prospects for future cooperation.

A considerable amount of time would be devoted to heart-to-heart talk. Valentin believed that the control must establish a close personal relationship or, better yet, a real friendship, with the agent. But he never belabored the point when talking to his superiors; they might not have understood him.

The intelligence service has a standard model of the control-agent relationship developed during the Cold War years: the control must treat his agent as a drill sergeant treats a buck private. After all, an officer serves the most progressive country in the world. He has no time for social niceties; he has to have control! For his part, the agent is supposed to be in seventh heaven just by virtue of being chosen to execute orders issued by a representative of that great state. Quite a few agents had been lost only because KGB operatives diligently followed that precept. Fortunately, Valentin was by nature inclined to skepticism, and he played his cards close to his chest.

After midnight, Bill drove his van to the prearranged place where Sasha would be waiting. The box with the papers would be placed in the operative car, Sasha would depart for the Soviet residential compound, while Bill would drive Valentin to the spot where his Malibu was parked. Valentin generally got home around 2:00 or 3:00 A.M.

Sometimes, though, things didn't work out. One midnight, Sasha failed to appear at the rendezvous spot. Valentin decided that he was simply late, sent Bill home, and proceeded to wait. Hour after hour dragged by, but Sasha was nowhere to be seen. The unthinkable had happened: Sasha had gotten mixed up and was looking for Valentin elsewhere.

That night Bill had brought an immense batch of documents. To be on the safe side, Valentin lugged the huge garbage bag bursting at the seams with the catch away from the curb and leaned it against the wall of a McDonald's. From time to time he nervously peeked at his watch. Disaster was looming ever larger in his mind. What normal person would loiter at night on an American street next to a garbage bag? If a police car happened to drive by . . .

A couple of hours later he decided there was no point wasting any more time, caught a cab and came home, entering the house through the back door, and dragging the garbage bag full of papers behind him. His wife, reeling with fright, let him in.

That night, Resident Yakushkin did not get much sleep either.

"What happened?" he asked the next morning.

"There was some sort of a mixup," Valentin replied. He did not place the blame at Sasha's feet, he just couldn't. After all, they were not done working together.

Yakushkin had no trouble figuring out the situation and reacted positively.

"All's well that ends well," he declared, and never mentioned the incident again.

What a magnificent attitude! No boss of Kryuchkov's stripe would ever do anything like that. He would have started digging and ferreted out the truth about who was to blame. He would have punished Sasha severely and proudly reported the whole story to the center. And, as a result, the operation would have suffered.

Yakushkin took a different course. It is not that he was kind; on the contrary, he was a tough, sometimes even cruel, man. But duty was foremost in his mind, and he had the fortitude to shoulder responsibility.

Another time Valentin became the victim of bad luck. When Bill let him out of his van near the parking lot where he had left his Malibu, he found that his car had a flat. But no sooner did Valentin open his trunk to get a jack than he heard the loud sounds of hurried footfalls. Two muscular fellows were running toward him from the other end of the parking lot. Just a few seconds stood between him and disaster.

Valentin slammed the trunk shut, dashed into the car, turned the key in the ignition, and, its tires squealing, one still flat, the Malibu disappeared in the distance. He never learned the identity of those two guys. FBI? Hoodlums? It made no difference. It was an emergency no matter how you cut it.

Yakushkin shared that viewpoint. The next day he listened to Valentin's report in gloomy silence and laconically summed up the situation.

"We will not report it to Moscow. They will definitely order us to discontinue the operation."

If Androsov had been in Yakushkin's shoes, he would have reported everything. And why not? Moscow would have ordered him to drop the agent. Valentin would have been punished—to be on the safe side. And the resident would have happily reconciled himself to life on easy street, reading the *Washington Post* and doing nothing. A dream come true for a real communist boss.

The annoying mishaps forced Valentin to revise his countersurveillance tactics. To that end, he moved to the Soviet residential complex on Wisconsin Avenue.

On the day of a scheduled meeting with Bill, Valentin would crawl to the garage via underground service lines and hide in the trunk of the operative car. Then Sasha's wife would gather a few friends for a shopping expedition. Giggling and chattering merrily, the ladies would pile into the car and Sasha would solemnly drive them to a large mall. His passengers naturally had no inkling of the cargo in the trunk.

Early in the trip, Valentin felt quite cozy in the trunk. It was roomy and he lay on clean bedsheets thoughtfully provided by Sasha. The troubles began somewhat later.

Sasha would drop off the ladies at the mall with strict orders to come out by 11:00 P.M. Then he would execute an elaborate countersurveillance maneuver, find some secluded spot, let Valentin out, and go for a long drive through the Washington suburbs.

Later in the evening, Bill would drive Valentin to a prearranged rendezvous where Sasha was waiting. They would transfer the catch to the trunk of the operative car, and Valentin would squeeze into the trunk, which was no longer so roomy, to put it mildly.

Sasha would pick up the women at the mall, usually arriving long after the appointed time. But the ladies never complained. A shopping trip was almost like a holiday for them. On the way home they carried on a lively discussion of their purchases and generally made merry, while Valentin, curled up on a mound of dirty papers, was thinking deep thoughts.

Sometimes it seemed to him he was stuck in some surreal world. There, inside the car, everything was normal, the way it was supposed to be: mundane concerns, small talk about the purchases—in a word, the tiny but real joys of life. While here, in the trunk, a pile of dirty papers with charts and diagrams, smelling of spilled coffee and cigarettes. The two worlds were separated by a thin partition, but in fact there was a vast gulf between them—a normal life on one side and a secret war of two superpowers, two hostile systems on the other.

*   *   *

The next morning, Sasha would drive up to the Soviet Embassy on 16th Street and openly unload boxes supposedly containing food and soft drinks. The boxes were carried into the residency, and Bill's papers were taken out and subjected to primary processing.

Bill generally delivered such a huge volume of documents that there was no way they could all be sent over to Moscow. Valentin selected the most interesting papers, but most of the batch had to be destroyed on the spot, burned in an old furnace in the Embassy basement that was used in turn by the cipher officers of the KGB and GRU (military intelligence) residencies. When the furnace was not in use, even regular embassy staffers were given access to it.

The dreary basement put Valentin, huddled on his perch at the brightly burning furnace, into a philosophical frame of mind. Apparently some mysterious force was guiding his reflection on the fleeting and transitory nature of life, because a short time later, the cipher officer of the KGB residency hanged himself near that furnace. He had a nervous breakdown and decided that, compared to his life, death was a lesser evil.

As he perused Bill's material, Valentin never failed to marvel at how lackadaisical the American system of classified record-keeping was. Had they been subject to Soviet laws, many of the employees of the companies whose offices were cleaned by Bill would surely have been jailed for criminal negligence. Without a second thought, they threw into the wastebaskets documents the likes of which were kept under seven seals in the Soviet Union. The liberal American attitude revealed the difference in the concepts of secrecy between the two countries—and, more broadly, between the two systems. Democracy tends toward maximum openness; totalitarianism tries to classify whatever it can.

Among the documents Bill supplied, not a single one was

designated as classified; but, thanks to his effort, the KGB obtained an enormous amount of information on the following Pentagon projects:

- the MX missile, from the design stage to the shop drawings; the Soviet military-industrial complex was particularly gratified to learn the details of the proposed MX basing system, and the drawings of the truck to cart the missile around caused fits of delight among Soviet designers;
- air-, sea-, and land-based cruise missiles, particularly the Tomahawk;
- the latest-generation single-warhead Midgetman missile;
- the Trident SLBM, designed for the new generation of U.S. submarines;
- the latest strategic bomber, initially designated as a "penetrating bomber," but subsequently renamed the Stealth bomber;
- AWACS (Airborne Warning and Control System) and NAVSTAR systems;
- anti-aircraft missile complexes;
- analytical reports on war games and staff exercises of the U.S. Armed Forces.

The intelligence analysts were amazed at the volume and quality of material delivered by Bill. They simply could not understand how documents of that kind had ended up in the trash can. The impression was that, as far as some Pentagon contractors were concerned, secrecy pertained exclusively to their own proprietary information, and they didn't think twice about discarding the secrets of other organizations and agencies.

Bill did not obtain any classified National Security Council documents, but they were liberally quoted in the papers he dug up in the trash baskets. Using those references, Soviet analysts more than once managed to reproduce the originals in full.

He never brought shorthand reports on the closed-door hearings of the Senate and House Armed Services Committees, but quite often found draft documents that had been used at confidential briefings of committee members.

Often enough Bill brought material generated by DARPA (Defense Advanced Research Projects Agency), one of the most important divisions of the Department of Defense, marked by the KGB as one of the most important targets for penetration.

Valentin and Bill were particularly excited in anticipation of each major national holiday, especially Independence Day. They knew that on the eve of the holiday, noisy parties would be held at the Pentagon contractors' offices, and a record catch would follow each celebration. Who would worry whether there is any classified information in the papers on his desk when the bottles have already been opened and the bubbly is pouring into the glasses? At every holiday party, the KGB licked its chops in preparation for the harvest of an especially bountiful crop of information.

Once Bill was nearly burned on the eve of a holiday. He was walking toward the exit with his catch hidden in a rolled-up *Washington Post*, when the unexpected happened.

"Hey, Bill, could I borrow your paper?" one of the Boeing staff workers asked him.

His hands became clammy, his knees turned to jelly. But it didn't take him long to collect himself.

"Sure," he said. "Just let me cut out an ad I need."

He stepped into the next room, threw the papers into the trash basket, cut out an ad that he naturally did not need, and returned with a smile on his lips. It was no fluke that he had passed the IQ test with flying colors: He knew how to think quickly.

At that time, the KGB was charged with the task of processing all military-strategic information related to the U.S. and reporting its findings to the Central Committee of the Communist Party and the general secretary. All KGB divisions, the Soviet Military Intelligence Administration (GRU), and the intelligence services of the socialist countries were required to supply the military-strategic information they obtained to the KGB external intelligence service, that is, the First Chief Directorate, where it was analyzed, summed up, and prepared for transmission to the Kremlin leaders and the heads of the military-industrial complex.

Needless to say, only the most important information was sent over to the KGB intelligence service—the kind that was fit to be reported to the Kremlin leadership. KGB analysts at regular intervals prepared digests of the military-strategic information on the U.S. and NATO obtained by the Warsaw Pact intelligence community.

To put things into proper perspective, in 1982, Bill's documents accounted for over 50 percent of the overall volume of information in that category. He single-handedly obtained more military-strategic information on the U.S. than all the fraternal intelligence services put together. That fact was a source of great satisfaction—but also suspicion. It was too good to be true.

Could it be that Bill was a plant after all? That question continued to haunt Valentin as well. It's not that he doubted the authenticity of the documents delivered by his agent. What Valentin couldn't fathom was Bill's incredible composure. He liked his agent and was concerned for his safety. But sometimes it seemed to him that Bill did not share that concern, which suggested the possibility he was a plant, because a plant naturally had nothing to fear from either the FBI or the CIA.

But Valentin's agonizing over that question was for naught because, strange as it might seem, he had no say in the matter. It came under the purview of the center, which represented the collective mind of all staffers and outside experts with varying degrees of expertise in the agent-running business.

With respect to Bill, the answer was an unambiguous no. The most resounding vote of confidence in the agent came from the managers of Soviet weapons design institutions, who were the main beneficiaries of the information delivered by Bill. Their verdict was that a plant would never deliver anything like the material supplied by Valentin's agent. That the documents were not classified did not bother them in the least. "We have seen more than enough classified documents to be able to distinguish the real stuff from a fabrication," they averred.

Yet the center was not totally satisfied. According to the rules of the intelligence service, any agent, even the most reliable one, was to be checked out at regular intervals. It was decided to test Bill's veracity using the good offices of the fraternal intelligence service of East Germany.

At that time, "our German friends" ran a valuable and reliable agent who was employed by the Bohum Aerospace Center in West Germany. He was asked to evaluate Bill's material on the latest technologies used in the Stealth bomber, which bordered on the fantastic in the minds of the Soviet military.

A long pause ensued, which cost Valentin some frayed nerves, followed by a gratifying response: the German agent attested to the authenticity of Bill's information. The intelligence bureaucrats calmed down and moved Bill to the category of valuable agent. Little did they know that an event had just taken place that could easily end their euphoria.

Once Bill brought a document describing the performance of one of the latest U.S. cruise missiles. It contained a lot of figures—except for one. Where the accuracy of the missile was supposed to be, the document showed a neat hole. Somebody had diligently scratched out that figure and then thrown the document away, apparently believing that without that detail, the document was no longer classified.

"Congratulations on exposing a plant," Resident Yakushkin said gloomily after perusing the document. "Nothing can be more indicative than that; the document is seemingly classified but it lacks the most important thing. It is alluring enough for us to walk into a trap, while preventing damage to U.S. national security."

"Please observe that only one numeral was scratched out," Valentin said mildly. "What is the largest single-digit numeral?"

"Nine," Yakushkin replied hesitantly, unsure what his subordinate had in mind.

"Right. So the maximum number that could be in this place was nine, that is to say nine feet or close to three meters. Which means that the maximum deviation of the missile from the target does not exceed three meters. And who cares if the accuracy is even greater? Considering the yield of the warhead, a three-meter deviation is, for all intents and purposes, dead center."

"You are right," Yakushkin said in delight. "That's what you'll write in the cable: three meters."

Thus did the Soviet military find out the accuracy of American cruise missiles and was profoundly grateful to the intelligence service. But probably to this day they have no idea where that figure came from, or how Bill had once again managed to dispel all suspicions about him.

Many Soviet design institutions working for the Ministry of Defense eagerly awaited each batch of papers delivered by Bill. Thanks to his effort, the Americans, unbeknownst to them, were lending a hand to Soviet weapons designers. They rummaged through the contents of the trash baskets of Pentagon contractors, checking their plans, designs, and calculations. Some papers, crumpled and evil-smelling, were more precious than piles of the most secret documents.

Actually, Bill was in a position to get hold of information treated as classified in the U.S., but he stayed away from such documents in deference to Valentin's wishes. But the fact that the agent delivered what was officially designated as "pulp" while being constantly within reach of incredible secrets was a source of nagging dissatisfaction for headquarters. The hottest heads advocated going further. For starters, it was decided to bug the Boeing conference room.

Bill brought a sample of the conference room drywall, and

the center fitted it with a tiny listening device. It was thought that Bill, master carpenter that he was, would have no trouble skillfully installing the eavesdropping contraption so that nobody would be the wiser, enabling the KGB to listen in on Boeing's strategic designs and, by extension, on the Pentagon's.

Valentin disliked the idea. He believed that as long as the Soviet military-industrial complex was perfectly happy with Bill's pulp, there was no point seeking extra excitement, needlessly endangering the agent. He did his best to delay the execution of the "technical penetration" operation. Then an event happened that whetted the center's appetite still more.

Bill brought a draft memo addressed to Ketron management from a company guard. It said that, on the eve of a holiday, the Ketron janitor (thank God, it was not Bill) was cleaning the company premises and saw that a safe stood open. The janitor reported his finding to the guard on duty, who ascertained that the safe belonged to one of the Ketron officials, who had forgotten to lock the safe when leaving the office.

The guard called the official at home but was not able to reach him until around midnight, when the latter returned from a protracted party. The official welcomed the news with a stream of invective and went to bed. It was not until the next day that he took the trouble to come to the office to lock his safe.

As Bill handed the memo to Valentin, there was a distinct impish sparkle in his eye. The incident suggested that the Ketron people treated the secrecy requirements in a highly lackadaisical fashion. Given a little imagination, it opened up broad vistas for intelligence.

But Valentin was of a different opinion. Having absorbed the contents of the memo, he told Bill: "Never, under any circumstances, touch any classified document even if it stares you in the face. What you bring us is more than enough as it is. Let's not play with fire if we don't have to."

Valentin tried to shield his agent from danger, and to his surprise, the leaders of the Soviet military design institutions weighed in on his side. These powerful allies were still so thoroughly satisfied with what they were getting from Bill, they were willing to pay him any amount of money for his so-called pulp. Such a powerful lobby proved too much for the center to contend with, and the daredevil plans were shelved.

In fact, the captains of military industry were eager to express their gratitude not only to Bill, but also to his controls, and lobbied hard to have them decorated.

Valentin received the Order of the Red Star. Many intelligence bureaucrats also decorated themselves, even though they had not the remotest idea of who Bill was or what it was he was doing. At that time, Kryuchkov was not yet interfering in operational matters, but he had already put his stamp on the process of reward distribution, which became cynical in the extreme.

The unwritten rule was that an intelligence officer could only be decorated after his boss had been. According to another rule, intelligence officers could be decorated for operational achievements only once every five years or longer. And if the five-year minimum has not been satisfied, forget about any reward, even if you have stolen the CIA director's personal safe. So the intelligence service decorated either the wrong people, or the right people for the wrong reason, or the wrong people for the wrong reason, as operatives joked among themselves.

Valentin did not expect to be decorated. Apparently the bureaucratic machine failed in some link. But when it came to Vladimir, Valentin's successor as Bill's control, the system reverted to form. He was thrown the puniest of decorations, while the most valuable awards went to people personally valued by Kryuchkov.

As for Bill himself, he worked selflessly and almost never took the money offered by Valentin. He took risks for the sake of his ideals. Little did he know that on many occasions the risk was not justified, because some Soviet design establishments used the information supplied by the agent to satisfy the selfish personal interests of their managers.

Some of Bill's material was buried in the analytical unit and never went anywhere. Thus, the intelligence bosses suppressed the Pentagon study on the effects of the Mount Saint Helens eruption, which turned out to be very similar to a nuclear explosion. Smart minds at the Pentagon took advantage of the rare opportunity, conducted research, and came to the conclusion that the immensely powerful electromagnetic pulses generated by the nuclear explosion would paralyze all operating communication, command, and control equipment and reduce practically to zero the potential for a counterstrike using strategic bombers.

The Pentagon study delighted the analysts, but displeased the leadership of the service. At that time, the Soviet Union was furiously developing a new generation of strategic bombers. Gigantic appropriations had already been authorized, lucrative orders placed, bonuses and awards distributed . . . all for naught, and just because a piddling study called into question the rationale for the project. Who needs such intelligence? And so, to get rid of this damnable question, the report was shelved and forgotten. No report—no problem.

Neither was the Politburo apprised of the National Security Council document setting forth conditions under which the U.S. might be provoked into a large-scale military response (besides a direct Soviet attack against America), such as:

- a Soviet attack against West Germany;
- loss to the West of Middle East oil sources;
- a communist coup in Mexico;
- annexation of South Africa into the communist camp.

The intelligence service leaders were shocked at the evidence of America's self-restraint. The KGB had indefatigably, day in and day out, year after year, shouted from the rooftops about Washington's ominously increasing expansionist aspirations, warning that "the imperialists are willing and ready to play with fire, with or without pretext." And here was an NSC document laying out what in effect amounted to a defensive doctrine. So what had the KGB external intelligence arm been doing all those years? Could it, by any chance, be true that it had been feeding disinformation to the Soviet leadership? Or maybe it was another instance of its stark incompetence? What a pain in the neck that document was!

Also suppressed was all evidence of the Pentagon's attempts to streamline its expenses and get a bigger bang for the dollar. On the other hand, all information about new major funding for Pentagon projects was given the green light and used by the USSR Defense Ministry as leverage in its fight for more money. In other words, had the Pentagon been nonexistent, the Soviet military-industrial complex would have had to invent it. The mainstay of the Soviet totalitarian system was the myth of the growing aggressiveness of "American imperialism," which could easily be sustained in a country separated from the rest of the world by an Iron Curtain.

Ironically, the national leadership fell victim to its own propaganda. Many people in the Soviet Union, and in the West as well, assumed that the recluses in the Kremlin were kept well informed about what was going on in the world. Nothing could have been further from the truth.

The daily volume of classified information alone sent to each Politburo member—on top of their other duties— amounted to at least one hundred pages. There was no way those octogenarians could read, much less understand, such a vast amount of material. They read even the newspapers perfunctorily, concentrating on the coverage of their own speeches and travels. But if the KGB chairman or the chief of intelligence delivered a report, that was a different matter entirely. It was very mysterious and, hence, credible.

That's how the amount of information made available to the Soviet leaders—and, consequently, their thought processes—came to be controlled by the KGB, which brazenly took advantage of its powers.

Valentin already had some inkling of the true state of affairs, which has since become common knowledge. As he worked on Bill's material, his deductions came to be supported by irrefutable evidence. As a result, he began questioning his own part in the unfolding events; doubt persistently gnawed at him. Bill delivered information in an ever-increasing flow, and Valentin couldn't help wondering who benefited from that cornucopia. His musings, which he naturally kept strictly to himself, led him to surprising conclusions.

It appeared that Bill's work brought benefits to a group of KGB bigwigs and leaders of the military-industrial complex, while causing additional hardships to ordinary Soviet men and women who were required to make new sacrifices on the altar of their country's military might.

For the United States, it was a win-win situation. By that time the Soviet economy had already gone into a tailspin, but the Soviet military-industrial complex refused to face reality. They saw Bill's material as their ticket to military parity with the U.S. in all areas, in all types of weapons, disregarding evidence that their policy merely exacerbated the economic woes of the USSR, inexorably dragging the country into an abyss. America, whose president castigated the Soviet Union as the "Evil Empire," couldn't have asked for more. While ostensibly working for Soviet intelligence, Bill was actually helping the United States to achieve its strategic goal: bankrupting the Soviet economy.

Could Bill be a strategic plant? Valentin asked himself that question time and time again—and always answered it in the negative. His train of thought followed a simple logic: if Bill was indeed a plant, then he was a perfect plant that could only have been set up by a perfect counterintelligence service. But the latter was a figment of the imagination, because in the real world any counterintelligence service was a bureaucratic organization with all its vices and failings. And an imperfect special service could never mount a perfect operation, such as burrowing into the KGB network to plant their agent.

Valentin was certain that preparing the quantity of material delivered by Bill, much less obtaining official permission to transfer it to the KGB, was beyond the capacity of either the FBI or the CIA as he knew them. He felt that such a feat could only be pulled off by a unique trio working together: Bill, the FBI director, and the U.S. president—an improbable, unfeasible troika, as unlikely as the operation of planting Bill himself.

Valentin believed Bill when he said, "I don't help your military because I think they are better than the Americans; I do it because they are weaker and yet unafraid to challenge America." Valentin hoped that his agent's material would force the Soviet leaders to drop out of the arms race to achieve military parity with the U.S., a race that was killing the country. For Valentin, that would have been the highest imaginable reward, far outweighing any decoration. And he did live to receive that reward.

In the summer of 1983, Yuri Andropov, successor to Leonid Brezhnev as head of the USSR, demanded from KGB intelligence an assessment of the U.S. strategic nuclear capability. The report was based exclusively on the material supplied by Bill, primarily DARPA projects that the agent was able to procure.

Needless to say, the papers left a great deal to be desired. Much of the information was fragmentary and dissipated among scraps of different documents. Valentin and the intelligence analysts had to create, in effect, an entirely new document summing up everything they were able to glean from the trash basket pickings at Boeing and a number of other Pentagon contractors. Thank God, the project was entrusted to real pros, who were honest in the bargain. They prepared exactly the kind of report that they had long believed was urgently needed. It took them about two months.

That day, Andropov's gigantic office resembled a wartime general staff situation room. Numerous diagrams and blueprints were hung on the walls; the table was piled high with maps and reference books.

The report was presented by an intelligence analyst who was a friend of Valentin's. The issue was difficult and required specialized knowledge, which is why Kryuchkov wisely decided to defer to an expert. Andropov listened intently, his face twisted into a sour grimace—whether caused by another bout of kidney problems or by a foreboding that the Soviet Union was doomed, it's hard to say.

The crowning point of the report was a discussion of the most promising basing modes for the U.S. strategic missiles. The analyst spoke as simply and clearly as he could. The intelligence service had an iron-clad rule going back to Brezhnev's time: the higher the destination of the information, the simpler the terms in which it should be couched. For the Politburo, reports were written in language understandable even to an idiot.

According to Bill's material, the Pentagon was working on the following projects:

Variation No. 1. Land-based strategic missiles are stationed on aboveground launch pads. Upon receiving a signal that a Soviet nuclear strike is under way, the missiles disperse in all directions and, after traveling about a mile, miraculously burrow into the ground by means of a series of directed explosions and cover themselves with a layer of dirt so thick as to give total protection against any nuclear attack. Invulnerable to the Soviet missiles, which destroy the now empty launch pads, they are ready to deliver a devastating counterstrike.

Variation No. 2. Land-based strategic missiles are installed inside solid rock at such a depth that they can withstand even a direct hit by a nuclear warhead. Upon arrival of a launch order, a series of directed explosions, maybe even a small nuclear explosion, open a shaft through which the missiles fly into the open.

After the speaker was done, Andropov slowly walked to the diagrams illustrating the proposed basing modes for the U.S. strategic missiles, and stood still, deep in thought, amid a tense silence occasionally broken by someone's cautious cough. Stooped and sickly pale, Andropov looked very much like a defendant who has just heard a stiff sentence. Finally he turned and asked Kryuchkov: "How reliable is the information?"

"One hundred percent reliable," said the chief of external intelligence. "All previous material supplied by this agent has been authentic and entirely satisfactory to our military designers."

"It's over, then," Andropov said barely above a whisper. "We can't do anything at this level of technical sophistication. Further military competition with the Americans is pointless unless we are willing to destroy our economy completely. We have to come to terms with the U.S.—even at the price of major concessions. And the sooner we do it, the less we'll have to concede. We must prevent them from embarking on these projects before it's too late. Also, we'll have to revise our military doctrine. In light of what we've just heard, a first strike against America would be suicidal. We'll be lucky if we manage to retain some deterrence potential. Besides, as far as I understand, the Americans stress precisely the counterstrike capability—otherwise, there would be no point in their being so concerned about the missile-basing issue. It looks as though we've considerably exaggerated their aggressiveness all along."

It was a historic moment, marking a dramatic revision of the strategic doctrine and foreign policy of the Soviet Union. Gorbachev merely implemented the plans Andropov had drawn up but had not had the time to carry out. He was to die in a few months.

It goes without saying that the cardinal revision of the

Soviet foreign policy was not simply a result of Andropov's epiphany. Considering the sorry shape of the Soviet economy there could be no more dreams of building a socialist paradise throughout the whole world. Unlike Brezhnev in his twilight years, Andropov was lucid and capable of soberly assessing the situation. And that was probably his real service to his country.

By that time, Valentin had been recalled back to Moscow. Now he was head of the Washington Section of the North American Department, coordinating the activities of the Washington residency and its new chief, General Androsov.

The biggest contribution Androsov could have made to the Bill project was staying away from it. Yakushkin, smart man that he was, had done exactly that, and as a result had achieved considerable success. Unfortunately, the new resident decided to take charge. His first instruction was for Bill to take more care in selecting his material and deliver fewer papers—only the most interesting stuff—as a means of reducing the risk both to the agent and to his control. It was a dangerous mistake.

The simple truth was that Bill had no time to sift through and select material. While cleaning offices, he was constantly watched by the guards. His real work started when he entered the elevator with sacks full of papers.

Bill would stop the elevator between floors, dump the contents of the sacks on the floor, and furiously rummage through the papers. He would quickly select documents that he deemed to be of the greatest interest and roll them up in a newspaper to take home. Needless to say, he could not stay in the elevator for any length of time without arousing suspicion. He had to strike a balance between a desire not to miss anything important and the lack of time. He preferred to bring home as much as he could—let the people at the Soviet Embassy sort the papers out and decide what they needed and didn't need.

Constrained by Androsov's command, Bill faced a dilemma: either to prolong his dangerous stays in the elevator or to bring the whole catch home to sort it out at his leisure. Not surprisingly, the agent chose the latter option. From that time on, he would prepare a small batch of papers for transfer to the control and keep the rest at home.

Pretty soon he amassed a huge cache of stolen documents. What was he supposed to do with them? Previously, he had simply thrown them away—but that was before he had become a Soviet agent. Now if he was found out, the situation was far more dangerous.

Androsov, however, gave little thought to the agent's plight. He went right on exercising guidance, and in the spring of 1983 ordered that Bill be switched to dead-drop communication, theoretically a safer method. No personal contacts with Bill anymore. From now on Bill had to leave his papers in special hiding places and take from there instructions from his KGB handler. The theory said that it was safer. But in practice, maintaining contact via dead drops is so technically complicated that breakdowns in communication are inevitable, particularly at the outset. The new resident had no inkling of that—just as he had no inkling that a breakdown in communication was but a step away from a total failure of the operation.

Sometime later, Bill loaded some papers into a container three yards from the spot that Vladimir, Valentin's successor as his control, had indicated during the briefing. Try as he might, Vladimir failed to locate the package. There followed two weeks of anxiety and tension until Bill himself found and removed the papers.

All's well that ends well, right? Wrong! After that mishap, Valentin was tormented by a suspicion that during the fateful fortnight the FBI had found the papers and reloaded the drop to start an operative game with the KGB.

Failure was in the air, and finally it did happen.

In mid-October 1983, the radio intercept unit of the Washington residency determined that a surveillance operation was under way in downtown Washington. The FBI surveillance teams normally communicated in code, but that time they spoke in plain English, and their talk left no doubt who their target was: Bill.

That same night, Vladimir drove out to post a danger sign for his agent. Having reached the prearranged site, he was stunned to find out that Bill had already posted one. Apparently the agent had spotted the tail and decided to warn his control. Somehow he managed to leave the warning in spite of massive surveillance, even though it is unclear how an amateur could contrive to lose professional tails for a minimum of two hours—the amount of time it would have taken Bill to get from his home to the site. To this day, Valentin has a gnawing suspicion that the FBI committed its "blunder" by design.

All contacts with Bill were terminated, and sometime later the KGB learned some of the details of what had happened. The Peruvian residency managed to locate one of Bill's relatives, who said that one day the FBI had raided Bill's house and found an enormous hoard of stolen papers. He was interrogated for a long time but then was released, after which he vanished without a trace.

Interestingly, Valentin is still not sure who recruited whom: whether he persuaded Bill to work for Soviet intelligence, or whether Bill took advantage of the Soviets to scale new heights in his hobby, garbology. Nor is it clear exactly what led to the agent's downfall—Androsov's innovations, or his own mistakes of which the KGB was unaware.

Valentin found some consolation in the fact that Bill had not lost his freedom. He had paid a minimum price for cooperation with the Soviet intelligence. Valentin believes that the FBI either failed to discern the enormity of the security breach or decided to keep the whole affair under wraps. In truth, Bill had enjoyed no access to classified information, and merely passed on to the KGB the contents of trash baskets that were carried by the ton to the garbage dump or recycled. Had they attempted to put Bill on trial, his co-defendant would have been the entire information

security system of the United States. And there is no point
indicting the system. It will never be perfect, being forever
at odds with the two pillars of American society: economic
efficiency and a democratic, open national character.

I listened to Valentin in amazement. The events he was
relating to me had occurred only a few years back but
seemed to me to be part of another, long-ago era. It was as
if he had been employed by a different intelligence service.
The conditions under which I had to labor would have absolutely ruled out Bill's recruitment. Had Androsov, my
resident, been involved from the start, he would have
nipped the whole thing in the bud. I had reason enough not
to doubt this.

Once I had come into the residency carrying an issue of
National Geographic magazine, and bumped into Androsov.

"Do you like geography?" he asked me with an almost
courteous smile.

"No," I said. "It's just that an official contact I met at
lunch pressed it on me as a gift."

The resident's face changed dramatically. I had never seen
him that way, either before or after the incident. "How dare
you accept this magazine, you damn fool?" he yelled, sputtering and stamping his feet.

Stupefied, I looked at him and tried to fathom the reason
for such an extraordinary outburst of fury.

"Don't you understand they could conceal a classified
document between the pages and catch you red-handed?"
Androsov shouted. "Never, under any circumstances, are
you to accept any material from anyone, do you hear me?
Just you try to disobey, and off you'll go back to Moscow on
the first plane out!"

That was typical of the conditions that prevailed at the
residency. Boxes full of Boeing documents, when a mere
magazine was a no-no? Are you kidding?

Bill's story and the end of Valentin's career as an operative were a dire warning to me to give up all my ambitious recruitment plans and bow to the "spirit of the new times." But I made exactly the opposite resolution: to recruit, if not Socrates and Sputnitsa, then someone else—even if it killed me. Having committed myself, I decided to stay the course to the bitter end in order to find out—from my own experience rather than second-hand, from others' tales—the higher meaning of intelligence as practiced in the Soviet Union. As Napoleon used to say, "If the bottle is open, it has to be emptied."

I had one more incentive. In the final analysis, Valentin had worked for the Kremlin patriarchs. But now the country was being led by a different team with Gorbachev at the head, and I hoped the new leaders would be able to put intelligence information to much better use. It was a rather flimsy hope—every passing day on the job merely served to feed my skepticism. But what Russian officer ever shies away from a game of Russian roulette?

A month later, on the last day of my vacation in Moscow, I visited General Yakushkin to pay my respects.

"If you feel that Socrates can be recruited, you have to pursue the matter," the old general told me. "It is your debt of honor."

That was the last time I heard anyone in the intelligence service mention that expression. The "last of the Mohicans" took it with him on his way out.

5

I RETURNED to Washington in the spring of 1986. The very day of my return I went to the embassy. The working day was drawing to a close, and there was little reason for me to turn up at the residency after having spent nearly ten hours in the air. But Androsov appreciated all manifestations of zeal, and I had decided to play the game, which was absolutely essential for survival.

Each officer returning from vacation was eagerly awaited by his colleagues at the residency. Everyone was dying to learn the latest events at the center in Moscow, the latest rumors and gossip, trying to assess how the recent developments might affect their own career.

Androsov appeared and led me into his office. He proceeded to interrogate me in detail about the latest news from the KGB headquarters, and I told him about Motorin's arrest. The resident did not seem to be surprised.

"Now, I hope, you see how important it is to be prudent. It's clear now that the FBI people know a lot about our activities here. Remember, caution is the word. As a matter of fact, when are you planning a rendezvous with Socrates and Sputnitsa?"

"Very soon," I said.

"Don't forget to keep me posted on the results. I am especially interested in Sputnitsa's journalistic plans."

"You mean her career plans, or something specific?" I asked.

"Well," Androsov said reluctantly, "I mean what articles she is planning to write in the near future. Of course, only if she raises the point herself. On no account should you ask her."

There's something dirty here, I thought. Why would he be interested in Phyllis's articles? I definitely smelled a rat.

I went home to get some rest. It was crystal clear to me how to proceed, and I certainly wanted no part of Androsov's instructions.

The treachery of Colonel Yurchenko and Major Motorin had forced me into a technically difficult position. Now that the FBI was aware of our intelligence techniques and knew who I really was, I had to violate all the rules of the game if I was to outwit the Americans. The traditional lengthy counterintelligence routine using one's own car and the residency operative car did not seem effective anymore.

I decided to conduct the bulk of my countersurveillance maneuvers, prior to rendezvous with Socrates and Sputnitsa, on foot or using public transportation. This technique was unusual for the KGB operatives in the Washington residency and gave me an edge of surprise. Of course, there was no guarantee that I would succeed in throwing off the tails, which is why the core of my plan was to get through all the preliminaries with the prospective agents in two or three meetings and, if they still showed promise by then, to bring them to the Soviet Union to make them an offer of collaboration with the KGB.

Development of a prospective agent usually takes months

if not years, and any counterintelligence service knows that. Two or three meetings are absolutely nothing to go on; let the FBI try to figure out what happened within such a short time frame, I reasoned.

Still, I had to contend with the possibility that the FBI might upset all my designs. I realized that the Washington residency was doomed. With the help of Yurchenko and Motorin the FBI knew the identities of all the KGB operatives in the residency, and the only questions were how the residency would be destroyed and when. It was quite possible that the fate of the residency was being decided at the very pinnacle of the U.S. executive branch, taking into account the future of Soviet-American relations.

But the problem was that the FBI could at any time, without waiting for White House guidance, completely neutralize me by a simple technique. The FBI could approach me several times with recruitment offers.

Under a standard operating procedure of the Soviet intelligence service—which the FBI surely knew by now, thanks to the double agents—following each attempt at recruitment, the targeted KGB officer was required to submit an exhaustively detailed report to the Moscow headquarters. With inevitable clarifications, days, if not weeks, would be devoted to paperwork at the expense of actual intelligence work. And if the operative was thus approached on several occasions, he could forget about spying. In such cases, Moscow followed a logic that was simplicity itself: all right, today the officer reported the contact. But where is the guarantee that he will not be approached again and again until he succumbs to the recruiters' blandishments? It's better to be safe than sorry; bring him home.

Not to report about the contact with the FBI was suicidal, and Motorin's case was a gloomy reminder that it's better to return home than to do something foolish.

And so I nervously waited to be approached.

I met Socrates and Sputnitsa three days later in a tiny French café in Georgetown.

"We have a little surprise for you," Socrates said, handing me a postal envelope. "Read it; it's curious."

I opened the message and began reading. It was a letter to Assistant Secretary of Defense Richard Perle, signed by the president of the Heritage Foundation. The letter stated that the Soviet threat was a bluff, but one useful to American conservatives as a trump card in domestic politics. For this reason, Gorbachev's peaceful initiatives were to be declared a "menace" that had to be vigorously opposed. The president of the Heritage Foundation stressed the need to go on building up America's military might and doing everything to promote President Reagan's Strategic Defense Initiative.

The letter was written in a confidential tone, the way two like-minded people would conduct personal correspondence. I was somewhat taken aback by the letter's bluntness; not once did he mention U.S. national priorities, concentrating exclusively on the interests of the conservative political community.

"What is it?" I asked in bewilderment after I read the letter to the end.

"We got it in the mail a week ago," Socrates said.

"But there is no return address on the envelope."

"Exactly." He smiled.

"Who sent it?" I asked.

"We would also like to find that out," Sputnitsa observed.

Don't be a fool, my inner voice woke up. Don't you see that it has General Androsov's fingerprints all over it?

The letter literally shouted "Made in the KGB." Now it became clear to me why the resident had been so intent on finding out Sputnitsa's professional plans. He wanted to know if she could be sold on another of our forgeries.

But why didn't he tell me of his plan to carry out yet another active measure through Sputnitsa? I asked myself in bewilderment. Maybe he is checking someone out? No, it doesn't look like a check. If it is a purposeful action, it can have only one plausible goal: to trip Sputnitsa up, thereby derailing my attempt to develop her and Socrates. There is no way they would survive another public scandal.

Of course, it did not necessarily have to be a purposeful action; it might be just another example of incompetence. The Moscow headquarters could have sent a forged letter addressed to Richard Perle to the residency, with instructions to get it into print using any available means. And maybe Sputnitsa was the only one who would use that letter. So Androsov ordered her utilization yet again, on the principle that promptly complying with the headquarters' direction was the most important thing, while the future would take care of itself. In case of a scandal, he would command me to discontinue all contact with her. And everything would be fine. To hell with her, with the recruitment . . .

But what am I supposed to do now? I asked myself indignantly, trying very hard to keep my composure. Socrates and Sputnitsa are probably certain that I have something to do with this stupid letter. Thank you very much, Comrade Androsov, thank you for arranging this test for me. Even the FBI would have a hard time making things so difficult for me. Complete surprise is a guarantee of success of any test, and I have certainly been taken by surprise.

I was thinking furiously, all the while burying my face in the letter and pretending to study it in minute detail. The couple watched me intently.

"Well, it certainly is an interesting letter," I finally said. "Do you plan to use it?"

"No, of course not," Socrates said. "One scandal is enough for us."

"Maybe I should try to get it into print somehow?" I asked slyly. "Could it be a forgery?"

"Difficult to say," Sputnitsa said thoughtfully. "There is

only one way of checking its veracity: to ask the Heritage Foundation."

"No, I am not prepared to go that far," I said with a playful grin. "Still, you are experienced people. What do you think?"

"Experience tells us not to use anonymous letters anymore," Socrates said. "But if you wish, you can take it. Maybe someone in Moscow will find some use for it. Its basic idea is not bad, but the execution is too crude."

"All right, I'll think it over," I said, pocketing the letter. I had to take the damn piece of paper away from them; it was glaring evidence of an active measure stupidly conceived and equally stupidly botched.

Socrates and Sputnitsa appeared to be satisfied with my reaction to the letter. At any rate, the guarded expressions on their faces had disappeared.

"How long have you lived in America?" I asked.

"About a decade and a half," Sputnitza replied. "I even had a green card."

"Why haven't you been naturalized?"

"Because I don't want to," she said tersely. "I have my own country."

"And how did you meet each other?" I went on interrogating them.

"Oh, it's a veritable novel," Socrates replied. "Phyllis was the hostess of a popular radio program, a kind of talk show, in Scotland, where she grew up. At that time, I taught at Harvard. Once during a trip there, I heard her program. I was fascinated by her. So I pulled some strings and arranged to be interviewed on her program. She agreed, even though she mispronounced my name twice during the interview. Well, later we spent several days under siege in my folks' home—armed with a rifle!"

"Why the rifle?" I asked in surprise.

"Phyllis was married to a dyed-in-the-wool right-winger. I have no idea how she could stand him," Socrates went on.

"When he found out that we were in love, he swore to find us and for three days we hid out in my house. But we withstood the crisis, and later departed for America."

"Do you still teach at Harvard?" I asked.

"Not anymore. Life on a professor's salary is a bore." Socrates frowned. "So when I was offered a position with the Carter administration, I said yes without any hesitation. Even though I soon wished I hadn't."

"Why? That kind of job confers great prestige, doesn't it?"

"I was made in a different mold. My favorite college professor was a closet communist. We established a very close spiritual relationship. I treated him as a father. As a result, I turned into an inveterate socialist, but of a pragmatic variety. People of my ideological persuasion have a tough time finding a place in the sun in America. Besides, I am not an easy person to deal with. If I am convinced of something, I'll stick to my guns no matter what. Naturally, some people in Washington didn't like that at all."

"But how did you survive in such a place with your Socialist ideas?" I went on prodding my companions. They didn't seem to mind in the least.

"I kept my own counsel," Socrates replied. "Usually I would be done for the day by about eleven A.M. and spend the rest of my time conferring with Phyllis on the phone about our next spicy article. We had some earth-shaking publications in those days. Small wonder, since I knew so much . . ."

This fellow has a curious psychology, I thought. Before 11:00 A.M., he would work for the U.S. government and against it after 11:00. Amazing flexibility!

"And what do you do for a living now?" I asked him.

"I am a private political consultant."

"Do you advise the government?"

"No, only private citizens and nongovernmental organizations."

"Could you advise me?" Gradually, I was reeling him in.

It looked like an opportune time to step over yet another line separating a common journalist from an intelligence officer.

"Are you serious?" Socrates perked up. "What subject areas do you have in mind?"

"Well, you've probably noticed that the Soviet Union is currently trying to develop a new strategy in the area of foreign relations, including a new policy toward the U.S. Our national leadership is not monolithic by any measure; it's made up of several factions that are at odds with one another. We have our own hawks and doves . . . Lately, Gorbachev has been increasingly influenced by the doves, who advocate appeasement of America."

"It would be disastrous for your country," Socrates interjected.

"I agree, because I belong to the hawks," I said. For the umpteenth time I had to put on a mask. Everything I was saying at the moment was completely at odds with my actual feelings. I was merely baiting the hook in the hope that Socrates would bite. "But it's not easy for us to hold our own against the doves, because they have co-opted virtually the entire foreign policy establishment with its extensive American connections."

"But those connections are merely a channel for feeding you disinformation," Socrates remarked almost indignantly.

"I know. But it's important to make Gorbachev realize that. You have an enormous amount of experience and erudition. On top of that, you are a brilliant strategist, as I had ample opportunity to see during our last meeting. So if you agreed to share your ideas with me from time to time, I think we would be in a better position to influence Gorbachev and prevent the Soviet foreign policy, now that it has shed its crude pragmatism, from becoming too idealistic."

I finished my tirade and waited with bated breath. By intelligence standards, what I had just said almost qualified as a recruitment offer. To make one, I needed permission from both the resident and the center, which I didn't have. I could be severely punished, but I felt it was important to strike while the iron was hot.

"It's a deal," Socrates said, half seriously and half in jest. "Let's try to assess the effectiveness of my advice first, and talk about my fees later."

"Agreed," I said in the same half-serious, half-joking tone. At that time, it was the one most appropriate for both of us, because if anything unpleasant happened, the whole thing could be laughed off later as a bad joke. "I can guarantee that your advice will get to the very top of the Soviet leadership. Tass prepares material not only for publication, but also for top-level briefings. My stuff is used almost exclusively for the latter purpose."

"As I said, you've got yourself a deal," Socrates said, hugging Sputnitsa. "Let's go, dear, we still have work to do."

The next day, I stopped by the resident's office and, without a word, placed on his desk the letter Sputnitsa had given me.

"What's that?" Androsov asked with a sour expression.

"Your active measure," I replied dryly.

Frightened, he grabbed the letter and unfolded it.

"Hey, it's 'Zvon-2'!" (Translation: "Ringing-2," the code name assigned to the operation.)

"There won't be any *Zvon*," I said almost viciously. "As a matter of fact, Sputnitsa does her writing with Socrates."

"Well . . ." the resident mumbled. By the expression on his face, he didn't have a clue. At that point he had only one worry: how to explain to the center that an active measure code-named Zvon-2 had failed.

I did not wait for him to come to his senses, and took my leave. But I have to admit that my indignation knew no bounds. That moronic Zvon-2 had brought us to the verge of a scandal. What had the active measures service thought to achieve by sending its second forgery to Sputnitsa? Why hadn't they consulted the North American Department, as they were supposed to do, considering that Sputnitsa and Socrates were development projects of political intelligence?

Much later I found out that the whole story was the result of just one more botched job. The disinformation service leadership merely wanted to create a public row in order to demonstrate their effectiveness to Kryuchkov. They did ask the North American Department, but with General Yakushkin and Colonel Aksilenko gone, the department was in disarray and no one took the trouble of recalling that Socrates and Sputnitsa were our contacts. I was not even supposed to know about Zvon-2, which, if successful, would have placed that couple totally beyond our reach. In other words, yet another instance of crass stupidity, confusion, and incompetence.

A few days later, Androsov was recalled to Moscow as Yakushkin's replacement to be chief of the North American Department. The general's new appointment did not bode well; I had a premonition that soon the bell would toll for me.

As he said his farewells Androsov adressed me. "As for you, Comrade Lewis, we at the center will decide what to do about your contacts."

He couldn't have spelled out his intention more clearly: the Socrates-Sputnitsa project would be shut down—and soon.

Barely had Androsov departed when thunderclouds once again gathered over the residency. Gennadi Zakharov, an officer with the New York residency, was caught red-handed at a New York City subway station trying to buy college lab material from his contact, a Latin-American student, for a couple of thousand dollars.

In general, there was nothing unusual about that operation—except its timing. Soviet-American negotiations on another summit meeting were in the final stages. In light of that, the hunt for student lab material bordered on the insane.

The diplomats at the Washington embassy were aghast, the intelligence officers incredulous. To jeopardize a summit for the sake of such a trifle? How could it happen?

One theory was that thanks to Gorbachev's peace initiatives, the KGB's hold on him was weakening. It was becoming increasingly difficult to frighten the general secretary with the American threat, which the KGB had so successfully used to control his predecessors. The questions with which the Moscow headquarters bombarded the Washington residency clearly evidenced Kryuchkov's desire, if not to subvert, then at least to slow down the process of normalization of relations between the U.S. and the USSR. The objective interests of the KGB leadership lay in undermining the Soviet-American dialogue. And what could better serve that purpose than subverting a forthcoming summit?

Just a few weeks back, while I had been on vacation, such thoughts might have seemed absurd to me. But every passing day brought additional frightening proof that they were anything but imaginary.

A few days later, *U.S. News & World Report* correspondent Nicholas Daniloff was arrested in Moscow. He was nabbed in the midst of a rendezvous with a Soviet source who had brought him a map showing the disposition of certain Soviet military units in Afghanistan.

The speed with which the KGB carried out that operation indicated that it had been prepared before Zakharov was sent to meet the plant. The man in the street stood in awe of the efficiency of the KGB, but as an insider I knew only too well how things were really done at my outfit. Just to receive permission to apprehend Daniloff would have taken at least a week. Also, the operation had to be developed and planned, which also had to take a fair amount of time.

In a word, I had every reason for the troubling conclusion that, while Gorbachev tried to build bridges to the West, the KGB was playing an altogether different game. With Zakharov and Daniloff under arrest, the general secretary was trapped. He was required to show "firmness" in the face of "the nefarious designs of American imperialism." President Reagan, too, had to show equal firmness vis-à-vis Moscow's scheming. Both leaders became hostages of circumstances beyond their control. Both capitals resonated with thunderous declarations; the dawn of a new détente between the U.S. and the Soviet Union gave way to a new confrontation. It was terrifying to the people of both countries, but objectively served the personal interests of Kryuchkov and the entire leadership of the KGB.

And yet, Kryuchkov had apparently underestimated how serious Gorbachev was in his pronouncements about new political thinking. Like many other Soviet big wheels, the intelligence chief saw his leader's declarations exclusively as a political ploy aimed at strengthening the power of the elite—the *nomenklatura*. Kryuchkov's mistake nearly led him to disaster. The unforeseeable happened.

After a series of intensive contacts, Secretary of State George Shultz and Foreign Minister Eduard Shevardnadze announced that there would be a Soviet-American summit, in Reykjavik. They also pleasantly surprised the residency officers by agreeing to swap Zakharov and Daniloff. It was probably the first time in the history of the Soviet intelligence service that the government had stood up for one of its officers who had gotten into trouble.

This was surprising because in the USSR there were no indispensable people. This axiom has taken such deep root in the Soviet public consciousness that concern for individuals seemed not only out of place, but downright shameful. For example, the Soviet state had always treated its intelligence officers, not just with contempt, but with an incomprehensible sadism.

Prior to Nazi Germany's invasion of the USSR, Stalin's internal counterintelligence service had practically destroyed the entire Soviet intelligence network abroad. The guiding principle was that, after a few years abroad, an intelligence officer lost his ideological purity. In consequence, he was either liquidated in the country of his posting, or recalled home for "R&R"—to be executed or sent to the gulag.

The campaign of terror against his own intelligence service cost Stalin dearly, but failed to make him see reason. The intelligence officers who stole America's atomic secrets in the 1940s were marked men; they were to be executed in the event the first test of the Soviet nuclear warhead failed. Fortunately for them, the test went off without a hitch. The intelligence heroes were given the gift of life, while Lavrenti Beria, head of the NKVD, predecessor of the KGB, was awarded the country's highest military decoration: the star of Hero of the Soviet Union.

Many years later, when Khrushchev was at the helm, a few of the immediate participants of that intelligence operation were similarly nominated as Heroes. The award list was sent up to the Kremlin several times—only to be turned back on every occasion. It is said that Mikhail Suslov, the Politburo member who was the chief communist ideologist, was adamantly opposed to having the intelligence officers made Heroes of the Soviet Union. Small wonder, for such an award would have shown that the country owed its A-bomb to the intelligence effort, rather than the vaunted "advantages" of the Soviet political system or the "party's wise guidance."

A paradoxical situation emerged: the intelligence service had made an invaluable contribution to the strengthening of the USSR, but by the same token it had induced an inferiority complex in the Kremlin. The Soviet leaders trumpeted the advantages of socialism, while secretly using foreign achievements stolen by the intelligence service from the "doomed imperialists." Of course, they had no alternative to stealing, but people at the top of the pyramid of power couldn't help smarting at the thought that the Soviet Union was moving toward parity with America thanks to massive reliance on such contemptible means. And the most successful intelligence officers had to pay for the anguish of their leaders. They were squeezed like lemons, then dumped as garbage.

I knew quite a few stories like that, which is why the firm stand of the new national leadership in defense of Zakharov came as a pleasant surprise. Gorbachev's actions commanded respect.

In August of 1986 the Reykjavik summit was around the corner, and I rushed to see Socrates. A great pretext had presented itself to test his readiness to serve as my "adviser." This time Socrates turned up alone.

He was agitated, and got down to business without further ado: "By agreeing to a summit, President Reagan has painted himself into a corner. His administration is knee-deep in enormously serious internal problems: the promised budget cut is up in the air; the military buildup program has bogged down in Congress; the president is forever vacillating between arms control and Star Wars; the tax reform has no popular backing; social reform is spinning its wheels. Given all these problems, the president badly needs a success in Reykjavik. You can't miss such a golden opportunity; you must take advantage of the situation. Demand maximum concessions, be a bully, show toughness. He has nowhere to go. A failure at Reykjavik could spell disaster for Reagan."

"It sounds good, but is he really that vulnerable?" I was openly skeptical, hoping to spur Socrates on.

"I have some ideas." Socrates paused for effect and gave me an enigmatic look. "The scandal around the sale of

American arms to Iran is just beginning. There are two powerful bombs that have yet to be exploded."

"What are they?" His excitement was contagious; I was beginning to get nervous myself.

"Number one. The proceeds from the sale were used by the administration to give military aid to the Nicaraguan contras, thereby violating an act of Congress that prohibits actions of this kind. Moreover, in the course of that operation, the CIA helped the Medellín cartel to smuggle illicit drugs into the U.S., where the money was converted into arms for the contras. In a little while, this sensational revelation will definitely be disclosed to the U.S. media, but at this point very few people know about it. Quite possibly, President Reagan has no idea of it, even though the affair has a good chance of turning into his Watergate. If Gorbachev springs this surprise on Reagan at the summit, there can be little doubt that the U.S. president will become far more malleable."

"The facts, Martin! Where are the facts?"

"There is an organization in Washington called the International Center for Development Policy. One of its employees is an ex-CIA officer who used to work somewhere in Central America. On the basis of his experience, he prepared a report on the CIA ties to the Medellín cartel. It contains everything you need: the names of the agents; the time and place of each meeting; a description of the Colombian-drugs-for-arms-for-the-contras operation."

"And the other bomb?" I could barely contain my excitement.

"Here it is," he said, handing me a thin folder. "It contains some newspaper clippings and my own commentary. The gist of the problem is this: part of the proceeds from the sale of arms to the Iranians has 'stuck' to the hands of a few Washington officials who were privy to the operation. Let me repeat, it's just the bare bones of a story, which Moscow hopefully will be able to flesh out. I think these two bombs will serve Gorbachev in good stead."

Listening to Socrates, I began to think. Who would be the recipient of this information back in Moscow? Who would use it and in what way? Would it help my country, or merely further somebody's selfish interests? I couldn't answer those questions. Still, I had to encourage Socrates for his efforts.

"Not a bad beginning, Martin. I am amazed by your strategic analysis. Let's hope it will be parlayed into something tangible."

"I'll keep my fingers crossed. And remember, you should bring overwhelming pressure to bear on the Americans."

I was about to say goodbye when he stunned me with a query: "Do you have any idea how your former foreign friends are doing in Moscow?"

"What friends?" I asked in surprise.

"Well, for example, Philby, or perhaps Howard, the former CIA officer who recently fled to the Soviet Union?"

Is he planning to become one of them? I thought. Judging from his expression, it doesn't appear to be idle curiosity. I'd better play along.

"I'm afraid I don't know, but I think they are doing just fine. Our government knows how to be grateful for a job well done."

"They must be drawing good pensions," Socrates observed. He sounded as if he was trying hard to convince himself that it was indeed so.

"No question about it," I assured him. "They belong to the elite of our society, which is shielded from the problems besieging common Soviet men and women. Come to think of it, why don't you both travel to the Soviet Union and have a look?"

"We've planned to do just that for a long time, but somehow never have gotten around to it," he said.

"Are you serious about such a visit?"

"Absolutely."

"Then what's stopping you? Listen, I think I might be of some help to you."

That night I tossed and turned in my bed, too excited to sleep. Socrates showed such promise it was frightening. Now I was almost completely sure he was not a FBI plant. No plant would ever supply a Soviet intelligence officer with information of such incendiary potential. Whether it was authentic or not was totally irrelevant. Even if it was a fake, the FBI would never have dared palm it off on Soviet intelligence.

Besides, Socrates had actually suggested that we conduct an active measure—"flesh out the bare bones." Which meant that he had no problem dealing with a likely KGB officer.

And his question about Howard and Philby, what was that about? He had asked it as though planning to flee to the Soviet Union for good. So by and large, everything seemed to fit nicely into my original assumptions.

The next day, I planned to pay a visit to the International Center for Development Policy. At 11:30 A.M., I asked the Tass bureau chief to let me go for a couple of hours and, as usual, he readily complied. I got into my car and set out for Childrens Hospital, where my son had been hospitalized the previous year with a broken arm.

My FBI godfather and his faithful Impala were nowhere to be seen, but it gave me little satisfaction. Overt surveillance has its points, my inner voice was grumbling as I wound my way through the dense traffic on Washington's miserable roads. At least you know where you stand. And now? Maybe there is no tail, but maybe you just can't see it.

The hospital is located on Michigan Avenue, in Northeast Washington. As usual, the hospital grounds were nearly empty of people and cars. The red-brick, four-story garage was in the far end. I parked my Chevy on the upper level, on the open roof of the building, and looked around. The coast was clear. Time to start the operation.

I got out of the car, took a new pair of shoes from a plastic bag and put them on. The old shoes went into the trunk. Then I thoroughly wiped my hands with alcohol, pocketed the open flask to throw it away some distance from the garage, and put on a brand-new blue jacket. Such jackets were in vogue in Washington at the time, and one could hardly devise a better disguise.

Having thus changed my appearance, I slammed the car door shut, walked to the edge of the roof, and descended to the street level by way of the fire escape. The only exit from the garage was on the opposite side, so I could assume with a fair degree of certainty that nobody would be waiting for me here. My watch read 12:34 P.M.

There was a bus stop about three hundred yards from the garage. According to the schedule, the next bus was to depart in six minutes. So far so good.

There were six bored passengers on the bus. The driver closed the door behind me and turned the key in the ignition. The countersurveillance routine continued.

I took the last seat in the back of the bus and looked out the window intently. There were no outward signs of surveillance. If I am still being followed, then the tail ought to board the bus at the next stop or the one after that, I thought, preparing for the next ploy.

At the next stop, only one passenger got onto the bus—a black woman. Given her age and impressive girth, there was no way she could be surveillance. I started edging toward the exit.

Another stop. Two young guys entered. Can't be a tail, I thought. Two are too many for a half-empty bus. On the other hand, though, one shouldn't overestimate the opposition. They're also prone to blunders. The driver was about to close the doors when I, seeming to wake suddenly from a deep slumber, dashed outside like a bullet. A cab was driving on the opposite side of the street. I flagged it down.

"The Shrine of the Immaculate Conception, in Northeast," I told the cabbie.

The majestic shrine was nearly empty. Someone was playing the organ. A huge mural depicting Jesus Christ stood out like a bright spot in the semi-darkness.

I intended to spend a couple of hours in the cathedral, killing time and once again going over the plan for my subsequent course of action. But a few minutes later, it became clear that a church is not the best stage for a spy drama. It predisposes one to think of the eternal, compared to which all mundane issues pale into insignificance.

My God, what are you doing? And whom are you serving? I thought. But the Lord bade Moses to spy out the land of Canaan, didn't he? Which means that, in principle, intelligence is good work, isn't it . . . ? The whole point, it seems, is its objectives. Almost all spies sent by Moses brought back false information about what they had seen, and were severely punished by the Lord. Only Caleb and Joshua told the truth and were rewarded.

Blessed are they which hunger and thirst after righteousness. But who in my country needs the truth? Androsov and Kryuchkov? They couldn't care less.

Maybe Gorbachev does? I speculated hesitantly. Let's hope he needs the truth. It appears that he has launched something good.

I sat on the bench, closed my eyes, and immersed myself into the enchanting world of organ music. I had to wait a while longer.

At 3:00 P.M., I stood up and walked to the exit. I went down into the Brookland Metro station and took the first Red Line train. Its destination did not interest me in the least. I was totally preoccupied with the most important task of the moment: in the remaining time available to me, I had to decide whether or not I was under surveillance and take action accordingly.

What I did at that stage of the countersurveillance routine would have terrified the resident: I rushed out of the train at each stop, when the doors were already closing; took the next train only to repeat the ploy at the next station; switched lines; moved from one platform to another.

It is known in the trade as "crude countersurveillance." In principle, the purpose of countersurveillance consists not merely in determining, with a sufficient degree of confidence, whether one is followed or not; the maneuver must be executed so subtly as to be unrecognizable to the tail. But when the chips are down and the stakes are high enough, sometimes even crude ploys have their uses. The officer no longer thinks about disguising his maneuvers; the paramount task is to find out and then to elude the tail.

I had been thoroughly schooled in tricks of that nature. My instructors at the intelligence school strongly believed in their effectiveness. They felt that American counterintelligence officers, spoiled by all the technical marvels at their fingertips, were uncomfortable at low-tech tasks, such as surveillance on foot.

About an hour passed. I was dog-tired but still couldn't tell with certitude if there was anyone on my tail. Intimidated by all those breathtaking stories of the technical superiority of the American special services, I was afraid that my godfather was simply watching my maneuvers in the Metro on the screen of his monitor at FBI headquarters.

I left the Metro at Union Station, where it is always easy to lose oneself in the crowd, hailed a cab, and gave the address of the F. Scott Fitzgerald Theater in the Northwest quadrant of D.C. The ride would take about half an hour, during which time I hoped to rest a bit and collect my thoughts.

"Are you a foreigner, sir?" the cabbie unceremoniously barged in, and I recognized the painfully familiar Russian accent that most immigrants from the USSR cannot shed to the end of their days.

Damn it, just what I need now, my inner voice groaned. What if he is a former prisoner of conscience?

"How did you know?" I asked admiringly, with as nice a smile as I could muster at the moment.

"Taxi drivers are observant people, and former Soviet cabbies are doubly observant."

"Oh, you are from Russia? And how are things back there?" I hastened to ask him. Under the circumstances, it was better for me to listen than to answer the questions of my ex-compatriot.

The trick worked. Flattered by his passenger's attention, the cabbie talked nonstop. Before long, I knew his biography, all his numerous relatives still living in Odessa, his philosophy, and his plans for the future. The cabbie's biggest problem was that in America he had to look for fares all the time. In the Soviet Union, where he had also driven a taxi, everything was different, because cabs there were as much at a premium as everything else.

Yes, sir, life was easier in Odessa. Yet he wanted to have a better life, and so he came to America. But he didn't like what he saw in his new country. Surprisingly, it was not easy to have a better life. It required an entirely different outlook, one that was altogether alien to him.

The cabbie complained about everything: the poor earnings in Washington; the high prices; the meager tips; the lack of friends; the difficulties with English; and the roads in D.C.—although he readily agreed that the roads in Odessa were hardly any better.

Oh, those Soviets, I thought. Are they ever satisfied with anything? Look at this poor bastard, for instance. He doesn't like it here, so why not pull up stakes, go back to Odessa, and resume building a paradise on earth. But no, rather than returning home, the poor martyr prefers to suffer and soldier on in the imperialist hell.

It was time to say goodbye. I told the cabbie to drop me off at the first restaurant I saw, gave him a generous tip, and asked him innocently: "How long ago did you choose freedom?"

While my former compatriot was trying to penetrate the meaning of the question, I disappeared into the restaurant. I studied the menu, lit a cigarette, looked outside, saw that the ex-citizen of Odessa was gone, and walked outside. I hailed another cab and without further adventures reached the International Center for Development Policy, which was located at the opposite end of the city, in the Southeast section.

The receptionist, a young woman, sat behind a huge glass partition, probably bulletproof. I was impressed with such tough security measures, the likes of which I had previously encountered only at the British Embassy. After she learned that I was a Tass correspondent, she asked me to wait and called someone on the phone. I waited in tense silence.

"Hi, how are things in Moscow?" a middle-aged man came out and gaily greeted me in Russian.

I introduced myself and briefly told him the reason for my visit: "I need your report on the CIA ties with the Medellín cartel."

"Let's go and have a look," the man said politely, revealing no surprise whatsoever. I followed him upstairs to the center office.

Some ten minutes later, I had the report in my hands.

"May I use this document in print?" I asked.

"Of course, you may," the American said. "We have been thinking about ways of disseminating it ourselves."

"But it is as yet unknown outside your organization, isn't it?"

"Yes, it is."

"I have to apologize if my question strikes you as impolite, but how reliable is your information?"

"One hundred percent reliable," he assured me. "It was written by a former CIA officer who enjoyed direct access to the source material. Why don't you ask him yourself? There he is, talking to that gentleman."

I had no desire to introduce myself to a CIA officer, even a former one, and hastily bade him farewell.

The next day at the residency, I thoroughly studied the report. To make a long story short, I had in my hands a document of incredible destructive power, except for one small, but important, "but": it contained no irrefutable evidence that the CIA was involved in what the document described as a complicated cocaine-for-weapons operation centered in Central America. The CIA involvement was the key to the whole issue. Without such a smoking gun, the information was useless in the sense that Socrates had in mind.

That day, the residency sent to Moscow a long cable with a detailed summary of the report of the International Center for Development Policy and Socrates' oral communication that part of the proceeds from the sale of American weapons to Iran had been stolen by certain Washington officials.

A couple of weeks later, the active measures service responded in a way that left me puzzled. Usually, the cables sent by headquarters were dry in form and stern in content. Moscow had always been lavish with criticism, and on those rare occasions when headquarters had wished to express its satisfaction, it did so in an extremely reserved manner. During my intelligence career, I had read a lot of operative files, but I had never come across anything like that cable. In tone, it reminded me of the "Ode to Joy," and was almost cloyingly effusive by the standards of the Soviet intelligence service.

I was informed of the "profound satisfaction" that the active measures service had derived from the "detailed, timely and well-reasoned material on the cocaine-for-weapons-for-contras operation," and was congratulated on "a major success." The cable ended with this instruction: "Watch for the response to our active measures devised on the basis of your material."

I had no choice in the matter other than to obey. In view

of Moscow's enthusiastic reaction to the information that had come my way courtesy of Socrates, I had a premonition of a forthcoming dramatic denouement.

The promised active measures were not long in coming. On October 5, about ten days after the arrival of the headquarters cable and just six days before the Reagan-Gorbachev meeting in Reykjavik, a plane piloted by one Eugene Hasenfus was shot down over Nicaragua. Digging through the debris, our "Nicaraguan friends" found interesting documents, including some papers cooked up by the KGB active measures service. The news that the CIA was involved in illegal attempts to help the contras made the front page all over the world. The U.S. media enthusiastically jumped onto the bandwagon, and on the eve of the Reykjavik summit a major scandal broke out in Washington. Thus did the Soviet intelligence service take measures to endanger the meeting between the general secretary of the Soviet Union and the president of the United States.

Later, I found out some of the details of how the information Socrates gave me regarding the drugs-for-weapons operation had been put to use. I had quite a few contacts in the active measures service who personally designed operations on the basis of information provided. These intelligence officers had a pretty good idea of the motives behind the orders for a specific active measure. The bosses could never hide their designs from their subordinates.

Prior to the Reykjavik summit, the intelligence service— indeed, the entire KGB—was horrified to realize that its influence on Gorbachev was rapidly dwindling. Since the former Soviet ambassador in Washington, Anatoly Dobrynin, had been appointed secretary of the Central Committee of the Communist Party, he had all but monopolized Soviet policy toward Washington. The trend spelled disaster for the KGB.

Kryuchkov had long hated Dobrynin. When the Washington residency was headed by General Yakushkin, several

American politicians made an attempt, on the eve of presidential elections, to establish a communications channel to the Kremlin via the KGB. As a result, the prestige of the residency—indeed of the whole intelligence service—got such a big boost that Yakushkin once casually remarked: "We are in a position to influence the outcome of the U.S. presidential elections, you know."

But it didn't take Dobrynin long to deflate those ambitions. He declared firmly and decisively that all political connections to America should run via his embassy, while the residency should confine itself to spying.

In view of Dobrynin's influence with the Soviet leaders, the intelligence service had to swallow this bitter pill in silence. And so it did, but the humiliation stuck forever in its craw. Dobrynin became an enemy, the epitome of "those doves entrenched in the Ministry of Foreign Affairs who carry water for Washington." That's what the intelligence brass thought of the activities of the Soviet foreign policy establishment.

As secretary of the Central Committee, Dobrynin took the most important issues of Soviet-American relations directly to Gorbachev. As a matter of fact, this was how the idea of an impromptu summit at Reykjavik was conceived. Gorbachev and Dobrynin took a walk one day on a sandy beach in the Crimea, and decided to waylay President Reagan with a sudden proposal for a dramatic reduction of the strategic arsenals in exchange for an end to the SDI.

Kryuchkov jealously watched Dobrynin's stock going up, but was powerless to do anything about it. And then along came Socrates with his blockbuster message.

Since the end of World War II, the Soviet policy toward the U.S. could be summarized in one sentence: If America has no domestic problems, they must be created. Let the Americans focus on their internal affairs, instead of trying to interfere with our efforts to build a glorious future. The active measures service had always played a prominent role in the implementation of that policy. The active measure prepared on the basis of the information supplied by Socrates followed the general script.

According to the plan hatched by the external intelligence brass, the downing of Hasenfus's plane was intended to send a signal to the Reagan administration that Moscow knew much more than it let on. The real fireworks were reserved for Reykjavik.

On the eve of the summit, Kryuchkov gave Gorbachev a detailed briefing. Among other things, the intelligence chief told the Soviet leader that the CIA maintained ties with the Medellín Cartel, and that certain Washington officials had skimmed the proceeds of the arms sale to Iran to feather their own nests. I was told that the intelligence chief presented the damning information as indisputable, irrefutable facts.

The information served up to Gorbachev by the active measures service looked very much like an attempt to blackmail the U.S. president into a trade-off: our silence in exchange for an end to the Strategic Defense Initiative. It was assumed that, with the damaging information up his sleeve, Gorbachev would try to strong-arm Reagan—at least, this is precisely what any of his predecessors would have done, and Kryuchkov cautiously tried to plant the idea in the general secretary's mind. The intelligence chief's idea was that if Gorbachev could be persuaded to follow his cue, the U.S. president would have to strike a defiant pose; the Reykjavik summit would be a bust; Dobrynin and the Soviet foreign policy establishment that had promised Gorbachev a triumph would be seriously compromised; and the KGB would be able to regain its influence over the general secretary.

So here is what was actually at stake: not the outcome of a titanic struggle of the two superpowers; not the national interests of the Soviet Union; but, rather, a puny interagency pissing contest, a measly bout of bureaucratic in-fighting within the bowels of a system already dying, though as yet unsuspecting of its impending doom.

The active measure did not succeed as planned. The intelligence service had hoped that the U.S. press would pick up and run with the theme of the illegal aid to the contras, but nobody expected that the bombshell would go off with such a bang. Within a mere six days, between the downing of Hasenfus's plane in Nicaragua and the Gorbachev-Reagan summit, the U.S. media disclosed so much about the affair that precious little was left for Gorbachev to add in Reykjavik, except to raise the extremely delicate issue of corruption involved in the sale of American arms to Iran.

Fortunately, in that instance Gorbachev proved more cunning than his "chief spook." Reportedly, he did disclose the information to Reagan during their prolonged meeting behind closed doors, but presented it as a goodwill gesture, a manifestation of his concern for the political fate of the U.S. president.

The general secretary also promised that the KGB would refrain from fanning the flames of the Iran-contra scandal. The active measures service received the corresponding order immediately after Reykjavik, when it was already in the midst of an operation capitalizing on the corruption information supplied by Socrates. Thanks to Gorbachev, the KGB was quietly restrained.

On October 12, the U.S. media declared that the U.S.-USSR summit had failed. Victory! The top brass of the KGB rubbed their hands with glee. But a mere two days later, high U.S. officials unanimously pronounced Reykjavik a major success even though it had not resulted in any arms control agreement; its true achievement consisted of the fact that the American and Soviet leaders had developed a mutual trust.

Kryuchkov managed to find a way out of his quandary, passing himself off as one of the chief architects of the Reykjavik success. After all, wasn't he the one who had provided Gorbachev with the information that formed the foundation of mutual trust? Sometime later, he was promoted to the rank of four-star general. For the first time in the annals of the KGB, its external intelligence arm had an official of such exalted rank at its head.

Kryuchkov's hangers-on who came to offer their congratulations noticed their chief's somewhat strange deportment. He sat in a deep armchair like a pharaoh, vacantly staring at the ceiling. It was the look of a person who was out of his mind with joy.

All his life, Kryuchkov had been a zealous servant, doing someone else's bidding. But at that moment, he came to the conclusion that he could lead, not just the intelligence service, but the whole country. It was on that day, it seems, that he embarked on the path that would lead to the August 1991 coup and his imprisonment as a coup leader.

But leaving aside the events surrounding Reykjavik and the concerns of the intelligence brass on the eve of the Soviet-American summit, one has to admit that from a purely professional standpoint, the intelligence service pulled off a truly daring operation. I was surprised to find out that Soviet intelligence was still alive. The world might yet see that the KGB had mid-level officers secure in their skills and yearning to apply themselves to a worthy cause. To succeed, they did not need much: just a go-ahead order and no further interference from the communist bureaucracy above.

On the morning of October 21, a mere eight days after Reykjavik, I entered the Tass bureau and was surprised to see my colleagues uncharacteristically glued to the TV screen.

"What's up?" I asked.

"Shhhhh," Oleg Polyakovsky hissed and pointed at the screen. "Listen carefully."

State Department spokesman Charles Redman, slightly stuttering with excitement, was reading a statement to the effect that a large group of Soviet diplomats suspected of being KGB spies was to be expelled from Washington. He named only four names, and said that the list of the others would be handed over to the Soviet Embassy.

It's over, then, I thought. What will happen now?

The air in the residency was thick with gloom. Comrade Smell from the external counterintelligence section was particularly incensed, thundering against that spineless Gorbachev with his proclivity to endless appeasement of the Americans, whose arrogance knows no bounds.

When he saw me, Comrade Smell's eyes narrowed and glinted maliciously.

"I wonder what kind of services you have rendered to the Americans?" he hissed viciously.

"Get off my case." I waved him off.

"No, I'm serious," Smell persisted. "Tell me the truth. How come you are one of a mere handful to be spared by them?"

I looked at him guardedly and suddenly realized to my horror that he wasn't joking. Only three other intelligence officers were staying; the rest were packing up. A more dreadful situation could hardly be imagined. By remaining in Washington, I would automatically become suspect in the eyes of General Androsov. His inflamed imagination would certainly conjure up the most apocalyptic visions, similar to those voiced by Comrade Smell.

The only option available to me was to do nothing. Under any circumstances. Nothing at all. Ever.

In fact, everything could be explained easily enough. After the loud Daniloff affair, the U.S. apparently decided to leave the Russian correspondents alone in the hope that the Soviet authorities would repay the courtesy and spare the American journalists in Moscow. Because I was a Tass correspondent, as well as a KGB officer, I was permitted to remain in the U.S.

*　　*　　*

On November 1, practically the entire Washington residency was shipped out to Moscow, while I went into a depression—but not for long. On November 25, President Reagan announced at a press conference that he "was not fully informed on the nature of the activities undertaken in connection with this [Iran] initiative," and that his national security adviser, Admiral John Poindexter, and National Security Council aide Oliver North had been fired.

Then the president yielded to Attorney General Ed Meese, who stunned America with an admission that the proceeds from the sale of arms to Iran had been channeled, probably illegally, to the Nicaraguan contras.

The two statements signified the onset of the acute political crisis that became known as Iran-contra.

And just three days later, the CBS Evening News reported an interesting item: on November 27, Thanksgiving Day, the offices of the International Center for Development Policy had been ransacked. Nothing was missing, but the unidentified vandals had smashed the computers and destroyed some files.

I was shaken by the news. Most Americans wouldn't give it a second thought, but I knew better. Only two days after the administration had publicly acknowledged the contra connection, there was a mysterious break-in at the organization where I had learned the details of that operation! Moreover, nothing was stolen, they just destroyed some files—precisely those files from which I had learned about that very contra connection! The incident might be seen as a coincidence by some, but not by me.

I recognized an act of belated revenge. Clearly, in spite of all the countersurveillance tricks, my visit to the International Center for Development Policy had been registered. The Reykjavik summit had shown the results of that visit, and on Thanksgiving Day, one of the culprits of the "information leak" had been punished. I was next. As for Socrates, no matter how long and hard I asked myself whether he had been burned, there was no unambiguous answer. One thing was clear: under the circumstances, all contact with him had to be suspended.

That night, I was on duty at the Tass bureau and had to write a report concerning the CBS Evening News show. I didn't know whether or not to mention the break-in at the International Center for Development Policy—although, in reality, I had little choice in the matter. The next day, that news item could make the newspapers, in which case I would have to answer for an attempt to conceal information. I wrote a complete report, knowing full well that General Androsov, as new chief of the North American Department in Moscow, began his morning routine by perusing the Tass reports on the news shows of the American networks.

The very next day an urgent cable arrived at the residency. Androsov almost hysterically ordered the suspension of all contacts with Socrates and Sputnitsa. For once, we saw eye to eye on an operational matter, making identical assessments of the meaning of the break-in and its possible consequences.

A new resident, General Ivan Gromakov, came to Washington, but his arrival had little impact on the life of our now small community. We had to prove to the center that, despite the devastation of the residency, we were busy as ever. Prove it on paper, that is. Gromakov was an eminently suitable candidate to accomplish that task. A Russian teacher by training, he was a master of the epistolary style. Under his guidance, paperwork grew to unprecedented proportions. Finally, I got sick and tired of the window dressing, and turned my attention almost completely to journalistic pursuits.

But before long fate brought Socrates and me together again.

In January 1987, the U.S. was shaken by yet another episode of escalating violence. In the space of just one month, nine Westerners, including three Americans, were taken hostage in Beirut, bringing the total number of hostages held in Lebanon by Shiite radical factions to thirty, of whom eight were Americans. A powerful U.S. naval task force was being deployed in the southern Mediterranean: twenty ships headed by two of the world's largest aircraft carriers, the U.S.S. *John F. Kennedy* and the U.S.S. *Nimitz*. Once more, hostilities were in the wind.

The residency was confronted with a legitimate question: What were the objectives of the American armada? Was it preparing for a counterstrike? If so, when and against whom?

In April 1986, in eerily similar circumstances, the U.S. had struck at Libya to punish Qaddafi for his support of international terrorism. But this time the mad colonel did not seem to be involved. The hostage crisis broke out in Lebanon, and the American task force was being built up near the Lebanese shores.

The Reagan administration badly needed to show its resolve—if possible, quickly and without casualties. Beirut was a poor candidate; an armed action on the part of the United States could easily provoke the terrorists into killing their hostages. But the huge naval task force had already been deployed to the Mediterranean. Moscow was gravely concerned that under the circumstances Libya would again be used as the scapegoat to demonstrate American resolve.

In the middle of February, I was summoned by Gromakov.

"We have three hours to state unambiguously whether or not Libya will be targeted for another strike. Kryuchkov's orders. Can you think of something?"

"Do you think the White House has an unambiguous answer to this question?" I asked sarcastically.

"It doesn't matter," Gromakov replied. "We have been ordered to provide an answer, and we have to comply."

The resident apparently saw a shadow of a doubt in my face, and increased the pressure: "We have a mutual assistance pact with Libya. All right, I know that last spring we swallowed the attack on Qaddafi—after all, we were caught by surprise. But this time, the tension is building up gradually, and we have to come up with some response. Our fleet is stationed in the Mediterranean next to the U.S. Sixth Fleet. Usually they play a cat-and-mouse game with each other, but what's to be done now? Suppose the Americans launch a bunch of missiles and our ships do something foolish . . . In fact, under the NATO doctrine, an attack on one of their ships shall be perceived as an act of war."

Still I kept silent, and Gromakov decided to massage my ego.

"This is the first important assignment we have received since the devastation of the residency. Moscow knows very well the sorry state we are in, and if they appeal to us for information, it means that the country desperately needs it. Will we acknowledge our own impotence?"

I hated the word "impotence."

"The only person to whom I could appeal for help in this instance is Socrates," I said.

"He is exactly the one I had in mind," Gromakov said animatedly. "Unfortunately, we have no other option."

"But surely you know that the center has forbidden me to see him!" I exclaimed.

"Do we have any alternative?" the resident said with a gesture of resignation. "Remember, it's an extraordinary situation."

"Okay, I'll do it," I said, hating myself for following the dictates of emotion rather than reason.

"Don't forget, the cable to the center has to be sent within three hours," the resident reminded me as I walked to the door.

I was driving to a rendezvous with Socrates, feeling like a kamikaze pilot climbing into the cockpit, knowing it will be the last mission of his life and yet determined to accomplish it no matter what. There is no alternative, I was thinking. Our fleet is on station in the Mediterranean, and my government is faced with a crucial decision. It's not by accident that Kryuchkov gave us only three hours to come up with the information. It had been a long time since an assignment from the center had been so tough and demanding.

On the other hand, I knew that, whether I succeeded or failed, my career was set in concrete. I was going to be recalled to Moscow very soon in any case. Setting out to see Socrates, I was violating the center's directive. Androsov would never miss such a golden opportunity to kill two birds—myself and Socrates—with one stone.

I would not do it for the sake of my career, but for the sake of my soul, as a Russian saying goes.

I left my car about a mile from Socrates' house and called him on the phone. As luck would have it, he was at home.

"Martin, I have to see you on a matter of great urgency."

"When?" His voice betrayed some surprise. In the past, we had arranged our meetings well in advance.

"Today," I said.

"Where?"

"At your place, if possible. I received an urgent assignment from the home office, and have spent the whole day driving about the city. So I am afraid to arrange a meeting at a restaurant because I don't know when I'll be free."

"Okay," Socrates agreed. "You can come anytime you like."

Which will be pretty soon, I thought, and began walking toward his house at a brisk pace. I had to arrive as soon as possible. No matter how profound an intelligence officer's trust in his agent, an ineradicable suspicion always lurks in some remote corner of his mind: What if the agent is a plant? In that case he must call the FBI and report my call, I was thinking. While they ponder the situation and talk it over, I'll show up. The most important thing is not to give them time to nab me in his place in the midst of an attempt to obtain information.

When he opened the door, Socrates' mouth also flew open with surprise. It was barely half an hour since my call.

"So fast?" he asked me.

"You wouldn't believe the crazy roller coaster I'm on. The situation changes with breakneck speed," I muttered, trying to look like a person who had lost his head in all the fuss and bustle. "I need your help."

"I'll be glad to oblige," Socrates said. "Come in and make yourself comfortable."

"What are you going to drink—tea, coffee, or Pepsi?" asked a smiling Sputnitsa, who had come out to welcome me.

"Makes no difference as long as it's fast," I said. "I'm dying of thirst."

"Well, what happened?" Socrates asked me, sitting down in a rather tattered armchair.

"I got a request for information from the Tass central office," I said. "They want to know if Libya is going to be hit again. The situation looks quite serious."

"You think this time your side is prepared to do something to deter the Americans?" Socrates asked doubtfully.

"Judging by the tone of the cable I got, yes, I do."

"That would be great," he said pensively. "The administration has gotten so insolent it's time it got its comeuppance."

"Can you help?" I asked.

Socrates thought for a moment, then jumped up to his feet.

"Let me give a call to a friend at the Pentagon. Wait here."

He went into the other room, and soon I heard him talking on the phone. I could only make out snatches of phrases and words: "aircraft carrier," "Tomahawk," "situation room," "Soviet carrier," "special group is in continuous session . . ."

If he is a plant, now is the time for them to nab me, I

thought. In my mind's eye I could see two hulking fellows with cold eyes and steel biceps descending the stairs and walking toward me.

I was by no means paranoid. A few years back, two of my colleagues had been apprehended—one in New York City, the other in Washington, D.C.—under similar circumstances. The grievous experience of my predecessors did little to soothe my nerves.

Finally Socrates reappeared, his eyes betraying the now familiar gambler's sparkle.

"Take out your notebook," he said, all business. "The decision as to whether or not to strike—and, if so, then whom to strike—has not yet been made. A special group of high administration officials is in continuous session in the situation room. In general, a consensus is emerging in favor of making a show of force but not using it. Libya is on the short list of potential targets, but so far they haven't found a suitable pretext to attack it. In short, much depends on Qaddafi, or rather on whether he will be able to keep his mouth shut, and on your country, too."

"Where do we come in?" I asked, making notes on my pad.

"The Kiev carrier group is steaming toward the U.S. Sixth Fleet," Socrates said. "It is extremely important that the Soviet ships refrain from any action that might be construed as provocative by the U.S. Navy. You know how such things happen: some hothead pulls a daring stunt just to show off, the Americans feel they have to match the Russians stride for stride . . . In short, the navy brass should be deprived of a pretext to go to the White House for permission to meet the provocation head on."

"To sum up, there will be no strike if Qaddafi and the Soviet Union show restraint, right?" The center expected a clear-cut and definitive answer, and I sought to dot all the i's and cross all the t's.

"Right," Socrates replied firmly.

"How reliable is the information?"

"Straight from the horse's mouth: the Department of the Navy."

I could hardly think of a better source under the circumstances. Socrates was definitely telling the truth. He simply had had too little time to concoct a plausible lie. Everything had occurred too fast. Besides, if the center entertained any doubt, it had other resources at its disposal.

Having arrived at that conclusion, I changed the topic.

"Martin, chances are I will be leaving the U.S. shortly. Probably for good."

"Why so soon?" he asked with surprise. "You've been in Washington less than two years."

"I have a great job lined up in Moscow, but I can't tell you anything more for fear of jinxing a marvelous opportunity. Anyway, if you want to visit Moscow, let's make arrangements right now."

I had a feeling that recall orders would be coming any day now. But I wanted to continue to work with Socrates. General Androsov was afraid of recruiting Socrates in America? Fine. Then I'd bring him to Moscow. No FBI there, and the CIA is not much of an impediment either. Let him strut his stuff.

"Well, as a matter of fact, Phyllis and I would really like to visit the Soviet Union," Socrates said.

"Okay. I can arrange an official invitation for you from some unit of the Academy of Sciences," I promised.

"I'd rather you arranged a journalistic invitation to Phyllis. I would prefer to stay out of the limelight," he remarked.

"Will an invitation from the Soviet Novosti News Agency be good enough?"

"Sounds great."

"See you in Moscow, then."

It took me just a few minutes to prepare a cable on the Americans' intentions toward Libya. The residency had no other information on the subject.

"Thanks," the resident said with feeling. "Socrates has done us a great turn."

Feeling delighted for Socrates, I went to my cubicle and in one sitting wrote a lengthy analysis of my relationship with him. The conclusion was unambiguous: an attempt had to be made to recruit him. There could be no doubt about Androsov's attitude, but I wanted to go on record with my own opinion. I still hoped that someone in my country needed intelligence.

A few days later, I was recalled to Moscow.

6

I ENTERED the KGB external intelligence headquarters situated in a picturesque area in the south of Moscow. All of the world's intelligence services, and almost everyone in the nearby residential area of Yasenevo, knew the identity of that building. Yet all access roads were marked with road signs reading "Sanitary Zone," while at the entrance a modest door plate tried to convince unsuspecting visitors that they were entering the "Scientific Information Center."

The North American Department occupied one half of the fifth floor in one of the wings of the building. The employees of this department, widely regarded as an elite outfit, were engaged in political spying on the main enemy of the USSR—the United States of America. According to regulations, the rest of the departments were required to coordinate their activities with the North American Department, so its purview extended far beyond North America and, in effect, encompassed the whole world—anywhere on earth where Americans showed up.

Almost all of the rooms in the department looked the same: fifteen square meters (about 160 square feet), furnished with filing cabinets, standard-issue desks and chairs. Depending on the circumstances, each room was occupied by two to four rank-and-file operatives or one mid-level manager. There were no computers or other high-tech devices except for the transistor radios that carried the Voice of America broadcasts in the morning, and easy-listening music during the day. The windows looked out on a forest that gladdened the eye with the blinding whiteness of snow in winter, and with the gorgeous green of verdant foliage in summer.

The duty officer immediately took me to the general. He dwelt in an office about three times as large as the others, which was further distinguished by two extra amenities: a large bank of telephones on the desk and a portrait of Mikhail Gorbachev on the wall. Junior-grade officers preferred to adorn their walls with photographs of scantily clad beauties from Western magazines.

General Stanislav Androsov, appointed department chief several months earlier, seemed to be fully acclimated to his new position. His bearing bespoke his confidence, his eyes glistened with barely concealed triumph. He had never looked that way when he was running the Washington residency. A mere four months, and look at him—he is an entirely new man, I noted with surprise. As the saying goes, position makes a bureaucrat.

Also present in the office was the deputy department chief.

"You understand, of course, that your sojourn in America has come to an end," Androsov said derisively. "But life is not over, so let's turn over a new leaf and start fresh. Go to your room, sit down at the desk, and write a report about the whole Socrates affair. And remember, a sincere confession is your only chance."

The general's tirade struck me like a bolt from the blue.

I had expected a tongue-lashing for disobedience, but Androsov was playing for much higher stakes. "A sincere confession is your only chance" bordered on an accusation of treason, no less! Is he crazy? I asked myself in horror. What a sick joke!

But the general was not joking. He worked himself into a towering rage. His deputy, thoroughly cowed and bewildered, cut a pathetic figure. Appointed just three days before, he had no idea of what was going on and cursed the stars for landing him in such a mess.

"Have you received the information about the U.S. military plans concerning Libya supplied by Socrates?" I asked calmly. I had a hard time restraining my emotions. It was that information that I obtained during my last meeting with Socrates. It had been demanded—urgently!—by none other than the chief of intelligence. It was my ace in the hole and I used it without hesitation. But to little effect.

"We sure have," Androsov replied with a sardonic smile. "Except that it went straight to Internal Counterintelligence rather than the analytical service."

For the first time in my life I felt a chair shaking under me. My mouth was dry. The general was not joking—of that I had no doubt. He was on a fishing expedition, looking for treason, and his little game could cost me my freedom—or worse.

It followed from his words that he had the Internal Counterintelligence Department—the local inquisition of the intelligence service—on his team. There was practically no hope against that kind of opposition. It is easy to get into the clutches of Internal Counterintelligence, but to extricate oneself in one piece is all but impossible. Once those fellows launch an investigation, they feel duty-bound to go all the way. "Give us a body, and we'll always find treason in it," was the way some cynics in Political Intelligence formulated the motto of the internal inquisition.

I used to smile at such somber jokes, but now I was in

no mood for macabre humor. I am lost, it's over, I thought, trying desperately to concentrate. I had to jog my brain out of its state of paralysis. My fate was hanging in the balance.

"Don't you realize that Socrates is a plant the Americans used in order to feed us disinformation and to soften you up for subsequent recruitment?" It seemed that Androsov was about to burst out laughing.

"But didn't Socrates report that there would be no second U.S. strike against Libya?" I parried weakly. "To the best of my knowledge, the second strike has never happened."

"It hasn't—so far. But it may come tomorrow, or the day after. So you might say that your fate is being decided right now in the Oval Office of the White House or in the Pentagon," the general said sternly. "It seems to me you fail to appreciate the real depth of our responsibility. We had a naval task force stationed in Tripoli harbor as a deterrent against the Americans. But then the threat of a second strike became too real, and it had to put out to sea. Now, imagine for a second that the intelligence service reports, on the basis of your information, that there will be no second strike. The task force stays put in the harbor like sitting ducks, and all of a sudden the U.S. launches a missile strike against Tripoli, and our ships are accidentally hit. It would be a disaster! Americans blow up a Soviet naval vessel. It's an act of war, pure and simple! It becomes impossible to forecast the course of subsequent events. And all because of your information from Socrates."

"But the second strike never came, which means that Socrates was right." Listening to the verbiage of that chair-bound spy, I felt my composure slipping.

"But what if it had?" Androsov asked derisively, fixing me with his watery eyes.

"Why, then, did the chief of intelligence categorically give the residency three hours to give him an unambiguous answer as to whether or not the second strike was coming? The way I see it, you had no intention to respond."

"Gorbachev demanded that answer from the intelligence service." A sly smile played on the general's lips.

"And what did you tell him?" I asked, feeling a surge of burning indignation.

"I told him that the residency was in a shambles, and so we were not in a position to provide an unambiguous answer. Let the military brass decide what to do about their naval task force. It's their problem."

What a hypocrite! I thought. One minute he's holding forth with such tender concern for the fate of the Soviet task force, and the next minute it's somebody else's problem.

"That's the kind of answer anyone at the Soviet Embassy in Washington, including the janitor, could provide," I observed. It was clear that I had nothing to lose and going on the offensive was the only option. "What do we need a residency for if its information does not even reach the analytical service?"

Androsov became livid with rage.

"You yourself are to blame for everything," he hissed, barely able to contain himself. "We warned you many times that Socrates is a questionable character."

"I don't remember ever hearing you say anything of the kind when you were the resident," I shot back. "When you had to report recruitment successes, Socrates was regarded as a genuine asset. It was not until you became head of the North American Department that the center sent us a hysterical cable about him."

"You are mistaken," the general said, speaking barely above a whisper, his lips stretching into a thin strip and turning white. "I always instructed you to exercise maximum caution with regard to Socrates. There were ample reasons for that. If everything you wrote about him is true, then he is simply a madman."

"He probably is. Frankly, I doubt the normalcy of individuals who agree to cooperate with any foreign intelligence service." It sounded too defiant, but I wanted to rock the boat some more before delivering the decisive blow.

"You are going too far," shrieked Androsov, and his deputy nervously shifted his weight in the armchair. "Our best assets were ideologically driven."

"When was that, if I may ask?"

"It makes no difference," Androsov replied with the air of an affronted deity.

I kept silent, staring at Gorbachev's portrait. The general secretary looked back at me from his lofty perch.

"How did Socrates obtain the latest information from the Pentagon?" The general continued pressuring me.

I made a superhuman effort to remain calm.

"We were at his place. He just picked up the phone, called a friend at the Department of the Navy, asked him if the United States was going to strike Libya a second time, and the guy told him everything I reported in my cable. It's all in my report."

"I know very well what's in your report," Androsov said ominously. After a brief pause he resumed the onslaught. "So, are you going to tell the truth? Answer me. During you last rendezvous with Socrates, were you approached by FBI agents? Did they offer you money? Did they try to talk you into committing treason?"

There it was, the dreaded word: treason. Finally it had escaped the general's lips; but instead of fear, I felt a surge of fury. It was time to put an end to this farce and regain the initiative.

"To start off, I'd like to solemnly declare that the American intelligence services did not attempt any provocation against me. Nor did they make any attempt to establish contact with me."

"Aha, so you understand what we are talking about," Androsov said with gusto.

"Of course. That's why I am prepared to answer any questions you may want to ask, but I insist that the interrogation include a lie-detector test. I agree to accept its results unconditionally." Having baited my hook and cast it into the water, I held my breath, waiting to see whether or not he would bite.

The general fixed me with his famous fish-eye. His deputy receded even farther into his chair and looked for all the world like a child caught with his hand in the cookie jar.

"Are you indeed prepared to take the lie-detector test?" Androsov asked suspiciously.

"I am not just prepared for it; I insist on it," I replied.

The general grunted with satisfaction and nodded agreement. Now was the time for a little eye-opener.

"Following our latest debacles in Washington, I think all personnel of the intelligence service should take the lie-detector test on a regular basis," I said. "As a matter of fact, the Americans have introduced this practice at their State Department. Why don't we follow their lead? I am prepared to blaze the trail, but only on an official basis."

"What do you mean 'on an official basis'?" Androsov asked suspiciously.

"It means that I'm going to submit a report to the chief of intelligence, requesting permission to undergo a lie-detector test and suggesting regular polygraph testing of all intelligence employees. Without exception. I have nothing to hide, but let's all of us bare our souls to our motherland." That was my best shot. Having delivered it, I stared intently at my boss, trying to gauge his reaction. It was not hard to do.

His face fell. He realized that I would not permit myself to be quietly strangled. But he detested public executions. In general, Androsov was averse to all extremes; he hated everything that had the qualifier "too" attached to it: too noisy and too quiet, too intelligent and too stupid. Moderation was the overriding principle in his life, with just one exception: his flaming passion was making all kinds of funny little pieces from plywood with a fretsaw.

There was no way Androsov would allow me to submit a report suggesting general polygraph testing. The generals would be the first to howl with horror. Unlike me, they surely had a lot to hide. They would eat him alive if he were to allow such an initiative to proceed. Worse still, what would the chief of intelligence think of a department that gave rise to such dangerous initiatives?

Whew, looks like I won—this time, I thought. A hardened bureaucrat has walked right into my trap. He will never let me write that report, and without the report the case of my treason will simply fall apart. I will just refuse to answer his stupid questions by saying: "Why, Comrade General, how can you say such things? I am suspected of treason, but you are the one who is afraid of the lie-detector?" Pretty soon people will start whispering that the generals are afraid to take the lie-detector test. Could it be there is a special reason for their reluctance? And before long, a full-blown scandal will break out—first in the intelligence service, then its echo will roll through the entire KGB! The Central Committee of the Communist Party won't be happy! Faced with such a prospect, one should think twice before proceeding with the search for treason.

I hoped that was the thrust of Androsov's thinking—and so it apparently was.

"You may go," the general muttered in a voice suddenly drained of all life. "Enjoy your month-long vacation, and after that we'll decide what to do about you. As for your polygraph idea, we'll think about it."

"Right," I said and stepped out into the corridor.

The deputy department chief hurried behind.

"You are too presumptuous," he squealed in an unnatural voice. "Do you understand who it is you are talking to? The chief of the department, that's who."

"Why should you care?" I snarled at him. "It's none of your damn business."

"None of my business?" he asked in amazement. "You were being rude in my presence, thereby discrediting me."

I sighed heavily and entered one of the offices occupied by

the Washington Section of the North American Department. It was here that the operational files of our residency were kept; where my reports on the meetings with my American contacts arrived; where the directives to the Washington residency on what I was to do—and, more important, what I was not under any circumstances to do— were generated. In a word, it was the nerve center, the brain of the Washington residency.

At one time, that brain had throbbed with frantic activity, but now it looked rather dreary. A young officer was listening to the Voice of America, another was immersed in an English textbook, and the old-timer Fyodor, who was to join the residency shortly, was intently studying brochures of Washington stores.

"What are you running here, a funeral parlor?" I joked awkwardly.

"Believe it or not, you hit the nail right on the head," Fyodor said listlessly. "Motorin was executed the other day."

I gasped. I knew that Sergei Motorin, an ex-operative with the Washington residency, had been arrested on charges of treason and I had expected that he would be punished severely. But I could not have imagined that the time would come when we would be batting the breeze while Motorin, a fun-loving prankster, would be rotting in some unknown cemetery with a bullet in the back of his head.

"Was he tried?" I asked gloomily.

"A military tribunal," Fyodor replied. "That's when the whole story of his treason was laid bare."

"Why don't you tell me about it."

Fyodor settled himself into his chair and began his tale: "All right. As you know, Motorin had some problems with his operative work. It so happened there was a very good reason for that: he lived in mortal fear of being recalled home ahead of time. He preferred a well-fed America to a Soviet Union on a permanent diet. Very little was needed to push Motorin over the edge, and the required impetus was supplied by the FBI, which had been watching him very intently.

"According to the surveillance data, Motorin was unusually keen on material things. You know how some of our compatriots experience a genuine psychological shock upon entering an American store: the pupils of their eyes dilate, their excitement mounts until it reaches a level bordering on insanity. That's what happened to Motorin. The FBI duly noted it and targeted him for aggressive recruitment."

"But what was the actual hook?" I looked at Fyodor's desk groaning under the weight of the Washington brochures and felt a surge of annoyance.

"Once he had made a terrific deal," Fyodor chirped on. "A small store on F Street was selling substandard electronics at bargain-basement prices. Motorin managed to talk the owner into bartering a decent-looking stereo system for two cases of vodka that he had bought at a discount at the Soviet residential compound. As you know, deals of this sort are a no-no for Soviet citizens abroad. Sometime later, an FBI agent approached Motorin on a quiet Washington street and showed him photographs featuring our heroic intelligence officer trading vodka for electronic equipment. Motorin looked at the photographs and told the G-man to go to hell. The American submissively said okay and beat it. A few days later, the same agent again approached Motorin and was again rebuffed. But the FBI refused to give up. Its representative would regularly encounter Motorin in secluded corners, show him the photographs, and ask him to reconsider. Apparently the Americans correctly guessed that Motorin had failed to report the incident to the resident. Had he done so, he would have been kicked out of Washington with the speed of a cannonball. Since he was still there, it meant that he had kept his mouth shut, which in itself was a grave crime. Finally there came a day when the FBI agent told Motorin sadly: 'Sorry, Mac. I like you, but there's nothing I can do. My boss has presented me with an ultimatum:

unless I obtain your agreement to cooperate with us, I'll be fired and these photographs will be sent to your resident. They were taken by my colleagues during our previous meetings. It seems as though your options are quite limited, because your residency knows my identity as an FBI agent. How will you explain to the resident why you met me on so many occasions and never reported the encounters?'"

"How many times have you told this story?" I asked Fyodor; his narration was too smooth to be spontaneous.

"Lots of times," he acknowledged candidly. "Well, listen on. At that point Motorin must have felt the noose tightening around his throat. If he had reported the first recruitment attempt, he might have gotten away merely with a one-way ticket home. But now the likelihood was high that he would be accused of secretly cooperating with the FBI. Indeed, how can one prove one's innocence in the face of photographic evidence of nine meetings with a known FBI agent—meetings, moreover, kept secret from the resident?"

"Fyodor, you are torturing me! Don't keep dragging it out," I groaned.

"Well, to make a long story short, Motorin capitulated," he said with feigned sorrow. "Cooperation with the FBI in fact helped him improve his standing at the residency. An American counterintelligence operative was put in touch with him as a potential asset, and the wheel of fortune started spinning at breakneck speed. The 'recruitment campaign' was played out like a brilliant chess game. Androsov, who at the time was the resident, naturally had no inkling of what was really going on, and was in seventh heaven. Motorin was sending to Moscow informational cables composed by the FBI, and reporting back to the Americans on the successful completion of their assignments. The FBI asked him to study his residency co-workers, and he tackled the task with great enthusiasm. Each night guests crammed his apartment; whiskey and gin flowed freely; tongues loosened and started wagging. Many of them drank themselves into a stupor, while Motorin listened carefully and clicked his Nikon, a gift from his FBI control. Later, he would confront his associates with the photographs showing them in a very unflattering light, watching their reactions. If their eyes registered fear, he would report the name of the next victim to the FBI, and a new recruitment effort would be put under way."

"And that's it?" I asked suspiciously.

"I wish it were," Fyodor said with a melancholy sigh. "You'll probably recall that early in his tour of duty as resident Androsov had a brainstorm."

"You mean the map?" I asked.

It had been a disaster waiting to happen. Androsov ordered a huge map of Washington and its suburbs displayed in the anteroom of the residency. Each operative leaving on business was required to mark on the map the time and place of the operation and his code name.

When rumor of the innovation reached the center, many old-school intelligence officers were appalled. The then chief of the North American Department, Yakushkin, was beside himself with fury, but his ranting and raving went nowhere: the idea of the map had been approved by the chief of intelligence himself, Vladimir Kryuchkov.

Only an idiot could have failed to realize that the map was a time bomb. Naturally enough, it became the object of Motorin's rapt attention.

"Right," Fyodor exclaimed, enjoying my startled reaction. "Each morning, Motorin would drop by the residency and commit to memory which of the operatives were to meet their contacts, where and when. Barely an hour later, the information would reach the FBI, which was thus spared a great deal of time and effort. Indeed, why go to the trouble of tailing Soviet agents when it's easier just to wait for them at their destination? Within a few months, practically all the contacts run by the residency became known to the Americans. They could have destroyed the entire network in one fell swoop, but refrained from dealing the decisive blow for fear of compromising Motorin. An opportunity finally presented itself with the defection to the U.S. of Vitaly Yurchenko, our former chief. A lot of things, if not everything, could be laid at his doorstep. Our assets began collapsing one after another."

"Do you mean to say that Yurchenko had nothing new to tell the Americans?" I asked in surprise. Fyodor's story was a revelation to me. Yurchenko's defection was followed by the collapse of the entire KGB network in the U.S. There was the utmost certainty at the Washington residency that the assets were burned by Yurchenko. But then, nobody at that time knew of Motorin's treason . . .

"Anyway, judging by what transpired at the trial, my impression is that Yurchenko in fact merely confirmed what the Americans had learned from Motorin," Fyodor declared authoritatively. "Be that as it may," he went on, "Androsov found himself stripped of the network of agents laboriously built over the years by his predecessor, Dmitri Yakushkin. Ironically, the sum total of what the FBI paid to Motorin was $10,000, while the plant he had supposedly recruited was paid $30,000 by the center. So to add insult to injury, the Americans even made a tidy profit."

"But I just don't see how, after all that happened, Androsov managed to get himself appointed head of the North American Department. He was promoted and given control of intelligence operations in the whole of the United States." I couldn't believe it. What happened was that Motorin was able to destroy the entire network of agents in the U.S. with the help of Androsov's ridiculous map, with the result that the former was executed while the latter was promoted.

"Ask me another one," Fyodor snapped halfheartedly. "Yakushkin was chosen to take the hit; don't you know, he had been too tough on Motorin, thereby propelling him into the embrace of the FBI."

"But what about the map?" I all but yelled.

"They swept the whole story under the rug." Fyodor's thin red mustache stretched into a cynical scowl.

Again, for the umpteenth time, I was struck by the absurdity of it all. Maybe common sense is just an illusion, after all?

"How was Motorin found out?" I finally asked after a long silence.

Fyodor came to life again.

"He was burned by a leak from the CIA. At that time Motorin was back at headquarters, working at the active measures service. Of course, they set a trap for him and watched him unload a drop in the Kuntsevo Cemetery, where they lay in ambush. And can you imagine this coincidence? One of the participants in the ambush was a former operative driver of the Washington residency, who had often driven Motorin to operations. You should have seen his face when he watched Motorin unloading the drop. They were so shocked that they failed to arrest Mortorin then and there. So the next day Motorin was called upstairs and told to take a car and go collect a package at Sheremeteyevo Airport. As soon as he got into the car, they nabbed him, and he broke down on the spot."

"What did Motorin look like at the trial?"

"Awful," Fyodor said softly. "He was like a dried mummy. During the investigation he had gone completely gray, and they had dyed his hair. He spoke like he was in a deep hypnotic trance, confessing and confirming everything. There were some humorous moments, too. The members of the tribunal were intent on uncovering the deepest root causes of his moral degradation, so to say. And all of a sudden it came out that he had brought a water bed from America. So as far as the tribunal was concerned, that was the smoking gun confirming beyond any doubt his fall from grace. How do you like that?"

"Not much," I said gloomily. "You mean he didn't even try to argue, to defend himself?"

"Hey, what's wrong with you?" Fyodor was genuinely taken aback. "It seems bourgeois democracy is bad for your memory. Arguments? What arguments? During the investigation at Internal Counterintelligence, Motorin was pumped full of mind-altering drugs and forced to confess everything they wanted to hear. And at the trial those so-called confessions were presented as irrefutable proof of his guilt. What defense do you expect under such circumstances?"

"But couldn't he retract the phony confessions at the trial and tell the judges how they had been extracted from him?"

"Listen, it's clear now that America is bad for your mental health," Fyodor said confidently. "Trial? What trial? His fate was decided in the peace and quiet of the generals' offices. And on the eve of the trial he was told that his only chance to save his life was to confirm all the findings presented by the investigators and to repent. They promised him his life if he would behave, and he believed them. He simply had no other alternative. In his closing statement the poor guy said: 'I hope you will take into account the fact that I have fully repented and spare me. I have two small daughters.' But once the trial was over, they had no longer any use for him. And who the hell cares about his little daughters?"

"All right, Motorin confessed under duress, but he was actually guilty," I said. "But using such methods, even a totally innocent person can be made to confess to any imaginable crime."

"Sure," Fyodor said weightily. "If Kryuchkov wants you to confess that you were the one who killed Trotsky, don't worry, they'll make you confess. Moreover, the military tribunal will accept that confession as proof of your guilt, because its members and Kryuchkov play on the same team."

The room went silent. I felt as though I were suffocating. I needed a breath of fresh air. Gloomy thoughts raced through my mind, coloring everything black.

The wise Fyodor had brought me crashing down to earth. How could I have been so naive as to think that I had outwitted Androsov and broken free? How stupid of me! Those guys in Internal Counterintelligence couldn't care less about my chess moves. Their expertise was in breaking bones rather than playing chess. "Just give us a body, and we'll find treason in it." No, I had not gotten away with it. Of course, Androsov was a timid bureaucrat and could be neutralized. But he had already shared his nonsensical suspicions with Internal Counterintelligence, and the latter was very difficult to shake off. Like it or not, I would have to prove that I was not guilty. Motorin's plight was a dreadful reminder of what might happen to me if I failed to do it.

"Well, carry on with your intelligence work," I told Fyodor on my way out. He again reached for his brochures as I left the room and walked toward the elevator. At the exit from the building, I showed my pass to the warrant officer on duty and felt his stern, suspicious gaze on me, the way the righteous look at the stray sheep.

Stares of this nature never failed to elicit a specific reaction on my part; in the cross-hairs of the guards' honest and righteous eyes, I always felt my imperfections and had to stifle a powerful urge to repent every possible and impossible sin and become a monk. With some effort, I suppressed the urge rising from the deepest recesses of my much-tested intelligence officer's soul, and emerged into the compound surrounded by a tall concrete wall.

Here nothing had changed. The winter was warm, and I could hear the slaps of tennis rackets hitting the balls from the court. The small soccer field from time to time exploded in refined shouts. Behind the glass walls of the indoor swimming pool, the powerful and not-so-powerful torsos of intelligence officers cut the smooth mirrorlike surface.

Schools of fat carp darted about, and wild ducks languidly swam in the fountain—a proud innovation of Kryuchkov, who loved to enjoy the idyllic scene from the window of his office. His ducks were thoroughly domesticated, but woe to the poor devil who might have an innocent but unfortunate desire to play with them. Instantly, an enraged warrant officer would come running and publicly upbraid the villain on behalf of the service chief.

The trees surrounding the fountain were adorned with dead crows hung by their feet from branches. They had been shot on Kryuchkov's orders and hung out for the edification of their brethren, lest they steal food from the intelligence chief's pet ducks. The gruesome landscape had prompted the local wags to come up with a malicious saying: "That's what awaits any intelligence officer who betrays his motherland." They believed that it was exactly this kind of allegory that Kryuchkov had in mind in ordering the display of the dead crows.

Nearby was another facility dear to Kryuchkov's heart: a pigpen—convincing proof that the supreme spy of the USSR wholeheartedly shared the philosophy of perestroika, and especially the idea of self-sufficiency in food.

In the fall, the pork from the pig farm, the carp, and the ducks would report to the kitchen, bringing some diversity to the generally scanty menu as one of the special privileges available to the service personnel. But those little joys also had an unfortunate side effect: the unruly wind constantly changed direction. And as soon as the wind would turn westerly, the stench of Kryuchkov's pig farm immediately enveloped the entire compound as a poignant reminder that even illusory privileges had a price.

The narrow alleys around the building were, as usual, full of joggers. The faces of some of them bore the stamp of lofty responsibility for the destiny of our motherland and the whole of progressive humanity. Watching them, I recalled the first time I had come to the intelligence service in the summer of 1982. Alighting from the special bus with drawn curtains on the windows, I had stared in fascination at the faces of the officers in the compound, thinking admiringly: My God, just imagine the secrets harbored by these guys! What great operations they pull off!

But pretty soon, the youthful romanticism had been dispelled and the faces of my co-workers no longer elicited my admiration, but rather irritation and annoyance. The scales had started falling from my eyes on the occasion of Kryuchkov's speech at one of the general meetings. The chief had created a sensation among his listeners when he acknowledged that only 30 percent of his employees really did any intelligence work, while the rest just enjoyed a free ride. Later I was to realize that the true situation was even worse than Kryuchkov was willing to admit.

I had spent just two years in Washington, and yet I had come home a changed man. How many illusions lost, how many seemingly unshakable stereotypes undermined!

Contradictory thoughts wandered through my mind. I could appreciate Androsov's predicament. After Motorin's treachery, he was terrified by the prospect of another FBI plant. And here was Socrates, a former U.S. government official, offering me the inside dope on the Pentagon's plans with respect to Libya. Incredible, particularly considering that, following the destruction of the KGB network, Soviet spying had become a leading topic of discussion in the American media.

But why should I care about Androsov's sensibilities? I thought. If the situation is that hopeless, they should just shut down the intelligence service and go home. But not him. He has no plans of going home. He is still in business; having destroyed the network of assets, he is now trying to ferret out treason. I've sure gotten myself into a mess. I know that I am innocent before my motherland, but nobody cares. I must prove my innocence to Internal Counterintelligence. Otherwise, sooner or later I will share Motorin's fate; they will stuff me full of pills and force me to confess that I've been a CIA asset since childhood, and no military tribunal will listen to my pathetic babbling about how I was forced to give that confession under duress.

It didn't take me long to figure out the one way out of the impasse. I had to prove that Socrates was genuine. To this end, he had to be summoned to Moscow and recruited.

I used to dream of recruiting an asset for the sake of the

country and for the KGB. Now I had to do it to save my skin.

In April of 1987, when the unwelcome vacation was mercifully over and I had returned to the North American Department, the U.S. still had not carried out a second strike against Libya, and that saved me, at least for a time. Help also arrived from another—and quite unexpected—quarter. I won the first Tass award as the best foreign correspondent for the year 1986.

As a matter of fact, I never devoted more time to my journalistic duties than was absolutely necessary to blend into the crowd of clean correspondents in Washington. It was all but impossible to succeed in journalism as well as spying, so I had to sacrifice my secondary interests on the altar of my primary mission. But after the Reagan-Gorbachev summit meeting in Reykjavik I made an extensive analytical report on Soviet-American relations that unexpectedly drew close attention of some Politburo members. The Tass general director, Sergei Lossev, remembered that and made me the best correspondent of the year.

Now Lossev was outraged by my sudden recall from the U.S. He had expected me to stay in the Washington Tass bureau at least two more years and had given a piece of his mind to my superiors in the intelligence service. Then he summoned me to his office in Moscow and made me an offer: "Quit your service and join my outfit. You won't be sorry, believe me. In about a year, I'll send you back to America."

There was no reason to doubt that that's exactly what would have happened. Lossev was a member of the Council of Ministers and a man of his word. I was grateful to him for his tempting offer, but turned it down without much hesitation. "One does not change horses in midstream," as Abe Lincoln once said, and I was used to heeding good advice. I quit Tass for good.

There was very little to occupy the time of the staff members of the North American Department, where I was now stationed. After the recent expulsion of the KGB personnel from the U.S. our residencies there were in complete disarray. The Moscow headquarters did not have time to coordinate their activities. Somehow, between reading newspapers and exercising, we managed to while away the office hours. The once-monthly party meetings with their moments of black humor brought some comic relief into the dreary atmosphere of boredom.

At one of them, General Androsov proclaimed: "Our personnel policies must be clear and unambiguous. We don't need brain surgeons, but neither do we want outright idiots. Our ideal is a pedestrian but diligent operative."

Whereupon he proceeded to staff the department in keeping with his outlook. The first reaction to the innovation came from the acting New York resident. This particular operative was almost my age. He had been given his position after the recent mass expulsion of KGB officers from the U.S. An intelligent, brilliantly educated man, he was a marvel of efficiency. The generals disliked him, but had to put up with him.

"You wouldn't believe the kind of people they're sending me these days," the young resident told me indignantly. "They behave like they're on Mars. Scared of everything, arrogant in their inferiority, ignorant fools who can't do a damn thing. God, how long it will take to repair the damage they're doing with their personnel policies!"

What's the use ranting and raving? I thought. Out of sheer boredom I decided to reread my own material on Socrates and Sputnitsa—only to be disagreeably startled yet another time. I was struck by the comments General Androsov had made in the margins of my reports about my meetings with Socrates. The pages were covered with sarcastic observations such as, "Comrade Lewis clearly gets carried away," "A bit premature to make such conclusions," "Where are the guarantees?" And to my assertion that, "It appears

Socrates is weighing the possibility of eventually moving to the Soviet Union," the general had responded with a blast of ridicule: "Sounds too good to be true."

I have always believed that doubt and skepticism are healthy elements in our line of work. Without them, intelligence would be an endless series of failures. What riled me was not the general's doubts, but the fact that he had never seen fit to discuss them with me.

The atmosphere around me in the North American Department was virtually charged with electricity. An intelligence officer recalled ahead of time from a tour of duty abroad was usually slated for severe punishment; he would be issued a reprimand, demoted in position or rank, almost surely taken off operative status. With me, however, everything was mysterious and uncertain.

No punishment came my way. I turned up at the office every day—but was given no work to do. I attended party meetings—but was barred from operational ones. My colleagues treated me normally, many of them even showed their sympathy—but cautiously, lest the bosses notice. As for the bosses, they gave me a very wide berth, as though I were a leper. Clearly, it couldn't last much longer. Sooner or later the bubble had to burst. General Androsov would not submit to a polygraph test with me, but he had to test me some other way. I waited patiently for the other shoe to drop.

Once, walking in the corridor of the intelligence service building, I encountered Colonel Victor Cherkashin, the former chief of the counterintelligence unit at the Washington residency. Now he was a department head at the RT Directorate (a Russian abbreviation meaning "territorial intelligence") of the External Intelligence Service, the First Chief Directorate. Unlike the CIA, the External Intelligence Service of the KGB was chartered to run intelligence operations against foreigners within the borders of its own country. Such operations were handled by a special subdirectorate—RT.

We batted the breeze for a while, and then Cherkashin suddenly said: "Why don't you transfer to my unit? The North American Department is on its last legs. There is a concerted effort to shift the brunt of our American operations to the RT Directorate. We need results, we are success-oriented. Isn't that what you are all about?"

Here it comes, the long-awaited test, I thought, and agreed with him on the spot. Androsov was glad to let me go, and a new entry appeared in my personnel file to the effect that I had been recalled from the U.S. ahead of schedule for fear of likely FBI provocations.

I knew full well that Cherkashin's offer was a well-prepared scheme to which Androsov and the Internal Counterintelligence Department were privy. A lie-detector test was only marginally useful; its results could not be considered absolutely reliable. They wanted to catch me red-handed, and that's where Colonel Cherkashin came in.

The RT Directorate had never run a single American agent. The directorate personnel could be roughly broken down into five categories: burned intelligence officers; recruiters; failures; callow youths; and ne'er-do-wells.

An RT position never carried much prestige, because its officers were not posted abroad. But after the KGB residencies in the U.S. had been demolished, the situation changed. The RT Directorate was charged with the task of creating a crack force of former "American" specialists to pick up the slack due to the degeneration of the North American Department. The American project was initiated and led by Colonel Cherkashin, who became my principal boss and—adversary!

We had known each other since we were both in Washington, where Cherkashin had been in charge of counterintelligence operations at the residency. He was regarded as a master of blackmail recruitment, and was known for his skill in loading and unloading dead drops. In a word, he was a true counterintelligence ace.

Motorin's treachery was a major blow to Cherkashin's career aspirations. Still, he did not lose heart. He hoped to expiate his sin through recruitment successes. I liked Cherkashin's attitude. Most officers of his rank preferred to atone for their transgressions by licking their superiors' boots.

When I reported to my new command, Cherkashin told me: "I believe that Socrates and Sputnitsa are good prospects for recruitment. We have already sent them an invitation to visit the Soviet Union."

"What invitation?" I asked in surprise. "And who has sent it?"

"As you and Socrates agreed, the invitation has been sent from Novosti News Agency. We have made the arrangements together with the North American Department."

He hasn't wasted much time, has he? I thought. Now I saw how they were planning to test me: Socrates would be brought to Moscow and interrogated about his and my ties to the FBI. Funny, but I had asked for it myself. On the other hand, though, I had little choice. I was under suspicion for treachery, and Socrates would either dispel the doubts or, alternatively, add more fuel to them.

In any case, Cherkashin was in a win-win situation. If my opinion was confirmed, Socrates would be recruited; if Androsov's suspicions were corroborated, I would be unmasked as an "enemy of the people." It was not for nothing that Cherkashin was considered a master at the counterintelligence game.

"Can I help in any way?" I asked.

"Not at this point. We'll do everything ourselves," Cherkashin assured me, and I thought that he was pulling for the second option.

It was a crazy situation that can only arise in a bureaucratic intelligence service. The primary objective of the

KGB external intelligence was to recruit U.S. citizens. But deep in their hearts the intelligence bureaucrats were certain that goal was all but unattainable. They couldn't voice their doubts so as not to call into question the very rationale of their existence. Therefore officially they exhorted field officers to recruitment deeds, but as soon as an officer would report a glimmer of success in that department, he immediately became the object of grave suspicions.

Hard as it was to find a prospective agent in America, it was nothing compared to the difficulty of persuading the intelligence bureaucrats that the candidate was not a CIA or FBI plant. Of course, if a man turns up at the Soviet Embassy in Washington and offers to sell U.S. naval communication codes or a sheaf of classified CIA or NSA documents, there can be little doubt that he is genuine goods. It is hardly surprising then that almost all known KGB agents in the U.S. volunteered their services rather than being turned. My colleagues at the North American Department remembered just one case when a field officer had found and recruited an agent through his own efforts. That was Valentin Aksilenko's agent, Bill.

Now I claimed a similar success with regard to Socrates. Alas, my communist bosses did not believe in luck. It was easy enough to see their point. After 1979, hundreds of KGB field officers, scores of colonels, and a handful of generals toiled mightily but fruitlessly trying to duplicate Aksilenko's feat. And here was a lowly captain impudently claiming that within a mere two years of his first tour of duty abroad he did recruit a U.S. citizen. And not just anyone, but an ex–U.S. government official, to boot! Clearly, he was either a brazen whippersnapper or a boneheaded gambler duped by the FBI trying to penetrate the KGB with a sophisticated plant.

I could have taken years developing Socrates and the bureaucrats would have been perfectly happy. This kind of activity placed no responsibility on them, for it was implicitly assumed that any candidate could turn out to be a plant. But it was a different story altogether if Socrates was to be officially registered as an agent. In that case not only the recruiting officer, i.e., myself, but also the bureaucrat (head of department or directorate) would have to stake his career on the proposition that Socrates was not an American plant and that the intelligence he provided was trustworthy. That meant lifelong responsibility. If years down the road, God forbid, it transpired that Socrates did indeed feed disinformation to the KGB, the first heads to roll would be those of the people who had recruited and vetted the agent. The intelligence trade has a thousand-year history, but try as it might it has never succeeded in coming up with a foolproof method of verifying a person's trustworthiness. Once recruited, an agent is subjected to unremitting and unending checking. An agent absolutely reliable yesterday may be turned by the enemy intelligence services tomorrow.

Boy, did the intelligence service bureaucrats abhor risk and responsibility! Of course, they weren't averse to acquiring an agent, but they preferred the attendant responsibility to be borne by somebody else. Colonel Cherkashin belonged to that rare breed of bosses who were prepared to shoulder responsibility. But he could not ignore the position of General Androsov. What if I miscalculated? Then Cherkashin would have hell to pay: How did you get into this mess? he would be accused. Didn't General Androsov warn you that in all likelihood Socrates was a plant?

I was sure that Cherkashin would be able to chart the right course in these turbulent waters. But there could be little doubt that as long as I was employed by my intelligence service I would have to prove my innocence. Reminders that Socrates' report about the U.S. plans toward Libya proved to be true would serve no useful purpose. There would be no shortage of skeptics who would argue that "this time the Americans purposefully gave us truthful intelligence as proof of the reliability of the source. But how can we be sure that tomorrow they will not use him to slip us strategic disinformation that will spell our doom?"

It was like a bad dream: poor intelligence was bad, but good intelligence was even worse.

7

SOCRATES and Sputnitsa were scheduled to arrive in Moscow on a Sunday in May 1987. The previous Friday I was shown a cable from the Washington residency that said that on Wednesday Socrates had called the Washington bureau of Novosti News Agency from Athens to find out if he was expected in Moscow. He said that the next day he was flying to Cyprus, and unless the invitation to the Soviet Union was confirmed within two days, he planned to return to Washington.

As it happened, Cherkashin had been overly optimistic in his declaration that "we'll do everything ourselves." During the two months since my departure from Washington, the North American Department had not gotten around to sending an official invitation to Socrates. Everybody was trying to avoid responsibility while actively debating how best to jump on the bandwagon if Socrates was recruited and how not to be punished if the recruitment plan failed.

There was a lively exchange of cables on the subject between Moscow and the Washington residency; the intelligence officers were furiously scribbling in their notebooks; the bosses knitted their brows. The project was in full swing. Only one small detail, a mere trifle, had been overlooked—sending the invitation to the invitee.

All of the managers were gone for the day, which meant that I could cut through the red tape. I got in touch with the Novosti representative in Nicosia, asked him to find Socrates and Sputnitsa, and hand them the invitation. He had to work fast; they were to leave Cyprus in a few hours.

On Saturday night, I received Cherkashin's directive to welcome the "guests." I was given a free hand, with the proviso that I was to behave in such a way as to make them clearly understand my KGB affiliation.

Socrates was in top form. Tanned, excited to the point of hysteria, he delivered one monologue after another, redrawing the map of the world; breaking up and creating military-political alliances; changing the balance of power to America's detriment.

Sputnitsa behaved somewhat strangely. With a rueful smile constantly on her lips, she pretended to listen to us, but I had the impression that she was in a state of some unusual kind of intoxication. Occasionally she joined our conversation, but rarely to the point. As soon as it became dark, she excused herself and went to bed.

"She must be tired after the trip," I ventured to observe.

Socrates suddenly frowned and kind of drooped. A veritable dynamo a mere second ago, he now looked like a man broken by the cruelty of fate.

We were sitting in a suite in the Hotel Budapest in the very heart of Moscow, drinking champagne. At my request, the suite had been bugged, and all conversations were being recorded. Considering the suspicions harbored by Androsov and Cherkashin, I had little alternative.

"Where do you work now?" Socrates asked.

"An interdepartmental committee for foreign policy analysis has been set up in Moscow," I replied. "It includes representatives of all agencies involved in the formulation and implementation of foreign policy, that is, the Ministry of Foreign Affairs, the KGB, the Defense Ministry, and a number of research institutions. That's where I am employed. Our charter consists in making recommendations for the Kremlin in regard to the optimum foreign policies and streamlining the decision-making process."

The story of the interdepartmental committee was made out of whole cloth. But having once mentioned the full name of that mythical organization, subsequently I referred to it simply as "the Committee," the most popular colloquial name for the KGB. I thereby fulfilled Cherkashin's request to make Socrates suspect that I was a KGB officer. Besides, a recruitment offer on behalf of a nonexistent organization had a tremendous advantage; in the event Socrates refused to cooperate with the Committee—a possibility that could not be ruled out—not a single official Soviet agency would be endangered. It was a case of "false-flag recruitment," in the trade parlance.

"You seem to be going places," Socrates observed, and his tone suggested to me that he was ripe for a heart-to-heart talk.

"And how have you been doing?" I asked.

"We are in trouble."

"We?"

"Phyllis and myself. She has been suffering from some neurological disease they haven't yet identified."

So that's what it was! Now I understood the abnormalities in her behavior.

Socrates went on, "She has been going downhill fast. What a brilliant brain is dying! Outwardly, it resembles sclerosis. She is no longer able to read or engage in journalism."

"But her articles still appear in print. How does she manage it?" I asked.

"For years I've been ghost-writing for her. All she does is put her signature under my articles. Nobody knows about it, not even her editors."

"You mean you are the real author of all Phyllis's stuff?"

"Yes, practically all of it . . ."

That was a real eye-opener. Phyllis had been seriously ill and I had not noticed that. The Washington residency admired Sputnitsa's radicalism, while all along Socrates had been its exponent. If it's true, then he is as red as Trotsky himself, I thought. I could not believe it.

Socrates picked up a glass of champagne and began thoughtfully watching the sparkling bubbles.

"A month ago, Phyllis was fired from the British journal she wrote for," he said. "The editor thinks she lists too far to the left. The Yurchenko article we wrote was the last straw."

"Can I do anything for you, Martin?" I asked.

"What can you do for me?" He shrugged his shoulders uncertainly. "At the ripe old age of forty-plus, I feel almost like an old man. I am neither rich nor famous, my second family is on the verge of collapse . . . You didn't know, did you, that my first wife died of brain cancer. And now comes this second blow. It is said there are carcinogenic people who induce the growth of cancerous cells. Those who are in constant contact with them are at risk. Is it possible I am carcinogenic?"

"Cut that crap," I reproached him. "I think you need to find a good cause and immerse yourself in work to forget your troubles."

"Any ideas?" he asked hopefully.

"I can't help you in America. But in the Soviet Union, you could become an adviser to the Committee—unofficially, needless to say. Your ideas would go all the way to the very top, I can assure you of that. And of course, you'll be remunerated on the basis of the quality of your material."

"How serious is it?" Socrates came back to life. I was to

observe on many subsequent occasions that talk about money never failed to excite him.

"One hundred percent," I replied.

"Deal," he said firmly. "Since Phyllis was fired, we've been scraping the bottom of the barrel."

"Aren't you concerned that your work may be detrimental to the United States?" I asked.

"I don't regard America as my country," Socrates observed. "I've always felt like an alien there."

"Then why do you live there?" I asked in surprise.

"I am a man without a homeland, an eternal wanderer." He chuckled. "It might so happen that one day I'll ask you to arrange a safe haven for me in the Soviet Union."

"Speaking of safe havens, once you asked me how Philby and Howard were doing here," I interjected. "Do you want to find out straight from the horse's mouth? I can introduce you to them, if you wish."

"Nah, forget it." Socrates waved a listless hand. "I am wary of information leaks. You never know what might happen."

"But would you be willing to meet representatives of our Committee, if they express a desire to get to know you?" I asked.

"I am fully at your service," he replied.

The next day, I received a call from "Tatiana." That name was a code for the KGB eavesdropping service. Judging from their report, everything was going according to plan.

As soon as I had left, Socrates woke up his wife although it was 2:00 A.M.: "Phyllis, I think our friend works for the KGB!"

"I don't believe it," she said firmly.

"He offered his services to arrange a meeting with Philby and ex-CIA agent Howard for me."

"You were the one who expressed interest in them back

in Washington," she said. "So he decided to satisfy your curiosity."

"Maybe you're right on that score, but he also invited me to consult a committee," Socrates persisted.

"What committee?" Sputnitsa was bewildered.

"Some sort of interagency committee where he is employed. 'Interagency' is obviously a red herring, while 'committee' gives one a lot of food for thought."

"Did you agree?" Sputnitsa's voice betrayed clear concern.

"Do you have a better offer?" Socrates asked sarcastically. "You know full well how desperate our circumstances are. We are ostracized by everyone, we have no money and can't count on help from any quarter. But we must continue our journey, and continue it we will—whatever the cost. There is no returning to the past. I have no intention of crawling back to Harvard for a professor's cup of coffee. So our friend's offer is a very timely gift."

"Well, you'd better watch your step," Sputnitsa muttered and went back to sleep.

"In general, what can you say about my friends?" I asked Tatiana. The monitoring service sent us written reports on the conversations it recorded, but in many cases they said nothing about the mental state of the subjects. Small wonder, since the dry shorthand records gave no hint of the timbre of voice or the inflection, which frequently gave a more profound insight than the words themselves. But I had to hand it to the Tatiana girls: on many occasions they proved to be master psychologists. Direct communication with them was quite useful.

"Oh, your Socrates is a veritable tyrant!" the girl exclaimed. "He literally terrorizes his wife. The poor woman has an awful memory, and each time she forgets something, he gets mad and starts to yell . . . And his tight-fistedness verges on insanity. The bellboy brought their suitcases to their room and Phyllis gave him a couple of dollars as a tip.

Martin flew into a towering rage and cursed at her for a quarter of an hour."

"Judging by Phyllis's reaction to his suspicion that I am a KGB officer, she is absolutely sane," I observed.

"I have the impression that she is quite lucid as far as her immediate surroundings are concerned," the Tatiana officer said. "She also remembers quite well the events of the distant past. It is the recent past that gives her problems."

Having thanked her for the information, I sat lost in thought. Why did Socrates tell Sputnitsa that he suspected I was KGB? Certainly he was smart enough to surmise that the Committee was eavesdropping on him. He behaved as if he had come to the Soviet Union with the intention of turning himself over to us. Even back in Washington I had suspected that he was thinking along such lines.

When I reported to Cherkashin the results of my meeting with Socrates and Sputnitsa, he actually rubbed his hands in satisfaction. He was particularly impressed by my request to have the meeting taped.

"Everything is going extremely well," he said with an amiable smile that I had never seen before. "But how do we convince Androsov that Socrates is not a plant or a fake?"

"Let him talk to Socrates himself and show everyone how to go about intelligence business," I suggested. "After all, wasn't he the one who insisted on the need to check this guy out? So it's only natural that he should be the one to do it. The situation couldn't be more favorable; Socrates is now on our turf and prepared to see anyone."

"I suggested as much, but he categorically refused," chortled Cherkashin.

"Then let him delegate the responsibility to one of his subordinates," I said.

"He didn't like that idea either."

"In that case, who the hell needs him or his department?"

I didn't even feel the need to hide my exasperation. "Just think about it: an American comes to the very lair of communism to offer his services to the KGB, and an elite unit of the Soviet intelligence service, charged specifically with the task of looking for and recruiting just such people, is afraid of meeting him."

"Let's not digress into philosophy," the colonel interrupted my tirade. "Any other ideas?"

"How about you meeting with Socrates?"

"Oh, no," Cherkashin said hastily. "I have little knowledge of the case, and besides, I am busy right now."

"Then let's arrange a meeting for Socrates with one of our analysts acting in the capacity of a neutral arbiter," I suggested.

"An excellent idea," the colonel agreed. "Go ahead."

That same day, I introduced Socrates to Colonel Yuri Golikov, a former analyst with the Washington residency. He was a genius of political analysis and, like just about any genius, heartily disliked by his superiors. Upon his return from Washington, he was appointed an adviser to the analytical service, a position tantamount to political exile. When his boss delivered the "sentence," Golikov gave him a scornful smile and walked out of the office, slamming the door behind him.

When I suggested that he meet with Socrates, Golikov reacted like a hobbled mustang taken out for a breath of fresh air. He lived for his work.

The analyst spent almost five hours talking to Socrates one on one. In Colonel Golikov's view, Socrates was extremely well informed and had connections so extensive and so highly placed as to leave the entire Washington residency in the dust. The assessment could be relied upon; nobody had ever succeeded in pulling the wool over Golikov's eyes—he could see right through any lie.

Still, to make doubly sure, I asked the analytical service to provide an official evaluation of the information Socrates had provided to me back in Washington. I was prepared for any result, but the evaluation filled me with glee. About 80 percent of the information furnished by Socrates was sensitive and 76 percent valuable—incredibly high percentages. At that time, the sensitivity index of all the information procured by the Washington residency never exceeded 8 percent, and the proportion of valuable information was even lower.

"We must show it to Androsov," Cherkashin sniggered after reading the report of the analytical service. "It is beyond his wildest dreams."

Indeed, while persisting in his belief that Socrates was a plant, General Androsov never deigned to inquire as to the veracity and quality of the information he supplied, even though such an evaluation has always been one of the essential elements of source verification, the ABC of the craft that any junior-grade lieutenant is supposed to know.

"Prepare a report to Kryuchkov on Socrates' recruitment," Cherkashin ordered. "Time to bring this epic to an end."

Half an hour later, the document, written in keeping with all the rules of the game, was ready.

Top secret

To: Colonel-General
Comrade V.A. Kryuchkov
Director of the First Chief Directorate
of the KGB of the USSR
Report
on the recruitment of Socrates

Since the summer of 1985, the Washington Residency has been developing one Socrates, a U.S. citizen and a former White House official.

While observing the subject, it has been ascertained that he espouses manifestly anti-American views, believes in socialist values, and experiences feelings of frustration at his social and financial standing.

He has supplied political information highly graded by the analytical service, as well as some material that served as the basis of intense active measures designed to fan the flames of the Iran-Contra scandal.

Last May, the RT Directorate executed a secret operation to bring Socrates to Moscow. A number of operative measures involving intelligence officers, Soviet agents and technical means have been implemented with respect to the subject, who has been led to realize that he is dealing with KGB officers.

Said measures have served to corroborate the data concerning Socrates obtained by the Washington Residency. He has agreed in principle to cooperate with our service.

A comprehensive verification procedure has confirmed that Socrates is sincere in his relations with us. No data have been uncovered to support any suspicion that he cooperates with the enemy special services.

You are hereby requested to put Socrates on the agent roll of KGB External Intelligence.

Major-General ———
Head of the RT Directorate.

Cherkashin read the document, nodded his approval, and went to see the major-general who was the head of the directorate. That's how it used to be in the intelligence service: If one were to read a report, he would be awestruck. And only a handful of immediate participants knew the depth of the gulf between the bombastic reports and reality.

This was especially true with regard to "the comprehensive verification procedure." Actually Socrates left Moscow as much an enigma as when he arrived. To put him on the agent roll in such a state was sheer madness. An agent whose loyalties are in doubt is a walking time bomb.

The "verification" of Socrates in Moscow showed me—glaringly—yet another characteristic of KGB external intelligence. Its brass turned out to be totally impotent, not only on enemy turf, but even at home, where it did not have to contend with the FBI and where it had a virtually unlimited arsenal. Cherkashin was the sole exception, but he needed immediate results and was surrounded by incompetent bureaucrats. But Kryuchkov and his closest aides put their trust in documents alone.

As for me, I decided not to exercise any initiative, but to restrict my activities to those specifically ordered by Cherkashin. Being under a cloud of stupid suspicion, thanks to the fine hand of Androsov, there was little else I could do.

Before Socrates' departure, we agreed that next time he would come to Moscow alone, to work. Several days later, I was summoned by Cherkashin.

"Congratulations on a successful recruitment," he said solemnly. "You have proven your case. Kryuchkov noted in particular the fact that it's been a long time since we have recruited a U.S. citizen under the KGB flag. From here on out, the case is yours. I am the only person with whom you are to discuss anything relating to it. No one else will interfere."

He handed me the report and the Socrates file released by the North American Department.

"Androsov didn't want to part with it at first," the colonel added with a grin. "He insisted that 'we are the ones who have worked on his case.' It took some doing, but we finally managed to bring him around."

I returned to my office, opened the Socrates recruitment report, and stopped dead in my tracks. The upper part of the document contained Kryuchkov's decision, "Agreed," and his signature; and below it, right next to the signature of the RT Directorate chief, I saw Androsov's autograph. From a bureaucratic point of view it meant that the RT Directorate—territorial intelligence— acquired an agent in the person of Socrates, and Androsov jumped on the bandwagon at the last minute! The RT Directorate would have to bear responsibility for the agent's legitimacy, while Androsov would just get benefits.

I took a new folder, put all the documents inside, and wrote on the title page: "Operative Development Case No. 115131: 'Socrates.' " Little did I know that the most interesting events lay ahead. Cherkashin's compliment, "You have proven your case," gave me a warm feeling of satisfaction. But I knew it would be a mistake to trust a counterintelligence officer, and Cherkashin was a born representative of the species. All my senses shouted that the real test—not so much of Socrates' loyalty as of mine—had yet to come. I had to meet the challenge head on.

I analyzed the situation yet another time, went to see Cherkashin and said: "I think the circumstances warrant an in-depth verification of Socrates."

The colonel stared at me in silence for a long time. It is difficult to describe the sensation I experienced as his cold eyes focused on me like an X-ray machine.

"When is he coming again?" Cherkashin asked.

"In December."

"Start preparing the testing procedure. And this is for you." He took a piece of paper from a folder on his desk and handed it to me.

I went out into the corridor and immediately began reading the document. It was a report to Kryuchkov. Two days after Socrates had been recruited, Cherkashin reported his intention to test the agent by use of mind-altering drugs. Well, well, I thought, You can't be too careful with this fellow. Cherkashin is not Androsov, that's for sure. Now you'll have to prove to the end of your life that you are not an American agent, my inner voice observed philosophically. Wise guy! How could I argue with it? Cherkashin needed psychotropic drugs for one purpose only—to find out the most deep-seated secret: whether Socrates, or I for that matter, was an FBI or CIA agent. It was a dreadful method discussed by intelligence officers only in whispers. Everyone was certain of its absolute effectiveness. In theory, anyway—very few officers had ever carried out this test.

*   *   *

Meanwhile, the RT Directorate brass began bragging at all business meetings: "Comrades, for the first time in many years, the intelligence service has recruited American citizens under the KGB flag. And we are the ones who have pulled it off." I was upbeat, buoyed by the hope that my Holy Grail was around the corner; now, with a recruitment under my belt, I would finally be able to do some real work. Cherkashin's promise that no one would interfere in the Socrates case was reason for optimism.

Alas, Colonel Cherkashin did not keep his word. Immediately after Socrates was recruited, he completely abandoned work and immersed himself in the business of building his dacha, or country house. All day long Cherkashin would roam the city in search of construction materials. And on those rare occasions when he appeared at work, he would glue himself to the telephone, and one could hear excited exclamations resounding from his office: "Have you got the nails? What about cement? When do you expect the timber to be delivered?" I was amazed by these developments and could not understand what was going on.

The entire workload as regards American operations had to be shouldered by the RT Directorate deputy chief, Colonel Anatoly Bychkov, and the American section chief, Lieutenant Colonel Leonid Beresnev. Previously, Cherkashin had not permitted these "boys" to come near the serious matters. Now, after a long period of involuntary abstinence, they were champing at the bit. Six months had passed with very little activity. Socrates was expected in Moscow in about two weeks.

That morning, in December 1987, I was summoned to Bychkov's office. Very few senior intelligence commanders inspired such a murderous reputation among their subordinates. If anything united Colonel Bychkov's staff, it was their hatred for the boss.

He had been transferred to external intelligence from the Ninth Directorate, where he had been charged with the task of protecting the country's leaders. Rumor had it that while accompanying one of the Soviet leaders to Helsinki, Bychkov had earned a black eye: one night he went on a drinking binge and started roaming about the hotel, brandishing a gun and threatening to kill anyone who would dare make an attempt on his beloved boss. That incident, however, was merely a pretext to remove Bychkov from the protection service, where he was driving his colleagues insane with his incredible pigheadedness.

Bychkov was a strapping, jug-eared fellow with impressive silver hair, a heavy jawbone, and a perpetually slobbering mouth. Any hint of refinement or intellectualism provoked his violent reaction. Once a character reference of one of his subordinates crossed his desk. Among other attributes, the officer was praised for his intellect. Bychkov flew into a rage: "What is he, an officer or a miserable egghead?" The poor guy never found out why his once-promising career suddenly fell apart like a house of cards.

Bychkov failed to distinguish himself in the field. His very first foreign trip, to Canada, ended in an ignominious fiasco; he was burned by a plant and declared *persona non grata*. But that failure did not mar his subsequent career. As often happened under Kryuchkov, incompetence was rewarded with promotion. Within a short time, Bychkov was promoted to deputy chief of the RT Directorate.

In his new capacity, Bychkov immediately discovered huge untapped resources; to his great surprise he found out that tens of thousands of Americans annually visited Moscow, but for some strange reason not one of them had ever been recruited. The intrepid colonel laid the blame squarely at the feet of the "lazy bastards," his subordinates, and ordered that henceforth a recruitment plan would have to be drafted for each American applying for a visa at the Soviet Embassy in Washington.

Before long, the directorate was drowning in paperwork; everything else was put on hold. Of course, there was neither time nor resources to implement such sweeping plans. Every ounce of available energy was expended in drafting plans and writing explanations as to why the plans had not been translated into action.

Bychkov took a long time admitting the failure of his pet project, but after a while he came up with another idea of how to improve our performance. Each morning he would summon all of the section chiefs and chew them out (he proved a virtuoso at finding suitable pretexts for tongue-lashings). The thoroughly humiliated chiefs took their frustration out on their subordinates. The directorate trembled with the mass of negative emotions, but Bychkov was profoundly satisfied, patting himself on the back for his mastery at "educational work with the personnel."

"Let's get down to business," Bychkov said gravely. "When is Socrates coming?"

"In two weeks' time," I replied.

"You and Beresnev will work together under my supervision. We'll check him out with psychotropic drugs. You are all set?"

"Yes."

"Any doubts about his sincerity?" Bychkov narrowed his eyes in a show of shrewdness, jutted forward his heavy jaw, and pricked up his ears waiting for the reply.

"Actually, we should have answered this question before putting Socrates on our payroll," I remarked.

"We know better what questions to answer and when to answer them," Bychkov said, raising his voice. "Go and prepare the operation."

Use of specialty drugs was among the most delicate of intelligence operations. The documents related to such operations were marked with the "Special Importance" security classification, the highest level of secrecy classification in the country. The report on the use of a specialty drug could be signed only by Kryuchkov, and permission to execute such an operation was to be given personally by the head of the Technical Operations Directorate of the KGB.

Specialty drugs were developed by a laboratory at No. 1 Academician Varga Street, one of the most secret KGB facilities, off limits to all but the laboratory personnel. Interestingly, it was here that Kryuchkov would choose to call the decisive meeting of the plotters on the eve of the August 1991 coup attempt.

The laboratory produced a wide variety of specialty drugs, including poisons, narcotics, and psychotropic substances. Bychkov ordered the use of SP-117, concentrated alcohol, on Socrates. Judging by its number, the KGB arsenal included at least another 116 assorted potions.

Some three days before Socrates was scheduled to arrive, a laboratory staffer was dispatched to brief me. The small, portly man, his gay eyes mischievously glistening through thick spectacles, looked like he would be very much in his element at the doors of the gas chamber in a Nazi death camp. I nicknamed him "Aesculapius."

We retired to Beresnev's office, and Aesculapius started off by declaring that he was under KGB orders to direct the technical aspect of the operation.

"Is the drug dangerous?" I asked.

"Not at all," he assured me. "It is merely concentrated, unadulterated alcohol made of natural herbs. SP-117 works as follows: Two drops of the preparation are added to a glass of liquor. For best results, the subject should down the contents quickly, preferably in a single gulp. Then in about ten minutes he will be dead drunk. If he drinks more slowly, the state of inebriation will set in somewhat later. As soon as the desired condition has been achieved, you can begin the interrogation."

"Who is going to dispense the drug into the glass?" Beresnev asked.

"I will," Aesculapius replied. "Not into the glass, though. A bottle with doped contents will be delivered to the room. What kind of drink does the subject prefer?"

"Only champagne," I said.

"What about vodka?"

"He absolutely detests it."

"Okay, then, we'll dissolve SP-117 in a bottle of champagne, and you will be drinking vodka. Make sure there will be no mix-up; I remember a few cases of this nature. As soon as you find out what you want, I'll lace a cup of coffee with a certain powder. Make the subject drink it, and in ten minutes he will be absolutely sober."

"Do we really need it?" Beresnev asked.

"The powder is the key to the whole operation," Aesculapius replied with a peel of ringing, childish laughter. "If you allow the subject to emerge from his drunken state in a natural way, there is some likelihood that he may retain some recollection of what you talked to him about. But the forced sobering-up induced by the powder will blot out all memory of his experience."

"Are you sure it is not dangerous?" I asked again.

"I am prepared to stake my life that no harm will come to the subject," Aesculapius assured me. "In accordance with the instructions, I should be stationed in immediate proximity to the subject so as to observe his response to the preparation. You will have to think of a way to get me there."

"I am quite sure that your colleagues staked their lives that Captain Shadrin would be absolutely safe, too, and yet they managed to dispatch him from this world," I remarked.

"Captain who?" Aesculapius asked in surprise.

It had happened long ago. In the 1970s, Shadrin, a Soviet naval officer who was serving in Poland, defected with his Polish mistress to the U.S., where he became a Pentagon adviser. In a few years, our Washington residency caught up with the defector and, with the use of threats, turned him into a double agent. He proceeded to supply information, but soon the center began doubting his sincerity. Shadrin was summoned to Vienna, where he was given a shot of a specialty drug and taken in a van to East Germany. Unfortunately, they gave him an overdose, and Shadrin was found dead upon arrival in Berlin. As usual, the affair was hushed up, nobody was punished, and as far as the Americans were concerned, Shadrin was missing in action.

"Oh, yeah, sure." Aesculapius finally recalled the incident. "It was a serious blunder indeed. Well, what's to be done? We were just starting in those days and had merely a handful of reliable drugs. Now the situation is entirely different; we have at our disposal a slew of well-tested preparations for all contingencies. So there is no need to worry, everything will be okay." He said the last word in English.

"Just remember, if anything happens to Socrates, it's your head for sure," I threatened just in case. "Kryuchkov himself is watching the case, it's that important."

"Don't worry, he'll be perfectly safe," Aesculapius said with his mischievous grin.

It was a dreary December night as Beresnev and I set out to meet Socrates in his "deluxe" room in the Hotel Rossiya, with its view of the Kremlin. I cringed at the prospect of introducing Beresnev as my boss, especially after Socrates had met with analyst Golikov on his previous trip to Moscow. As bright as Colonel Golikov was, he had staggered the agent with his intelligence. Now Socrates was about to discover quite a different truth. What would he think of the Committee, knowing that it was managed by people such as Beresnev? I could only hope that my new chief would be relatively quiet.

I had come to know Beresnev when we both worked at the Washington residency. Prior to that he, like Bychkov, had been stationed for several years in Canada, but came up empty in both countries. Beresnev had gotten himself arrested trying to sneak a stolen pair of pantyhose past the security guards at a Washington store. A major storm broke out: a Soviet diplomat caught red-handed shoplifting!

Beresnev tried to pass himself off as a victim of an FBI provocation, but no one believed him. General Yakushkin listened to Beresnev's protestations with undisguised contempt and then said: "Let's assume that it was not a theft. But what kind of intelligence officer are you if you can be framed by means of such a penny-ante provocation? In Czarist Russia, in such cases military officers used to blow out their own brains, or at the very least resign their commissions."

"I swear I didn't steal the pantyhose," Beresnev cried, begging for mercy.

"Who cares about the pantyhose? The problem is that you are unfit to be an intelligence officer," Yakushkin said acidly. "If you couldn't steal a piece of lingerie, how are you going to steal U.S. state secrets? Get out of here! You disgust me!"

But when Beresnev returned to Moscow, he was picked up by Bychkov and made chief of the American Section of the RT Directorate. In his new capacity, Beresnev developed an unexpected talent; he turned himself into an unsurpassed master of the art of "jumping-aboard-at-the-closing-stage."

Beresnev mastered this simple technique in a snap, which earned him the nickname "Johnny-come-lately." Judging from the fact that he had emerged on the scene, he obviously felt that the operation with Socrates was entering the endgame stage and it was time to reap the rewards. I was far from sure that he was right, and full of foreboding that, blinded to reality by the gleam of the forthcoming medal, he would do something stupid. Actually, I did not begrudge my superiors their awards—as long as they left me alone to do the job. I was disagreeably surprised to find out that

Beresnev had set out to meet the agent without even feigning an attempt to familiarize himself with his file—it was like commencing surgery without having the slightest idea of what was wrong with the patient.

"Will our conversation be recorded?" Beresnev asked when we approached Socrates' room.

"Of course," I replied. "The girls from Tatiana are working full tilt."

"Next time see to it that the mikes are turned off," he said, frowning.

"Why?"

"Why jump at any opportunity to demonstrate our stupidity?" Beresnev said—and to my surprise I saw that he was absolutely serious.

The table in the room was sagging under a pile of Russian delicacies that most Russians could not afford. A pretty waitress sent by Aesculapius daintily poured vodka into two tumblers and filled a champagne glass with the bubbly. Beresnev and Socrates were discussing the issue of U.S. bases in Greece.

Having learned from the agent that there are such bases even in the outskirts of Athens, Beresnev said self-importantly: "At this stage, the Soviet Union will be fully satisfied if they are just moved farther away from the capital."

I could have screamed. Beresnev was clearly in over his head, teetering on the brink of failure. I had to intervene, and pronto.

"Dinner is ready," I said loudly.

"To our success," my boss proclaimed and downed his glass.

But no sooner had Socrates followed suit than Beresnev jumped in again.

"In principle, the Soviet Union is prepared to lend Greece

any kind of assistance if her government demands total withdrawal of American bases."

Socrates, who had not yet figured out that his interlocutor did not know what he was talking about, was so surprised that he forgot his champagne.

"What amount of economic aid can you offer?" he asked.

"As much as needed," Beresnev replied gravely, reveling in the effect his words produced.

"How about a little saber-rattling?"

"Sure, why not!"

Behind the agent's back, I was furiously making faces, trying to draw Beresnev's attention to the full champagne glass. Finally my boss deigned to descend from heaven to earth, and raised a second toast: "Research continues."

Socrates looked at him suspiciously, picked up his glass and proceeded to savor its contents. Beresnev was fussing about him, offering him now this delicacy, now another. For a short time silence reigned in the room, interrupted only by the monotonous sound of jaws at work.

Five minutes passed, ten minutes . . . Socrates was still sipping champagne without any visible effect. After another ten minutes, I decided it was time to consult Aesculapius, who was stationed one floor down, at the KGB watch suite.

"How about the fair sex?" I stood up and looked inquiringly at Socrates.

"Capital idea," he said animatedly. "And where are they?"

"Let me check." I went out of the room and down the stairs.

"What are we going to do?" I asked Aesculapius, entering his room. "Your drug doesn't work."

"I don't believe it," he protested. "It's just that your agent is sipping his drink instead of gulping it down. Don't worry, it'll work. Let's go, I want to observe him."

When I came back I saw that the show was indeed beginning. Socrates was visibly losing coordination; he slurred his words, his eyes were losing focus. Jerkily, he poured himself a full tea glass of vodka, downed it, and collapsed in a helpless heap.

"The shift is over," I said. It was a prearranged signal to Tatiana's people to stop recording and turn off the microphones. "And you"—I turned to Aesculapius—"wait downstairs. We'll call when we need you."

KGB rules forbid conducting an interrogation of a drugged subject in the presence of unauthorized witnesses. Even taping was not allowed, so as to leave absolutely no traces.

Lounging in an armchair, Beresnev was watching me with eyes that he had some difficulty keeping focused. Suddenly hot fury surged through me. Again, I had to go through the most dire test in order to prove my innocence. And all because I had achieved the nearly impossible—recruited a U.S. citizen? But I had to go through with it, to prove myself to whom? To a petty thief, a failed intelligence operative who by an inexplicable quirk of fate had become my boss? Or to Bychkov? Or maybe to General Androsov, who had run first the residency and then the North American Department into the ground? How long would this affront to common sense go on? This crowd had gotten so lazy that no one even wanted to check my trustworthiness; I had to do it myself. Oh, no, comrades, I've had it, I decided.

I sat down next to the agent and got the ball rolling.

"Martin, I helped you to become an adviser of our committee, so that you'll be able to improve your finances. Now it's your turn to lend me a hand. I need to establish contact with the CIA or the FBI."

Socrates reclined in the chair, snoring lightly. I had to shake him hard to bring him to his senses. His glazed eyes went around the room, stopped on a glass full of vodka. He grabbed it and poured its contents down his throat. Then he fixed me with unseeing eyes and muttered something unintelligible. The diagnosis was clear: inebriation in an extreme degree.

Apparently, the drug was only part of the reason, the rest

being considerable physical fatigue; Socrates had had no time to rest after the long flight from the U.S. So under the effect of the SP-117, he had not merely gotten drunk, but was utterly senseless. He was liable to say just about anything, which was more dangerous for me than for him.

If worse came to worst, all Socrates risked was losing the "honorary title" of a KGB agent, while I would have to contend with Internal Counterintelligence—an ominous prospect if ever there was one. But that night I had little choice. Either I would allay my superiors' dangerous suspicions, or all was lost—*La commedia è finita*. I asked one question after another, waiting with morbid fascination for the answer that would seal my fate.

"Martin, I am sick of the Soviet Union and everything in it. I don't want to live here anymore. Please put me in touch with U.S. intelligence. You have some contacts there, don't you?" I waited with bated breath.

Beresnev was watching us with fascination, looking like a novice joyously swimming in the murky waters of big-time espionage.

Socrates scooped up some caviar with his hand and smeared it on his beard.

"I can't do it," he said. "Buzz off, you're a psycho."

"Yes, I am a psycho," I admitted without remorse, "but you must help me. Remember, I helped you, even though you are crazy, too."

"It's a dangerous game," Socrates mumbled. "If you lose your shirt, come to Washington. I'll try to help you . . ."

"Will you put me in touch with U.S. intelligence?" I insisted.

"Go to hell," he said spitefully. "I hate their guts. Do you want me to hate your guts, too?"

What a brilliant reply! Beresnev hummed with satisfaction and poured the vodka. My head ached with stress. I was dying to pause for breath.

"Would you like to take over?" I asked Beresnev. He nodded his agreement.

"Who has sent you here? Who are you working for? The CIA? The FBI?" he kept asking with a scowl.

"Leave me alone," the agent moaned. "Where are the women you promised?"

"Why, he is not all that drunk," I noted with surprise. "Well, so much the better."

"Maybe you are working for British intelligence?" Beresnev continued his onslaught. "How much do the Germans pay you?"

"Shut up . . . I have a headache . . . pour me some more champagne . . ." Socrates muttered and dipped his face into the salad bowl.

"No, answer my questions!" thundered Beresnev. "What kind of mission have the Germans given you?"

I sat on the sofa, listening intently to the interrogation. Let Beresnev talk as much as he wanted. He must be left with the impression that he had conducted a highly sophisticated verification procedure, and very effectively at that.

For about two hours we interrogated Socrates about his alleged ties to the secret services and demanded that he put me in touch now with the CIA, now with the FBI. Socrates responded mostly with gibberish. In the process, Beresnev had consumed a solid meal and now was leisurely picking his teeth. It was time to end the show.

I took two bottles of brandy from my attaché case, poured their contents into the bathtub, and put them on the table. Then I took out a bra and placed it in an eye-catching position on the armchair next to Socrates. After a final once-over to make sure that everything indeed looked like the aftermath of a wild party, I called Aesculapius.

"The client is tired. Could you please bring some coffee."

About ten minutes later the same waitress entered our room with a small serving table containing three cups of coffee—two in one corner and the third one, designed for Socrates, in another.

"Martin, it's time to refresh ourselves," I said in a weary

voice. "Otherwise the ladies are going to leave. They are sick and tired of our boozing."

"Yeah, sure, let's have some coffee," Socrates said fussily and hurriedly drained his cup.

I immediately filled the glasses with vodka and handed one to Beresnev:

"Quick, we must make this look like an orgy."

No sooner had we swallowed the vodka than a small miracle took place; Socrates was sobering up fast, looking around with the air of a totally perplexed man.

"What happened? I fell asleep, didn't I? And where are the women?" he asked in bewilderment.

"They tried to arouse you, but failed and left," I said with a drunken grin.

"Pity . . . It never happened to me before," Socrates said disgustedly.

"Well, you must be dog-tired," I observed. "You didn't rest after your journey, and you've paid for it."

"What's this?" Socrates asked in surprise, pointing at the bra.

"Your trophy." I smiled and threw it at him.

"Boy, I can't believe we drank so much," he muttered, gingerly lifting the bra with two fingers. "Two bottles of champagne, two bottles of vodka, and two bottles of brandy? I can't believe it." Dumbfounded, he shifted his gaze from the table to me and Beresnev, then to the bra.

"You'd better believe it, my friend," I said. "You can't imagine the kind of drinking that goes on in our agency. Get used to it if you want to fit in."

"I think what I need is a lot of sleep," Socrates said almost plaintively. "I've come here to work, and must be in good shape."

"Tomorrow you are on your own the whole day. Rest well," I said. "We'll get down to business the day after."

As Beresnev and I were leaving the room, Socrates dropped onto the sofa. He was totally exhausted.

*   *   *

Beresnev and I stood under a streetlight outside the Hotel Rossiya, smoking greedily. A bitingly cold wind was lashing our faces unmercifully, but Beresnev's eyes glowed in triumph; he had taken part in a major operation.

"The test was a beauty," he said excitedly, his breath heavy with a mixture of vodka and champagne.

"I have this nagging feeling that something is not right. I don't know what, but we did something wrong," I protested. Having concluded the conversation with Socrates to my satisfaction, I could afford to have some fun at Beresnev's expense.

"You are out of your mind!" Beresnev exclaimed fretfully. "The checkup came off great. Socrates is clean as a whistle!"

"He didn't answer our questions, just mumbled unintelligibly."

"You read him wrong," Beresnev said. "He was so innocent that he was simply confounded by our questions about all those special services. Listen, I was really amazed at the kind of questions you asked. Weren't you afraid that, drunk as he was, he would end up saying, 'Okay, I'm a CIA agent; I'll put you in touch with Langley.'"

"What was I supposed to do?" I said with a touch of malice. "After all, I was under a cloud, wasn't I?"

"Cut it out, will you," Beresnev said with a smirk. "You can forget it now. As a matter of fact, I was under suspicion, too. Remember that stupid pantyhose story?"

"I sure do. How could you survive after catching all that flack?"

"Well . . . Don't you know the rule of thumb: somebody spits in your face, you wipe it off without a peep and go on like nothing happened."

"Like Jesus Christ?"

"No, like a piece of shit." Beresnev scowled and spat on the ground.

Apparently he did not even suspect what a profound truth he had just put forth. Just a few words, but they conveyed in a nutshell the life story of practically any Soviet citizen. I sighed deeply and said: "I wish Cherkashin had not ignored operational work."

"It was to be expected," Beresnev said significantly.

I eyed him thoughtfully. He was regarded as Cherkashin's buddy and doubtless knew a lot about him, including things I could not even suspect. Beresnev seemed torn between prudence and temptation. Professional caution demanded that he keep his mouth shut, while a desire to strut his stuff bolstered by a few drinks and the successful talk with Socrates propelled him in the opposite direction.

"Well, okay, here goes." He spat yet another time. "Just remember, you'll be mighty sorry if you let the cat out of the bag." He looked mysteriously around and dropped his voice to a barely audible whisper.

"Upon his return from the Washington residency to Moscow in the fall of 1986, Cherkashin was awarded the Order of Lenin—in secret!"

That was a mind-boggling piece of news. Not because Colonel Cherkashin was awarded the highest decoration of the Soviet Union, but because he was decorated in secret. Distinction of this kind was conferred on intelligence officers only in exceptional cases and only for exceptional achievements. Neither the next of kin nor the colleagues of the intelligence officer thus decorated were to know of the signal honor. Nor could he wear the medal, which was kept either in his office safe or at the personnel department.

General Gorovoy, the control officer of John Walker, who passed U.S. Navy secret communication codes to the KGB, was awarded the gold star of Hero of the Soviet Union. After Walker was exposed in 1985, some U.S. officials declared that he had done more damage to the country's national security than anybody else since World War II. So what did Colonel Cherkashin do to earn the Order of Lenin after allowing two officers from the Washington residency to go bad right under his nose? What could he have done to get that award?

"I don't believe it," I exclaimed vehemently. "Cherkashin was in charge of the external counterintelligence unit at the Washington residency and as such has to take the blame for the treachery of Motorin. Well, okay, ex-CIA agent Howard defected to Moscow and said that Motorin had been recruited by the FBI, so Motorin was executed, allowing Cherkashin to atone for his deadly blunder. But I'll be damned if I see how atonement for one's sins merits the country's highest distinction!"

"Howard had nothing to do with it," Beresnev said. "He came to the Soviet Embassy in Washington empty-handed and was shown the door as an agent provocateur. When he turned up in Moscow in 1985, all of us were thunderstruck. What the hell did we need him here for? On second thought, it was decided to grant him asylum and also to give him credit for betraying Motorin, though in actual fact he had not the remotest idea of his existence. A classic ploy: to ascribe a success to a compromised source as a way of providing cover for another, still active, agent."

"But if not Howard, then who?" I asked. "I always understood that Motorin was not burned owing to his own negligence, but because of a tip from Washington."

"That's exactly right," Beresnev agreed. "Let me tell you even more. Our external surveillance spotted Motorin at the site of a dead drop loaded for him by the CIA in Moscow a few months after Howard had turned up. Moreover, Motorin was not under surveillance; our guys had spent three days waiting for someone to turn up at the dead drop."

"Which means that they knew either the exact site of the dead drop or the identity of the CIA control who ran Motorin. So they could put him under surveillance and watched him load the dead drop," I said.

"A brilliant piece of thinking," chuckled Beresnev.

It appeared there was no way Howard could disclose the location of the dead drop loaded by the CIA for Motorin or the identity of the CIA operative. Not only is the communication procedure the most secret part of running an agent, but it is routinely revised prior to each new operation. Which meant that it could only have been disclosed by a CIA official who enjoyed direct access to Motorin's file early in 1986, when the agent was slated to unload the dead drop at the Kuntsevo Cemetery in Moscow. By that time, it was several months since Howard had defected. Could it be that Cherkashin recruited an asset at the CIA? I thought. And could he still be there? After Howard, not a single double agent has been uncovered at Langley.

"How do you know about Cherkashin's secret decoration?" I asked Beresnev.

"I read it in his personnel file. Recently, I was preparing his evaluation and called up his file from the personnel department. That's where it is all set forth in black and white."

"Was Androsov also decorated for that agent? After all, he was the resident in Washington at the time."

"What did Androsov have to do with it?" Beresnev asked in surprise. "For all intents and purposes Cherkashin enjoyed complete independence. He worked for the External Counterintelligence Directorate and bore sole responsibility for handling Americans who came to our embassy in the U.S. to offer their services to the KGB. As far as he was concerned, the resident didn't exist, because he had the right to report directly to Moscow."

"And how do you know that Motorin was burned because of a tip from the CIA?"

"From one of the surveillance boys who spent three days watching the dead drop loaded by the CIA. They had no idea that Motorin would be the one to turn up to unload the dead drop."

That's when I recalled one more curious incident. A few months after Motorin had been executed, Chief of Intelligence Kryuchkov conducted an operational meeting attended by some eight hundred intelligence officers. At the end of his speech Kryuchkov suddenly said: "We know there is a traitor in this audience. I am offering him his life if he surrenders. Otherwise he will be shot."

The audience erupted in indignation. Everybody was certain that it was some kind of sick joke. But it wasn't. Sometime later, a colonel with the intelligence service was arrested. Many years previously, he had been recruited by the American intelligence services while on a business trip to the U.S. He had maintained no contact with the CIA in Moscow and thus could not be caught red-handed. There had been no evidence against him so far as I knew. Now I realized that Kryuchkov had nothing incriminating on the colonel besides a CIA tip. That's why he had made that earth-shattering declaration, hoping to spook the suspect into showing his hand.

So it appeared that at least two agents the CIA ran within KGB intelligence had been destroyed through no fault of their own but through the efforts of a CIA mole recruited by Colonel Cherkashin. If true, it was a stupendous feat. To work with Cherkashin was a formidable, even dangerous, task, but the results one could hope for under his guidance made it worthwhile in my eyes. With Cherkashin at the helm, the Socrates operation opened staggering vistas. But why on earth would he withdraw from intelligence activities, for no apparent reason and of his own free will, handing the reins of power to amateur spymasters in the persons of my new bosses? I asked Beresnev this question.

"The usual thing," Beresnev replied with the air of a connoisseur. "He was elbowed aside and stripped of the agent who had earned him the Order of Lenin. There are lots of generals ready and willing to man the old feeding trough. Actually he was lucky to get his medal. It's an unwritten law of our service: the major forges a career for the colonel, the colonel for the general, and the general for the intelligence chief."

He was positively beaming with happiness. Obviously, he liked that "law." For the time being anyway.

"So what happened next?" I asked.

"Next, Cherkashin took umbrage and was promptly barred for life from foreign travel—just in case, lest he ever, God forbid, conceive a desire to spill the beans to the Americans about his agent." Beresnev could barely restrain his glee. "Then he turned his back on his duties and devoted himself full-time to the construction of his dacha. Sort of, 'Take your job and shove it.'"

"So, they've just destroyed yet another pro with their own hands."

"What do you mean?" he asked, pricking up his ears.

"Nothing. Forget it," I said vaguely. "Do you know the name of Cherkashin's mole?"

"The less you know, the more you live." He paused, then said, "Don't you dare express any doubts about Socrates when you see the bosses tomorrow. Remember, the control procedure was a success, the agent's sincerity was proved beyond any doubt. And that's the way it is."

We parted. The news of Cherkashin's extraordinary achievement and the demise of his operational career put me in a philosophical frame of mind. General Yakushkin getting the boot as chief of the North American Department; Colonel Aksilenko's removal as head of the Washington Section; the openly contemptuous treatment of Cherkashin, holder of the Order of Lenin, that forced the colonel to wash his hands of operational work—all reflected the general mores in the intelligence service. The pros pulled chestnuts out of the fire for bureaucrats, the latter then ate the pros. Moreover, they took such delight in tearing down their betters as if none of them ever realized that sooner or later the time would come when nobody would be left to work for them, and they would starve. It seemed to me that the bureaucrats in the intelligence service had already reached the rock bottom of degeneration and lost even the paramount instinct for any living being—the instinct of self-preservation. They fiddled with abandon while Rome was burning.

By the end of 1987, almost all KGB intelligence officers who at one time or another had run American agents had been taken off operational status. One of them, Hero of the Soviet Union General Gorovoy, was forcibly removed to the intelligence school, turning him into an internal dissident who never passed a major meeting without a scathing attack on Kryuchkov and his minions. The Hero of the Soviet Union could afford loud dissent. Others swallowed their humiliation and suffered bruised egos in silence. Not a pretty picture and a powerful disincentive to young intelligence operatives who would otherwise be expected to be champing at the bit. The maxim "initiative is a punishable offense" became a behavioral norm.

The foreign agents recruited by the KGB could not help being affected. Recruiting and running an agent is an art form, an evil art form, and like any art it is strictly individualistic.

As soon as intelligence bureaucrats invaded the agent-handling turf, it turned into a semblance of a Soviet collective farm, with inevitable failure looming on the horizon. The agent was no longer in a position to affect the outcome. He could be as smart and resourceful as a hundred James Bonds—and still would have no chance. Sooner or later he would be burned by the intelligence service to which in an unguarded moment he had entrusted his fate. In such a case, survival is strictly a matter of divine intervention.

I strongly suspected that the "unwritten law" of the intelligence service to which Beresnev had referred would pretty soon spell my doom—and Socrates' too. I was helpless to change the outcome, but I had no intention of lending a hand to the bureaucrats.

The next morning, Beresnev noisily barged into my office and yelled excitedly: "Write a report to Kryuchkov about Socrates' test. And remember, no expressions of doubt; the agent is absolutely sincere with us and has no ties to the

Western special services. Bychkov fully agrees and will countersign the report."

I took a sheet of paper and was about to start writing when I saw that Beresnev was still dawdling uncomfortably by the door. Judging by his expression, he was about to unburden himself of an important piece of news.

"One more thing," he finally screwed up the courage to say. "Your report should say that I alone conducted the checkout under Bychkov's guidance. You don't have to mention your participation."

Oh, Vanity Fair, how many people have fallen victim to your blandishments! Get ready to accept another victim; he is literally breaking down your door in his haste. Of course, Beresnev and Bychkov will feature prominently in my report. Let them hope that Kryuchkov will remember their names and reward them for their heroic deeds in the line of duty. I wasn't sure he would, though; hundreds of heroes of that caliber flashed before his eyes every day.

8

THE next morning Socrates and I were sitting in his hotel room facing a stack of clean paper and a typewriter with a Latin keyboard that I had managed to rustle up, with some difficulty, in our department. I faced a tough challenge: to make the agent write a report, that is to say to accomplish an intelligence assignment. Until he did it, he did not qualify as an agent in the true sense of the word. While developing him, I had been talking about using his services in an advisory capacity. Now I had to guide him in a smooth transition from consultations to intelligence reports, because consultations can be based on his personal opinion while an intelligence report requires real facts.

"What information? We were only talking about foreign policy consultations, weren't we?" Socrates made a show of bewilderment, even displeasure, but to me his eyes betrayed the truth: I believed he was prepared to do anything asked of him, so long as he didn't lose face. If he was to become a KGB informer, he wanted to have a plausible alibi. Above all, in his own eyes. It was exactly such an alibi that he expected me to supply.

"You are absolutely right, Martin," I agreed. "But let me initiate you into some of the ways of the Kremlin, or else you won't be able to see my point. One of the maddening characteristics of the Soviet bureaucrat is his certainty that there is nothing he doesn't know or can't accomplish—if only because he has read Marx and Lenin, or at any rate heard their names. Our task, yours and mine, is to inculcate certain ideas in his obstinate head any way we can, because in this case the ends do justify the means. If we call your memoranda 'consultations,' the Kremlin will take umbrage and the whole scheme will fall through. But if we serve up the very same material as intelligence, success is virtually guaranteed. Well, the choice is yours. I have already applied for funds to pay for your services."

When Socrates heard the reference to money, his eyes flashed and he apparently concluded yet another bargain with his conscience. I don't know how convincing my explanation sounded—and frankly, it made little difference as long as he accepted it as a basis for self-justification.

For two days running that December, we worked like crazy on his report. Socrates had a beautiful writing style and a fair amount of experience in compiling informational documents. But I had to teach him to compose intelligence reports in such a way as to conform to the strictest canons of the analytical service: above all, reliability, confidentiality, importance, timeliness, and concreteness.

Socrates worked fast, but evinced all the symptoms of mental anguish. The heartrending moans that he emitted at frequent intervals could have melted ice and broken stone. My God, what an indolent bastard! my inner voice marveled. Small wonder that in search of easy money he got entangled in the KGB net. At least he doesn't have to go to work every morning.

The questions posed to Socrates by the analytical service ran the gamut: the U.S. position at the Soviet-American arms control negotiations; the Reagan administration's policies toward the USSR and the hot spots around the world; the balance of forces in the administration and Congress as regards the key foreign policy issues; the election campaign leading to the 1988 presidential elections; issues relating to trade and economic relations between the USSR and the U.S.

Finally, Socrates tapped at the typewriter keyboard for the last time and threw himself back in the chair in exhaustion, while I grabbed the weighty stack of papers and rushed to the analytical service.

There had been a time when I was naive enough to think that the center eagerly awaited agents' reports and pounced on them as soon as they arrived. Nothing could be further from the truth. Under Kryuchkov, the KGB external intelligence service needed only information that could be put to good use in the incredibly convoluted game of bureaucratic politics.

The Intelligence Information Directorate, also known as the RI Service (the initials for *Razvedivatyelnaya Informatsiya*—"Intelligence Information"), occupied two floors of the left wing of the KGB intelligence service building. All KGB residencies abroad sent their information to this unit to be analyzed, pieced together, and processed into intelligence estimates for the country's supreme leadership. Outwardly, the RI offices differed from those of the operational subdivisions only by virtue of more numerous filing cabinets and by the stamp of eternal skepticism on the faces of the analysts themselves.

It was in one of those offices that I found an analyst named Sergei, whom I had long known and respected as a highly professional and independent-minded expert. Sergei's predictions regarding the course of events in the U.S. generally came true, while remaining largely unknown beyond the walls of the RI Service. Its leaders tried to steer clear of predictions, for fear of being called to account if any of them failed to materialize. Such a risk-averse attitude did wonders for the longevity of the leading analysts even past retirement age while driving Sergei nuts, for he saw risk-taking as the only real path to career advancement.

I deposited the traditional souvenir—a carton of Marlboros—on Sergei's desk, and opened the conversation with a traditional question: "How are things at the brain center?"

"Things are awful," he answered sullenly. "I can't remember when it was as bad as it is now. The U.S. residencies send us a flood of absolute junk, totally devoid of specific facts; just a bunch of abstract speculation, and ludicrously little classified information. Last year, for instance, it amounted to a pathetic eight percent of the total. And your outfit managed to scrape together all of three—can you hear me, three!—pieces of secret information related to the U.S. And, to make matters even worse, the precious few classified gems that you guys do obtain, which I include in my analytical reports, are more often than not scrapped by the RI brass."

I was smiling with the air of a person who had long known and accepted that life was unfair.

"Just have a look at this lousy sheet of paper." Sergei was warming to his subject.

He dove into his safe, took out a big bundle of papers, leafed through them, and extracted a document bearing the highest classification designation.

"This is an analysis of the balance of forces in the U.S. Congress following the latest off-year election," he thundered, waving the sheet. "Care to see what's in it? The first paragraph states that there are conservatives in Congress; the second avers that there are also Democrats; the third discloses that there is an unstable center prone to shifting now to the right, now to the left. And as a clincher, a strategic conclusion: in the final analysis, it is up to President Reagan to make all important decisions. What an awesome display of sheer brainpower! Of course, it's up to the president! Who else is to make important decisions, goddamnit!"

"Who is the author of this valuable piece of analytical work?" I asked.

"The chief of the American Department of our service ... As a matter of fact, this kind of analysis would have amply sufficed for Brezhnev; and if it had been leavened with a couple of fresh jokes, the old man would have had a ball. But we are in the midst of perestroika, and Gorbachev was outraged by the kind of trash that is served up to him under the guise of analytical reports and reviews."

Sergei nervously lit a cigarette and went on venting his feelings.

"Recently, the general secretary called on the carpet the managers of the analytical units of the Ministry of Foreign Affairs, the KGB, and Military Intelligence, and let them have it with both barrels. The Foreign Affairs people were cursed out for coloring the truth, the military for outright stupidity. As for our stuff, Gorbachev said he was at a loss as to why we bother to send him cables so murky nobody could decipher their meaning. The first paragraph says that the ceiling is white; the second begins with an expression of doubt, "However ... ," and ends with a confession that, come to think of it, the ceiling might turn out to be black after all. And that's all, end of message. No conclusions. Let the addressee make his own guess as to the color of the blasted ceiling."

"Has the blowout had any consequences?" I asked without much hope of hearing something new.

"None whatsoever." Sergei angrily tossed the folder aside. "The next day, the chief of the RI Service, Khrenov, called a meeting of the top brass. The general called on them, very gently, to improve the analytical quality of their reports and increase the number of forecasts. When he was done, the chief of my department took the floor: 'Comrade General, making forecasts is like walking through a mine-

field; one misstep—and all of us will be pensioned off.'
'Your position surprises me. Let's pretend that I have not
heard you,' Khrenov responded. And the next day, everything went on like nothing had ever happened.

"And to tell the truth, I understand why it doesn't. The
kind of information we get on political issues couldn't be
more pathetic. Believe me, in many instances we could
learn more just by reading American newspapers."

"You think spying is easy?" I reproved him good-
naturedly.

"Believe me, I appreciate your problems," Sergei hastened
to assure me. "I can guess how incredibly hard it must be to
recruit a source at a U.S. government agency or, say, in
Congress. But even if we assume the impossible—that such
a source miraculously does materialize—I am by no means
certain that the information he would supply would always
be used in our reports to the country's leaders."

"How is that?" I asked the analyst. "Who needs our service if our country's leadership has no use for classified
information coming straight from the U.S. administration?"

"I am not talking of the Kremlin leaders, but of the intelligence brass," Sergei replied with a sly grin. "You see,
lately I've had the impression that Kryuchkov is at a loss
regarding the kind of information he needs. To go on trum-
peting about the growing aggressiveness of the U.S. makes
no sense; one risks being accused of crass stupidity, as was
the case with Military Intelligence. But neither is there any
point in extolling the bright prospects of Soviet-American
relations, taking the cue from the foreign policy establishment, because a dramatic improvement of the climate between the superpowers would be tantamount to a death
sentence for the KGB. That's why we are painfully looking
for a new concept that could serve as a guide when preparing analytical reports. Although 'concept' is too grand a
word. Actually, it's just another round of insider politick-
ing. Meanwhile, until the dust settles, our service's leaders

affirm that bolder assessments of the U.S. situation can only be provided on the basis of classified U.S. government documents. As if there existed, at the White House or the Department of State, a single document containing a detailed description of the administration policy toward the Soviet Union. My bosses know full well that such a document is a figment of their imaginations, and they demand it for the sole purpose of justifying their own torpor."

"How painfully familiar," I said. "But the real question is—what are we going to do?"

"If only we had a good source . . ." Sergei sighed dreamily.

"We have one!"

"Who?"

"Socrates. You must remember his stuff from the Washington residency."

"Can we trust him?" the analyst asked dubiously.

"He has been accepted as an agent, that is, formally acknowledged as one hundred percent reliable. Beside, it has been recently reported to Kryuchkov that Socrates has been successfully tested for trustworthiness."

"What kind of information is he supplying now?" Sergei asked brusquely, his voice conveying a sense of urgency.

"You be the judge." I took a fat bundle of papers from my attaché case.

"You mean he himself prepares intelligence reports for you?" Sergei's pupils dilated with amazement.

"See for yourself."

"I am impressed," the analyst said. "But what about his sources?"

Without saying a word, I handed him one of Socrates' reports featuring about fifty of his most important past contacts.

Sergei snatched the document from my hand and pounced on it. A whistle of admiration escaped his lips.

"Wow, that's some list. Aides to leading senators and representatives; Senate Foreign Relations Committee staffers; people close to a presidential contender; arms control experts; the daughter of a CIA secretary! Congratulations, old man, you've left the entire Washington residency in the dust. Believe me, I am in a position to know."

"Any ideas?" I smiled.

"Yeah, I think so." Sergei thoughtfully rubbed his forehead. "I'm going to make a list of the most pressing questions of the moment for each of your meetings with Socrates. That way we'll be able to keep abreast of developments and go to the very top with our information. Your agent looks awfully good. Let's hope he'll help us breach the reinforced concrete wall of the stinking bureaucracy. I need it and so do you. But most important, so does our service."

"Are you sure somebody else needs it?" I asked skeptically.

"Absolutely," Sergei exclaimed with conviction. "Gorbachev is veritably suffocating for lack of solid information. He is being deliberately fed all sorts of junk. He is still not sure if the Americans will support his reforms—and he won't be sure for a long time, if he confines himself to the traditional sources. I wish he consulted me instead of reading Kryuchkov's reports . . ."

"Long live our Union!" I laughed.

A political intelligence report is an extremely delicate thing. It is not a specimen of military technology that can be touched, licked, smelled, even tried out on a testing platform. Nor is it an American government document that has to be passed on upstairs whether you like it or not, for fear of being accused of willful concealment.

A political intelligence report is a fragile alloy of real facts combined with its author's intellectual and even moral faculties. Feed a piece of news to two intelligence officers, and they will use it to produce two entirely different documents. One won't be worth the paper on which it will be written, the other will be a marvelous, sparkling gem of analytical skill.

But what's to be done if the report runs counter to the boss's forecast? Does one pass it on or not? And if yes, is there any chance that it will not be buried in the boss's office?

For a political intelligence report to make it upstairs it has to meet all sorts of informal criteria as well as the official requirements. Above all, it must buttress the viewpoint currently dominant at the top, as well as the personal views of a long list of functionaries, from the head of the relevant analytical service section all the way up to the chief of intelligence. Small wonder that only useless junk could successfully negotiate all those barriers.

Sergei was in the right place at the right time. We were a perfect fit. Socrates' information began to sparkle like a diamond. He was particularly adept at analyzing the U.S. position at the bilateral arms control talks. One major reason for his success was a set of excellent sources on that issue. Some of them were his Bethesda neighbors who had no idea that their natural openness was grist for the KGB mills.

About two weeks later, in late December, the farewell party on the occasion of Socrates' departure from Moscow was planned with a great deal of pomp. Beresnev donned his best suit, and for the first time hoisted spectacles on his nose.

"What shall I tell Socrates?" he asked.

"Well, tell him that we really appreciate his readiness to help us; that we never forget our friends and know how to show our gratitude; that we are very concerned about his safety. And above all, show maximum admiration for his towering intellect and maximum understanding and sympathy when he starts complaining of his cruel fate."

Beresnev diligently made notes on a piece of paper. But my last point elicited an unexpected reaction.

"You and your lousy psychobabble," he mumbled sullenly. "Rather than slobbering all over the agent, one must keep him on a short leash."

Beresnev smiled brightly as he knocked on the door of Socrates' room.

"I ordered a table at the restaurant," Socrates declared, letting us in.

"First, we must talk," Beresnev said sternly, and sat down in an armchair.

He made a short speech thanking Socrates for his contributions. When the speech was over and the handshakes exchanged, Beresnev said, "Let's make arrangements for the next meeting. We'll conduct it in . . . Damascus."

"Damascus? Why Damascus?" Socrates was taken aback.

"It's necessary," Beresnev said flatly.

"To whom?" The agent could not overcome his puzzlement.

"That's just the way it has to be done," my boss said, continuing his curt tone.

"But it will be dangerous for me," Socrates observed in confusion. "It would be better to meet in the Soviet Union. Here you are in full control of the situation. I will come via Greece or some other country. You will not stamp my passport with any visa so as not to leave any traces . . . Why go to Syria and expose ourselves? There are all sorts of dangers lurking in Damascus: the local counterintelligence, the Mossad, the CIA."

But Beresnev was deaf to the agent's demonstrably reasonable arguments.

"We have to meet in Damascus," he insisted.

"Well, okay." Socrates surrendered. "We'll have one meeting abroad."

Beresnev beamed as if he had accomplished an extremely difficult and important task.

"And now on to the restaurant," he commanded.

★　　★　　★

At our farewell meal, Socrates dropped a bombshell.

"What would you say if I tried to return to the White House after the next presidential election?"

"A wonderful idea," Beresnev exclaimed, but at that instant the orchestra erupted in an ear-splitting outburst of music, momentarily interrupting the general conversation.

Beresnev reached for the salad, while I leaned forward toward Socrates.

"Martin, you must be joking, of course."

"I am dead serious," he assured me.

"How do you plan to do it?"

"I have excellent connections on the Dukakis team," Socrates said. "Some of his closest aides are Carter administration alumni. If Dukakis wins—and I think he will—I'll have an excellent chance of getting a job with his administration."

"And are you setting your sights on a job at the White House or elsewhere?"

"We'll cross that bridge when we come to it," he said evasively. "The most important thing for me is to get a job in the national security area, in which case we'll gain access to vital intelligence. That's what you want, don't you?"

"But suppose George Bush wins the election. Then what?" I asked.

"I doubt it," Socrates replied skeptically. "However, in the unlikely case he does, I'll pull the strings I keep in reserve and get a job with the Republican administration."

"What reserve strings?" I asked with surprise.

"I have an excellent contact in Congress, the aide of a prominent conservative Republican senator. We share an interest in Pakistan. He has some business interests in that country and follows the events there very closely. Fortunately, Phyllis is pretty tight with Benazir Bhutto, and we have a lot to tell that guy. That's how we trade information."

"Don't be a fool, Martin," I said. "For a man with your

reputation to count on a Republican senator's support is foolhardy, at the very least."

"We'll see. Let's not try to hasten events," he chortled. "In the meantime, I am putting my money on Dukakis and don't expect to lose."

"How do you plan to get a security clearance?" I persisted.

"I doubt very much that, when the Democrats come to power, their security requirements will be as stringent as those of the Reagan administration. But even if I have to undergo one, what will it show? I've come to the Soviet Union on an absolutely legal basis; besides, it's not a crime. I don't really know, and don't care to know, your affiliation and that of your friends. So what can they charge me with?"

"Why do you go to all this trouble, Martin? Do you really need money that badly?" I did not hide my skepticism, and Socrates was a little embarrassed.

"Yes, I am on the brink of a financial disaster," he admitted gloomily. "But you are mistaken if you think I am bluffing in order to wangle more money out of you. It definitely looks as though sooner or later I'll have to leave America for good. And before then, I'd like to square a few accounts."

"Well, it's your life," I capitulated. "But if you want to make the most of our association moneywise, you'd better produce. The communication channel to the very top of the Soviet leadership is open; don't let this opportunity slip between your fingers."

"Any special reason why you want that meeting to take place in Damascus?" I asked Beresnev as we walked home.

"We have to train the agent in clandestine ways," he replied haughtily.

"But how are you going to process his information there?"

"Who cares?" He gave me a knowing smile. "We've already worked out a schedule of subsequent meetings with Socrates in foreign countries. First I'm going to Damascus, then to Cyprus, then to Singapore or Hong Kong. And Deputy Chief of the Directorate Bychkov will go for a control meeting to Monte Carlo."

"Why go across half the globe to Singapore or Hong Kong?" I asked in surprise.

"Because that's where the electronics are cheap," Beresnev answered simply.

That's how the rendezvous venues were selected by the intelligence service. Who cares about security as long as VCRs are cheap in Hong Hong?

Richer by $3,500 to cover his expenses, Socrates departed for the U.S., while the RT Directorate continued to resound with triumphant fanfare for a long time. The intelligence bosses were stunned by the news: Deputy Chief of the Directorate Bychkov was in the midst of a stupendous operation, trying to sneak an agent into the White House! Someone inopportunely recalled that Bychkov was about to be pensioned off, but was angrily put in his place by Kryuchkov: "Pensioned off at such a time! Are you out of your mind? Get him a two-year deferment."

Bychkov held his head high, his eyes gleaming triumphantly. Beresnev was promoted to full colonel. I was not forgotten, either; I received a promotion to the next military rank of major.

In all the jubilation, the most important questions were left unanswered: Are Socrates' plans feasible? Do they correspond with the interests of the intelligence service?

Socrates professed readiness to give it a whirl. Who knows? I never forgot that he had invited a Soviet diplomat to the White House as a Carter administration official. Had he been an agent even then, contact could have been maintained with him on an official basis, with only a handful of Soviet intelligence officers being the wiser.

There were no technically insuperable obstacles to keeping in touch with a White House mole. How to infiltrate one was the problem. I had strong doubts about the feasibility of Socrates' plans, particularly his expectation that he would get support from a pillar of conservative ideology in the U.S. Senate. Chances were that Socrates was simply trying to shake the Soviet intelligence service down for more money, dangling the lure of possible, though hardly probable, prospects. But no one asked for my opinion. It was time to report successes—and my bosses certainly needed no help in that department, especially given my doubts.

If Socrates were to be planted in the administration, the first order of business would be to get rid of Bychkov and Beresnev, and only then to worry about the FBI. Who would have thought that a Soviet intelligence operative had to contend with problems of this nature?

In spring of 1988, Beresnev returned from Damascus empty-handed and in a foul mood.

"What happened?" I asked.

"Your Socrates is no pushover," he replied sullenly. "I tried to work with him the way an agent must be treated . . ."

"And how must an agent be treated?" I asked in a silky voice.

"Well, the way an officer treats a private in the army . . ."

"And?" I could barely keep from laughing.

"He was really pissed off. 'One more command in this vein, and I'll kick you out of my room,' he said. Why on earth did I listen to Bychkov? Now we'll have to do something to get back into Socrates' good graces."

"Have you brought any information?"

"Information? You must be kidding." He made a wry face and waved with the air of a martyr.

That same day, I received a phone call from Sheremeteyevo-2 Airport:

"Are you planning to pick up your operational cargo?"

"What cargo?" I asked in amazement. "What are you talking about?"

"Well . . . Beresnev works for your outfit, doesn't he?"

"So what?"

"We are holding the baggage he brought from Damascus."

"Was he carrying contraband?" I couldn't understand what the customs people wanted from me.

"No, of course, not. It's simply that he went over the weight limit and refused to pay, insisting that it was operational cargo. That's why I'm calling you. If it is indeed operational cargo, tell your boss to call us or send us an official letter to that effect."

"And what does the baggage contain?" I asked.

"The usual stuff: a stereo, area rugs, clothes . . ."

"Why, of course, it's operational cargo." I laughed. "You will get your phone call, don't worry."

A mere thirty minutes later, Bychkov was on the phone, trying to spring Beresnev's baggage. Apparently, part of the "operational cargo" was earmarked for him. Cherkashin's share was a marvelous door lock for his dacha.

Who would dare to say that the Damascus meeting was fruitless? Socrates didn't do that badly either. He reported that he was working successfully on plans to penetrate the White House, and was rewarded for his labors by Beresnev to the tune of $7,000. Only the analytical service came off the loser. It was the first time the agent had failed to provide any political intelligence.

A couple of months later, army general Kryuchkov was appointed chairman of the KGB. To everybody's surprise, he was succeeded as chief of intelligence—head of the First Chief Directorate—by General Leonid Shebarshin, a career intelligence man and a consummate professional. Many officers couldn't believe that Kryuchkov could be that sensible. They expected the position to go to Androsov,

Bychkov—anyone but the accomplished spymaster Shebarshin. His choice ran counter to Kryuchkov's entire personnel policy.

Apparently, Kryuchkov realized that he had run the intelligence service into the ground and that only a super-
expert could save it from total collapse. Of course, that
super-expert could not be allowed to operate without supervision, but as KGB chairman, Kryuchkov was in a position to keep a watchful eye on the new intelligence chief.
Besides, Kryuchkov bequeathed to Shebarshin all his deputies, who were to preserve continuity of leadership at the
intelligence service. In short, Shebarshin's brief was to try
to resuscitate the intelligence service while staying away
from politics. Obviously, Kryuchkov saw politics as his own
strong suit.

About three months after the inauguration of George Bush
as U.S. president, Socrates arrived in Moscow, this time
accompanied by Sputnitsa. Her condition had markedly de-
teriorated, and she came to Moscow seeking succor and
solace. While she was undergoing tests in exclusive hospi-
tals catering to Kremlin personnel, Socrates and I got down
to business. After the Damascus fiasco the previous March,
Beresnev was keeping a low profile and only turned up to
butt in on us when we ate out.

As I had expected, my agent had failed to land a job with
the Republican administration. He was contrite and somewhat apprehensive. But pretty soon, much to his surprise, it
developed that the KGB was not in the least interested in
the reasons for his failure. They just couldn't care less. Of
course, the poor guy had no way of knowing one of the
cardinal precepts of the Soviet bureaucracy, to wit: trumpet
the anticipated success with as much fanfare as possible,
but if it fails to materialize or turns into a disaster, behave
as if nothing happened.

Apparently, nothing in his experience had prepared

Socrates for such a turn of events. Needless to say, rather than enlighten the agent as to the subtleties of the Soviet bureaucratic system, I twice made it a point to show him my tacit displeasure. Socrates realized that he had to make amends, and promptly produced another trump card: information on a secret meeting at the White House.

According to Socrates' report, during the post-inaugural honeymoon, President Bush called a meeting with a view to developing the administration's strategy toward the Soviet Union and Western Europe. Three leading Soviet experts sat in on the meeting, and one of them told Socrates the gist of the discussions.

According to the agent's information, President Bush remarked that the U.S. should welcome perestroika in the USSR, but only if it was not merely a propaganda ploy and the Soviet leaders meant business. Figuring out what was really going on in the Soviet Union would take time, with the implication that the U.S.–USSR arms control process would have to be put on hold for a while.

Bush emphasized that the chief strategic objective of the U.S. policy in Europe was to prevent the Social Democrats from winning the approaching elections in West Germany. An electoral failure of the ruling Kohl-Genscher coalition, a distinct possibility absent outside interference, could have a domino effect for the British Tories and also give a shot in the arm to the Papandreou-led Socialists on the eve of parliamentary elections in Greece. Such a disastrous turn of events would pull the carpet out from under NATO at a crucial point in its confrontation with the Warsaw Pact, and boost Soviet influence on the continent.

So, the U.S. was prepared to support genuine perestroika, and the outcome of the Cold War hung in the balance in Western Europe!

By all appearances, Socrates' report was a mother lode of first-class intelligence. Today, some might think it trivial, but at the time, in the spring of 1989, Gorbachev did not know the answer to the question of whether or not the

West, above all the United States, could be enlisted in the cause of perestroika. The question was of strategic importance to the Soviet leader, who had come to realize that the USSR badly needed radical reform rather than a mere facelift and was desperately looking for allies. And since he certainly could not count on any measure of support from the Soviet establishment, Gorbachev had little choice but to pin all his hopes on the erstwhile enemy, the West.

The Soviet leader was reluctant to embark upon radical reform without a clearly articulated message of support from the leading Western powers; meanwhile the West was waiting for Moscow to signal that perestroika was not just another hoax from the Soviet propaganda bag of tricks. Someone had to make the first move, and it appeared as though Gorbachev was preparing to take the plunge.

He pestered the intelligence services, demanding an unequivocal answer as to whether or not Western support would be forthcoming if he launched radical reforms. For its part, lacking quality sources of political information— above all pertaining to the U.S.—the intelligence apparatus bobbed and weaved, trying to shake him off with ambivalent pronouncements.

Gorbachev was furious, Kryuchkov became edgy—and then out of the blue came Socrates' report. It was exactly what the doctor had ordered: the information was strategic in nature, and it had not been leaked to the press. In short, it was a spy's dream, except for one thing: like much of the stuff supplied by Socrates, there was no way of verifying its authenticity.

To query the Washington residency was a waste of time; to approach President Bush for confirmation was hardly feasible. So the analytical service was the first and last resort.

"We'll prepare two special communications for Gorbachev," the analyst Sergei said confidently after reading the agent's report. "One on Soviet-American relations, the other dealing with U.S. strategy in Western Europe."

My head swam, the sweet taste of success like honey on my lips.

Of all information generated by the KGB's political intelligence arm, special communications were the *pièce de résistance*. They contained information of supreme importance and had the highest degree of classification; they were prepared for only a handful of the country's leading officials and printed on special paper in just two copies: one hand-delivered to the client, the other kept by the analytical service. Only the KGB chairman or his deputy had the right to sign special communications. People who prepared special communications formed an exclusive caste, for very few individuals in the entire intelligence service have ever so much as caught a glimpse of such documents.

By the late 1980s, the political branch of the First Chief Directorate annually produced an average of ten special communications dealing with the U.S., most of them compiled directly at the analytical service by analyzing and processing the many cables from station chiefs—residents. If a special communication was based on information coming from a single source, that person was assigned the highest classification of the information service, "a special source," subject to the highest degree of control.

In 1989, the entire political branch ran merely three special sources, none of whom supplied data on the U.S. Socrates became the sole special source on the U.S., designated as such by the political branch. The information he supplied was sent directly to Gorbachev. Then events began unfolding at a dizzying speed.

The very next Sunday, all members of the American unit of the analytical service were hastily summoned to work. KGB chairman Kryuchkov handed down an urgent assignment: to draft, on the basis of Socrates' data, a Resolution of the Communist Party Central Committee on the U.S. strategy in Western Europe. A few days later, it was approved.

All Soviet state agencies involved in planning or implementing foreign policy were ordered to oppose U.S. efforts in Western Europe. Henceforth, it would be one of the strategic foreign policy objectives of the Soviet state. In those days, a Resolution of the Communist Party Central Committee was the supreme law of the land.

It didn't take me long to find out the reason for such a dramatic turn of events; the analytical service was cozy with the Central Committee staff and was receiving excellent feedback. Having read Socrates' report, Gorbachev sent it for review to his closest foreign policy adviser, Politburo member Alexander Yakovlev. The latter asked Kryuchkov whether the information was reliable. "Unquestionably so," was the answer. To be on the safe side, they sought the opinion of Valentin Falin, head of the Central Committee Foreign Relations Department and a veteran of diplomatic service, with a long stint as ambassador to West Germany in his résumé. Falin produced a scathing critique of the agent's report, but was ignored. Curiously, two otherwise implacable enemies, Yakovlev and Kryuchkov, in this instance joined forces to maximum effect. A few days later, the resolution urgently drafted by the KGB on Kryuchkov's orders was approved and became official policy.

That's how major state decisions used to be made. Gorbachev gave an assignment to Yakovlev. The latter consulted Kryuchkov. Both ignored an experienced Germany hand, Falin, because Kryuchkov imagined himself to be a leading expert in the area. It did not even occur to them to consult the Ministry of Foreign Affairs or genuine experts. Experts? Who needs experts if Comrade Kryuchkov and Comrade Yakovlev see eye to eye on the matter in question? And *voilà!*—a new strategic direction of Soviet foreign policy.

It was most distressing that Alexander Yakovlev, the one member of the Soviet leadership whom I respected, had become involved in this dubious business. How could it have happened? I have no idea, but the smart money says that the Central Committee resolution was the end result of a convoluted Kremlin intrigue. People in the analytical service told me unequivocally that the whole thing was driven by internal politics—"a social order," as they put it.

I was astounded at the bizarre way in which the Soviet leadership reacted to Socrates' information. Gorbachev took heart when he heard that the U.S. was serious about supporting reform in the USSR; meanwhile the Central Committee of the Soviet Communist Party decided to go after the United States in Western Europe. Niccolò Machiavelli himself would be put to shame by this kind of statesmanship. Gorbachev is seeking an ally in the West while his Central Committee works overtime to play dirty tricks on that same ally—and elevates their foul play to the rank of state policy into the bargain.

But I was even more astounded at the process whereby the Central Committee resolution was conceived and produced. This procedure makes other grave mistakes almost inevitable. Forget about this particular resolution—let it be just an annoying mistake. But one couldn't help recalling the rueful comment made by the great Russian historian Karamzin, "Our land is great and bounteous, but there is no order in it." Still no order, anywhere. And that is what is frightening.

In making intelligence my career choice, I believed that it was the one field of endeavor guided by common sense. Full of hope, I worked hard to master the tricks of the trade. One of the select few, I learned how U.S. citizens are recruited; how they are run; how information is prepared for the supreme leadership of the country. And now I was seeing just how the leadership used that information. Having reached the most ambitious goals and seeing them at close range, I experienced only deep frustration.

The only conclusion one could derive from that experience was that my country has no use for intelligence. It is only needed by individual bureaucrats who utilize it to further their personal objectives. I had heard this earlier, specifically from Valentin Aksilenko. Now I had come to understand it based on my own experience. Had this episode with the Central Committee resolution happened some years earlier, I could have argued that this was just an infraction of the rule. Now I had enough experience to believe that this actually was the rule.

After that revelation, intelligence lost all its luster in my eyes. It was high time to think about resigning.

Unfortunately, the Central Committee resolution had far-reaching consequences. Barely a few months later, in the fall of 1989, Gorbachev went on an official visit to East Germany, during which he exhibited a complete lack of understanding of what was going on in that "fraternal country." He came to stump for the cause of renewed socialism—and brought about an almost instantaneous demise of the main bulwark of communism in Eastern Europe.

The reasons that Gorbachev was so poorly informed were clear enough. Under the rigid precepts of the Soviet bureaucratic system, once the ruling body, the Central Committee of the Communist Party, resolved that the Soviet Union's chief international priorities consisted of opposition to the United States in Western Europe, it became an immutable policy. Henceforth, other sources and documents were allowed only to corroborate the party line or elaborate on it, while information pointing in a different direction had virtually no chance of receiving a hearing upstairs.

According to several KGB friends of mine, who were assigned to the Berlin residency at the time, the cables that the station was sending to Moscow on the eve of Gorbachev's visit to East Germany stuck faithfully to the theme sounded in the Central Committee resolution: the situation in the country is complicated but manageable; once Comrade Gorbachev arrives and talks to the German people, everything will fall into place. The information was vetted for ideological purity by General Gennadi Titov, KGB resident in Berlin, hand-picked by Kryuchkov himself. Prior to the August 1991 putsch, Titov was appointed head of the KGB Second Chief Directorate (counterintelligence).

Later, Kryuchkov started a false rumor that Alexander Yakovlev was a CIA agent. Considering how much objective damage Kryuchkov himself visited on his country, a strong case can be made that he was the CIA Moscow station chief, a particularly valuable spy, who showed impressive skill running an extensive network of smaller-caliber American agents like Androsov and Bychkov.

The intelligence provided by Socrates enabled Kryuchkov to strengthen his political hand with minimal risk; after all, President Bush himself was concerned above all else with Western Europe, wasn't he? And if something untoward happened in Eastern Europe, it would only mean that the U.S. had miscalculated, right? Why, if the White House itself blunders, who are we not to make mistakes?

Thus was the political map of Europe being redrawn.

Such was my train of thought as, not long after Gorbachev's departure from Berlin, I stared at the TV screen watching East Germans gleefully tearing down the Berlin Wall. While the Soviet Union was busy erecting roadblocks to U.S. policies in Western Europe, the eastern part of the continent imploded.

But what about Socrates' report? Was it a piece of disinformation cooked up by American counterspies? A miscalculation of the Bush administration that failed to foresee the correct turn of events? Or maybe a figment of the agent's imagination? After all, he was smart enough to be able to concoct strategic "information" as a way of squeezing more money out of us.

The second theory, that Bush's team miscalculated, seems to be the most plausible one, but still, I cannot be sure. Only Socrates himself can provide the answer. "You never know"—these three words would be an appropriate epigraph to a truthful book about an intelligence service, any intelligence service, anywhere in the world.

Meanwhile, the RT Directorate was jubilant. Its leaders

had finally been initiated into the mystery of the special communication. Bychkov perked up and stopped thinking about retirement. Beresnev was awarded the KGB commemorative medal.

Socrates saw his remuneration rates soaring. This time he earned $15,000 for supplying valuable information. Another farewell dinner was awaiting us at the International Trade Center built by that well-known friend of the Soviet Union, Armand Hammer. This Western oasis on the bank of the Moscow River clashed with the dreary architecture of Stalin- and Khrushchev-era buildings, and looked like a brand-new Rolls-Royce in a junkyard. That night I was to serve the agent dessert in the form of . . . a Soviet prostitute. He had long been hinting that his strenuous endeavors deserved just such a reward.

I couldn't help but be astonished by the events that I was participating in. Socrates saw himself as a political mover and shaker, while in fact all he actually did was further the careers of a gaggle of bureaucrats. My bosses used him as much as he used me. I prepared the final version of the intelligence reports for which he was paid.

The next day Socrates and Sputnitsa departed for Greece.

9

A COUPLE of weeks later Socrates came back to Moscow.

"I've brought a secret message for Gorbachev from Greek Prime Minister Papandreou," he declared while we were still at the airport. He was literally shaking with excitement.

"What do you have to do with Papandreou?" I asked in surprise.

"I am his *éminence grise*, his personal adviser on American-Greek relations."

"Since when?"

"About three years."

"Listen, Martin, I like you. But the trouble with you is you regularly cause intolerable headaches to my superiors."

"To hell with your superiors." Socrates frowned. "Can you get the message to Gorbachev?"

"Of course I can."

"Let's go to the hotel, then. Great deeds are awaiting us."

I had nothing against great deeds. But for the short term

I had a more pressing concern: how to present Bychkov with another surprise?

One of the core tenets of the KGB holds that the service has to know everything about an agent, including who he sleeps with and how well or how poorly he acquits himself doing it. Needless to say, that doctrine was naive in the extreme. But my bosses religiously believed in it, so I had to tread very gingerly.

I put Socrates in his room and immediately got down to business.

"Martin, we have a funny proverb in this country: whoever pays the band orders the music. You might think it simple-minded on the part of my superiors, but they believe you are their exclusive property. Now like a bolt out of the blue, it transpires that you also have ties to the Greek government. Besides, you are a U.S. citizen but, last time I checked, unregistered as a foreign agent. I appreciate your problems and have long suspected the existence of some sort of Greek connection. Nothing wrong with that as far as I am concerned, but my bosses would be really pissed off to find out that you have kept so much to yourself. Let's look for a way out together."

Socrates was taken aback. In any other set of circumstances he certainly would have told me to go jump in the pond, but it was imperative for him to get Papandreou's letter to its destination. So he had to come clean, albeit reluctantly and behind an emotional smokescreen.

"You know that I had a lot of problems with my father," he began in a somber tone. "All my life I've suffered from an acute deprivation of fatherly love. Andreas Papandreou is a father figure, a surrogate father for me, I suppose. What an intriguing personality! Phyllis has been pretty close to his American wife since the time when he was in opposition to the 'Black Colonels' regime. He is a born politician. I thought that he was an ideal vehicle for my ideas. So I began working for him. It all began when George Shultz was getting ready to visit Athens," Socrates continued. "Tough negotiations on the subject of U.S. bases were in store; the Reagan administration was exerting enormous pressure on the Greek government. Objectively, Papandreou was the junior partner, hardly expected to stand up to Shultz. That's when I came up with a terrific idea: the U.S. secretary of state had to be maneuvered into a psychologically uncomfortable position, which was an easy thing to do. 'Look,' I said, showing Papandreou a videotape of several official functions in which Shultz had taken part. 'He always chooses tall chairs. He is a big guy who is very uncomfortable in a small chair. So let's put two chairs in the negotiation room: a large one for you, a small one for Shultz.' This is exactly what we did. You should have seen George Shultz at the negotiations. He looked like a penknife in an undersized holder. Flushed and angry, unable to concentrate on the subjects under discussion, he was totally preoccupied with his cramped legs. To make a long story short, Papandreou won a resounding victory, leaving the furious Shultz in the dust. And all because of an uncomfortable chair. After that Papandreou came to trust me. Pretty soon I became his principal adviser on American-Greek relations. There was hardly an important cable sent by the Greek ambassador in Washington to his government in which I did not have a hand."

"So it was the Greek lobby that you counted on to penetrate the White House if Dukakis became president?" I asked.

"To a certain extent, yes. As I have told you, I had long-standing ties with some people who were close to Dukakis. I was on excellent terms with a few members of Dukakis's foreign policy team. But, of course, the Greek lobby also was a potent factor . . ."

"Let's go on. If Papandreou's message is to reach Gorbachev, your Greek connection will have to be explored as thoroughly as possible. The most important thing is to convince my superiors that the CIA has nothing to do with it."

"Looks like it won't be easy," sighed Socrates.

"What do you mean? Do you have further surprises up your sleeve?" I asked apprehensively.

"Unfortunately, yes. Recently, I've been castigated by the Greek press as a CIA stooge."

"Martin, I'll positively have to demand a raise for handling you—you know, the kind of extra pay Russian workers receive for handling hazardous materials. One of these days you'll give me a coronary. All right. Let's talk now about Papandreou's message to Gorbachev. Give me some background on it."

"As you probably know, Greece is headed for parliamentary elections in which Papandreou's party is sure to take a bath. His downfall is a foregone conclusion—and all because of that damned stewardess! Papandreou fell head over heels in love with that young thing, an ex-stewardess. She even started to tag along to official functions. Wow, what a sorry spectacle! To make such a fool of himself! Sure, she is beautiful, but why take her to official events? What's wrong with keeping her as a secret mistress? Anyway, the damned broad has taken away all of his chances for reelection. Except for maybe one . . ."

"Meaning . . . ?"

"Gorbachev's official visit to Greece," said Socrates, and looked at me pleadingly. "It has to be set up within the nearest two months, otherwise it will be too late. Such a visit can be a clincher. That's how I put it to Papandreou."

"And what was his reaction?"

"He agreed and packed me off to Moscow."

"How did you let him know that you had access to Gorbachev?" For me, this was a question of paramount importance. I was afraid that my agent, trying to raise the stakes in the game, had let the cat out of the bag about his relationship with our service. But whatever else you could call him, Socrates was nobody's fool.

"I said that I had connections in Moscow's highest scholarly circles, such as, for example, the Institute of the U.S.A. and Canada—and those people are heavily involved in the decision-making process as far as Soviet foreign policy is concerned," he said smoothly. I realized that he had expected my question.

Still, I made another attempt.

"Did Papandreou ask for specific names?"

"No," he said firmly.

It's impossible! I thought. No one in his right mind would send a confidential message without inquiring about the channels through which the message would reach the destination. But let's put it aside for a while. Time to tackle the most important issue.

"So where is the message?" I asked.

Socrates sighed with a great show of contrition: "I spent the whole night composing it together with Papandreou's personal secretary, but in the morning the premier said that it would have to be done by word of mouth. It is easy to appreciate his position; an oral message is deniable, while a written document, if leaked, can be suicidal."

"Why?"

"Because as a quid pro quo for Gorbachev's visit Papandreou promises to do just about anything the Soviet Union desires."

"Such as . . ."

"Such as, for instance, kicking out all U.S. military bases in Greece within a short time after reelection. Or raising hell within NATO. You will readily appreciate the implications for the balance of forces in Europe. You would be fools to miss such a golden opportunity."

"We'll try not to," I reassured him. "Now, assuming that Gorbachev says yes, who will handle the practical details of his visit?"

"The Soviet Embassy in Athens and the Greek Embassy in Moscow should be kept out of it; they have provided sufficient proof of their ineptness. Besides, the negotiations should be leak-proof as much as possible until the very moment when the news of the visit will be broken. The remainder is up to your side. Just appoint any plenipoten-

tiary representatives to negotiate with Papandreou personally or with his most trusted lieutenants."

That was all I needed.

"Great," I said to Socrates. "Take a piece of paper, put it
into the typewriter and type up this letter to Gorbachev."

While he pecked at the keyboard, I was doing some thinking. I had no doubt that the agent's offer would scare our
communist leaders, who would see the CIA's shadow behind it. Personally, I was convinced that the American intelligence services were not involved—in this particular
case, at any rate. The fact that Papandreou was prepared to
conduct negotiations about Gorbachev's visit personally
was proof enough. Of course, Socrates planned to benefit
from this affair, but only a naive person would expect anything else. The Soviet Union is about the only place in the
world where one is expected to believe that burning midnight oil out of sheer loyalty to noble causes is normal. I
could spend much time weighing all pros and cons, but I
was certain that he was telling the truth and that his information had to be relayed to the Kremlin.

Papandreou's message as set forth by Socrates made a powerful impression. It was a plea for help from a desperate man
that ended thus: "A friend is seeking your support. Please
don't turn him down. We know how to be grateful. Your visit
to Greece will bring strategic benefits to the Soviet Union."

"Do you have a big personal stake in Gorbachev's affir-
mative answer?" I asked Socrates.

"For me it is the difference between to be or not to be," he
replied.

"Then you'll have to wait and hope." With these parting
words I hurried to the office.

I reported my conversation with the agent to Bychkov,
but to my surprise he failed to discern the bureaucratic
risks inherent in the information. To the contrary, he
beamed like a newly minted silver dollar.

"Sit down and draft a cable immediately," he said with
the air of a man who had just crossed the Rubicon.

"Whew," I thought, and went to my office.

This time the information provided by Socrates had to be routed through the Greek line of the analytical service, which had no idea of his existence as an agent. I drafted a cable and added that the information had been received from Papandreou himself via a trusted agent. It only remained for me to make up the list of addressees—but at that point I had an inspired idea to pass the buck to Bychkov.

"Write it down," he said in a voice positively resonating with trumpet calls and drumroll. "To Chief of Intelligence Shebarshin, First Deputy Chief of Intelligence Kirpichenko, Deputy Chief of Intelligence Leonov, heads of the analytical service, the active measures service, the external counterintelligence directorate, the Fifth European Department, the North American Department, and the C Directorate [undercover intelligence]."

I did as told, and ten minutes later the cable was sent under Bychkov's signature. The next day came the reply from the analytical service.

It said that our cable was completely at odds with the entire contents of Papandreou's file and that the information supplied by our agent smacked of a Western attempt at disinformation. The cable itself bore Intelligence Chief Shebarshin's comment: "This is likely to get us into very hot water."

Complete failure! Dark as a thundercloud, Bychkov glowered at me ominously, his eyes blazing with hatred, fury, and suspicion.

Total catastrophe! Socrates was a plant. And I was the one who had recruited the plant. Practically no chance to rehabilitate myself. Androsov's old suspicions are now augmented by new suspicions coming from none other than Shebarshin himself. Now nothing can save me. There is no way the Internal Counterintelligence Department will let me slip its clutches one more time. Might as well play Russian roulette.

Such was my train of thought three days later as I was walking to the deputy chief of the RT Directorate's office to answer his summons conveyed by his secretary. I was going to hear my sentence. Strangely, I was still certain that Papandreou's message was authentic. Fat lot of good this certainty did me now!

I sighed hopelessly and opened the door. Colonel Bychkov behaved enigmatically. Cheerful and smugly self-satisfied, he was strutting about the room, heaping mockery on Beresnev, who gloomily sat in the corner.

After some preliminary discussions Bychkov said: "Now for the good stuff. We've really cleaned their clock!"

"Whose clock?" I asked suspiciously.

"Everybody's!" snapped Bychkov. "You name them: the analytical service, the European Department, our Athens residency, the American Section, even Shebarshin himself—we've handed them their asses, all of them!"

"Something happened?" I did not believe in miracles and suspected that Bychkov was playing some kind of cruel joke on me.

"Papandreou personally confirmed that he had authorized Socrates to conduct negotiations about Gorbachev's visit to Greece." Bychkov came to a stop in the middle of the room and theatrically pointed his index finger upward. "And he told it to none other than the Soviet ambassador in Athens!" my boss ended triumphantly.

"But what about our entire Papandreou file?" I asked with a touch of sarcasm.

"A bunch of baloney!" Bychkov said contemptuously. "When the shit hit the fan, we were the only ones outside the barn. Prepare a request to transfer Socrates to the valuable agents category."

"On whose authority?" I asked guardedly.

"Cut out the idiotic questions," retorted Bychkov. "What's a valuable agent?"

"A person conscientiously working for the KGB, holding

an important position in the highest bodies of power and authority of the U.S. or NATO countries, and supplying important information on top-priority issues."

"Right," said Bychkov, and again raised his index finger. "Last time I checked, Greece was a NATO country, and Socrates is a personal adviser to its prime minister. We could not get him into the White House, but, fortunately, it transpired that he holds an important position anyway. As for his information, the analytical service has concluded that it does indeed qualify as extra-important. The analytical people have sent their apologies for their recent mistake. I've been ordered to appear tomorrow before General Leonov, Shebarshin's deputy. He supervises all U.S.-related operations and has agreed that Socrates should be reclassified as a valuable agent. Kirpichenko, first deputy chief of intelligence, also says yes. Can you imagine that they will hold an opinion different from their chief's?"

Contrast is a true key to experience. Up and down, up and down all the time; a pawn jumps forward and before you know it becomes a queen. Merely a few minutes ago, nobody would have put a red cent on my future, and now Lady Luck was again smiling on me. Even rank-and-file assets among U.S. citizens were few and far between, but nobody could remember the last time we had an American deserving of the valuable agent designation. I did not dare dream of such a stroke of luck. And even had a dream of this variety ever crossed my mind, I would have kept it to myself for fear of being ridiculed as a megalomaniac. Just a couple of years ago, however, I would have been delirious with joy.

Bychkov was summoned to an audience with Deputy Intelligence Chief General Leonov. Tall, with his head held high, at this instant he resembled a Teutonic knight. He brought not only a report but also a statement on Socrates' checkout by use of mind-influencing chemicals. He planned to astonish Leonov with an account of how he had handled the agent. Leonov had only recently been assigned to oversee the worldwide recruitment effort targeting Americans, and had never heard anything like this, or so Bychkov believed.

Beresnev and I sat in Bychkov's office, waiting for him to return. We were pretty sure that he would return victorious. Leonov was widely known as Kryuchkov's protégé, the brains behind the intelligence chief. If the KGB chairman himself implicitly accepted Leonov's advice, the new intelligence chief could hardly be expected to ignore it. Socrates' inclusion on the rolls of valuable agents seemed to be a cinch, and Beresnev was loudly discussing who would be rewarded and how. As his imagination got progressively inflamed, the generosity of expected rewards was growing by the minute. I was fending off mounting annoyance, from time to time glancing out the window to keep myself in check.

Two hours later, Bychkov triumphantly returned in all his glory.

"Piece of cake," he said with the air of a man who had done his duty. "Leonov went to report the case to Intelligence Chief Shebarshin. We have just a little more to wait."

"How did it go?" Beresnev asked, burning with impatience.

"Great," Bychkov replied smugly. "Leonov was particularly impressed by the story of how we tested Socrates with psychotropic drugs. He just sat there, oohing and aahing in disbelief. 'I've never heard anything like this,' he says. 'You guys are amazing.' He was also surprised that we had not reported a successful penetration of the White House."

"But we haven't penetrated it," I remarked in surprise.

Bychkov gave me a condescending look as if I was a hopeless moron.

"You must memorize, once and for all, the unwritten

regulations of our service," he said didactically. "Rule one: the boss is always right. Rule two: if the boss is wrong, refer to rule one."

He was certain that his words represented higher, eternal verities. Beresnev giggled subserviently.

"It's true that we have not been able to infiltrate Socrates into the Bush administration," Bychkov continued his inspired monologue. "That is to say, strictly speaking, we have not yet got there physically. But we must think in broad categories. Did the agent bring us intelligence from the White House? Yes, he did. Does he have access to sources capable of providing such intelligence in the future? Basically, yes, he does. So for all intents and purposes we have penetrated the administration. Leonov shares my assessment. And spare us your remarks," he added, giving me a suddenly nasty look. "You'd better remember the difference in the breadth of our visions. We know what to do and how to do it."

The telephone rang and Bychkov grabbed the receiver eagerly.

"Yes, Comrade General, that's me. It's Leonov," he whispered gleefully, pointing at the telephone.

Then the unexpected happen. As Bychkov listened, his face got longer and longer, his eyes lost their luster, an expression of utter confusion appeared on his face. Finally he replaced the receiver and stood transfixed.

"Leonov said, 'It's bumbling,' " he said with difficulty, his lips going white.

I bit my lip so as not to blurt out something untoward.

"What did he mean by that?" Beresnev asked.

"He went to the chief of intelligence," Bychkov said in confusion. "The chief read our report on the inclusion of Socrates on the rolls of valuable agent, then took out the cable about Papandreou's message, and said: 'Things of this nature must be reported to me alone, while you have broadcast the tidings of your valuable agent far and wide. It's bumbling. After such a blunder I can't sign this report.'"

I struggled desperately not to burst out laughing, and I am afraid it showed in my face. Bychkov fixed me with a baleful eye and hissed maliciously: "Who has sent the cable about Papandreou's message to all these people?"

"You have," I said almost meekly.

"What!"

"Remember I called you and asked who to send the cable to? And you dictated to me the list of names."

My answer threw Bychkov off balance, but he quickly recovered.

"So I made a mistake!" he bellowed. "But you should have stopped me. You are to blame for this mess!"

"I merely followed your directive: the boss is always right." A derisive smile appeared on my lips. I no longer felt the need to restrain myself. My resignation was a foregone conclusion.

Gorbachev didn't take long to respond to Papandreou's offer: no visit to Greece was in the cards. When I told Socrates, he aged before my eyes.

"It's the end," he said with the air of a sacrificial lamb. "Papandreou will lose the election, and I will lose my job. How will I pay my bills?"

"How much are the Greeks paying you?" I asked.

"Sixty grand per and a once-a-year free vacation round-trip air fare for my family. We fly the Greek national airline Olympic, first-class."

"You can earn as much from us if you go on providing decent intelligence," I remarked.

"I'm afraid of staying in America," Socrates confessed. "Sooner or later I'll have to seek a safe haven. I planned to move to Greece, but with Papandreou gone it will become dangerous as well. I have a lot of enemies there, too."

"So what are you going to do?" I asked.

"I wanted to talk to you about it for some time," Socrates said hopefully. "What if I move to Moscow? We could set up a high-powered lobbying operation to promote your country's interests in Washington. I have some relevant experience. Here is just one example. When Richard Perle resigned as assistant secretary of defense, he became a consultant to a firm that lobbies for the government of Turkey. According to the Greek intelligence service, the Turks promised to pay this firm a big bonus if it succeeded in pushing through Congress a bill to increase military assistance to Ankara. As you know, Congress approves the amount of aid to Turkey and Greece as a single package and in a certain fixed ratio. Turkey gets a little more, but Ankara wanted an increase in its share. Then Papandreou asked me if I could help block that bill. I tracked down two congressmen who were to decide the outcome of the voting in the House—the so-called swing votes. It transpired that Greek ships regularly underwent repairs in the district of one of those legislators, which meant jobs and a lot of revenue. I called him, introduced myself as someone working on a story for the Greek newspaper *Ta Nea*, and asked him to confirm that he was planning to support an increase in military assistance to the Turks. He got cold feet and promised to vote against the bill. I used roughly the same approach to secure the vote of the other legislator. Imagine, just a couple of phone calls, and all Perle's lobbying firm's hard work was nixed. We could do similar work for the Soviet Union."

"Listen, old man," I said skeptically, "of course, I'll pass on your suggestion. But I know our bureaucracy well enough. For them, it's too complicated. They don't know much about lobbying, and therefore there is almost no hope of getting their consent. Do you have any other ideas?"

"I've got it!" Socrates said excitedly. "You know, I have a source who is the daughter of a CIA secretary. Here's an interesting tidbit coming from her. One of the CIA top officials has a regular girlfriend whom he visits at her Georgetown home almost daily. Not long ago, he lost his wife to cancer. And recently, his girlfriend has been diagnosed with a serious illness. He is absolutely devastated. He loves her madly and in spite of everything still comes to see her."

"Very moving, but I'm afraid my superiors won't be moved enough to pay much for this piece of information."

"Let me finish," Socrates said irritably. "That CIA boss is a very religious man belonging to one of the most austere denominations. In his church, this unmarried relationship is a grave sin. His conscience torments him constantly, but he just can't help it. It won't take much to push him over the edge; a threat of exposure would be enough. Blackmail him! You will have more than enough information for that: his girlfriend's name and address, the schedule of his visits, his license plates. What else do you need? Install a secret camera in her house, bug it. If anything else is required, just tell me; I'll talk to my source and she'll pump her mother. We are in total control of the situation. Let's make our move. After all, he is one of the top CIA officials. Here is the lowdown on him." Socrates handed me a sheet of paper.

"Cool it, Martin," I counseled, pocketing the report. "Now is not the time to attempt an operation of that sort. I think you should save your friend and her mother for more realistic objectives."

I was driving to the office, pondering what Socrates had told me about the CIA big shot. The cold shoulder I had given him was a normal field ploy. He had no business knowing just how important his information was.

I had no idea what to do with Socrates' report. Clearly, it was a hot potato. An attempt to blackmail a top CIA official, as Socrates suggested, was too much of a gamble; the guy was just too important for us to succeed. But the CIA secretary, who was the source of that information, had gotten herself entangled in what was known in the KGB parlance as a recruitment trap.

The KGB handled such cases relying on tried and true techniques honed over decades of practice. The situation seemed near perfect for a recruitment pitch: Thank you, ma'am, for especially valuable information you have provided to us via your daughter. Here's your remuneration in the amount of half a million bucks. We'll be eagerly awaiting more information. Our next rendezvous will be held at such and such place, at such and such time. The amount of subsequent payments will depend on the quality of the information you'll be supplying.

Suppose the CIA secretary flew into a rage and told the KGB officer to go jump in the lake. No big deal! He should be able to handle her easy enough. I'm really sorry, ma'am, but if you refuse to be prudent we'll have little choice but to inform your boss that you have provided the KGB with a little dirt on him. After that your chances of landing a job anywhere will be nil; indeed, who will employ a person who has shown disloyalty toward her boss? And what about your daughter? She was the one who passed your information on to the KGB. Let's be sensible, ma'am. If you play ball with us, not only you save your daughter and yourself, but you'll get rich beyond your wildest dreams.

But even if the blackmail attempt fails, the KGB will not lose anything. The CIA secretary can be approached by an officer sent from Moscow specifically for that purpose who will depart immediately once the job is done. Socrates is prepared to stay in Moscow if the money is right, so he is in no danger. In a word, no disaster was in the cards, while success could bring incredible dividends. The CIA secretary could be in a position to know more than many field officers. With field work compartmentalized, each operative knows only what he or she absolutely needs to know, while a well-placed secretary would know the activities of at least a few field officers. At least that was standard operating procedure at the KGB.

Damn this info, I swore. What am I supposed to do with it?

I disliked dirty tricks and wanted no part of this stuff. It was right up the external counterintelligence alley, while my bailiwick was political intelligence. But Socrates handed his report to me and our conversation was taped by the girls from Tatiana, the eavesdropping service. Could I afford to sit on the information? Maybe it was yet another loyalty check. Did Colonel Cherkashin, an expert on the CIA, really forswear intelligence or maybe was he lying in ambush, waiting for me to show my hand?

I had no choice but to report to the head of my department, Cherkashin.

He read Socrates' report impassively. He was wearing his usual impenetrable mask—maybe even more impenetrable than usual.

"I'm going to see our bosses," he said. "We'll talk when I return."

Cherkashin was absent for about ninety minutes. During that time he was gone from the RT Directorate. If he indeed went upstairs, then it was either to the external counterintelligence directorate that dealt with the CIA matters or to the chief of intelligence. When he returned, our conversation was brevity itself.

"Who else knows about it?" Cherkashin asked, taking Socrates' report from the folder.

"No one," I said.

"Was your conversation with Socrates taped?"

"Yes."

"As soon as Tatiana sends over the transcript, you are to bring it to me personally. I'll keep his report as well. Nobody is to know about it. Erase it from your memory. You've never had any talk about a top CIA official, understood?"

Socrates was leaving Moscow in a foul mood. His ideas about the lobbying operation had met with a cool response, and the remuneration he received to the tune of $10,000 was a cold comfort. But Beresnev was on top of the world.

His next meeting with the agent was to take place on Cyprus.

That next meeting never materialized. The agent did not turn up. Beresnev sent a cable that he was staying in Nicosia for another week—for a standby meeting.

What standby meeting? I asked myself in amazement. He didn't arrange it with Socrates.

To be on the safe side, I looked up the communication regime for the Cyprus meeting in the file, and sure enough, Beresnev had forgotten to arrange a standby meeting. It was an amateurish mistake because the rules of communication with agents are the ABC of the intelligence craft, which is drummed for months into the heads of cadets at the Intelligence Academy.

Beresnev returned to Moscow in a depressed and sort of mysterious mood. The communication channel to Socrates no longer existed. I was racking my brains trying to find a way of restoring it when to my incredulous dismay it transpired that Deputy Chief of Directorate Bychkov decided to send the agent an official invitation to Moscow—via the Institute of the U.S.A. and Canada of the USSR Academy of Sciences. Under existing rules, the invitation was to be personally handed to the recipient -which meant that Socrates would be summoned to the Soviet Embassy in Washington.

"But you will burn him!" I blew up.

"It's none of your business," Bychkov cut me off.

It is difficult to describe the feelings I experienced watching how my agent was being led to the slaughter. It was a crime to officially invite Socrates to the Soviet Union for the second time—or, worse, to summon him to the Soviet Embassy. Once, he had been invited to come visit with Sputnitsa—in the spring of 1987. But at that time he had not yet been our agent and had not been collecting intelligence for us. Now the situation was entirely different. Another trip to the Soviet Embassy spelled disaster for him. There was no guarantee that he wasn't already under surveillance by the FBI. Why play with fire? Besides, there were a thousand other ways of getting in touch with him.

But try as I might to talk Bychkov into calling off his stupid undertaking, he stood his ground. His arguments boiled down to a simple proposition that his "horizons" were broader than mine and therefore his word was the ultimate truth. His decision was implemented.

Socrates was summoned to the Soviet Embassy in Washington and handed the invitation. In a little while, he came to Moscow. I was about to go and see him when Bychkov stunned me with an unexpected order: "You've done your part of the job. From now on, the agent will be handled by Beresnev alone. You are not to see Socrates under any circumstances whatsoever."

Apparently these guys have made a mess and are now trying to sweep it under the rug, I thought, and asked Tatiana to monitor the goings-on in the agent's hotel room.

This time, Socrates planned to stay for ten days. For a week Beresnev looked preoccupied but happy. The main events unfolded at the very end.

On Friday, near the close of business, Tatiana called me.

"Something must be done," the officer on duty told me excitedly. "Socrates is about to beat up that Beresnev of yours."

"What's going on there?"

"Let me read you the shorthand record.

"Socrates (yelling at Beresnev): 'You are an idiot!'

"Beresnev: 'How dare you!'

"Socrates: 'I'm just stating a fact of life. I'm sick and tired of your imbecilic toasts. I've come on business, but restaurant going is all that interests you. I am leaving next Monday, but we have yet to do any intelligence work. I am paid to do intelligence, not to chew the fat with you in restaurants.'

"Beresnev: 'You must obey my orders.'

"Socrates: 'What orders? Who are you to boss me around? With your talents? At thirty-four, I was a key official at the

White House; currently, I'm an adviser to Papandreou! And you are just a messenger boy!'

"Beresnev: 'Stop insulting me!'

"Socrates: 'It's impossible to work with you! I pose questions, you leave, and the next day come empty-handed. If you have problems with your memory, bring a tape recorder, tape everything, and take it to your boss. Why the hell do I need intermediaries such as you? Maybe you are trying to ruin our relationship on purpose. Tell your chief that I want to see him. I've come to work!'

"Beresnev: 'Well, we are working!'

"Socrates: 'No, we are not. All you are saying is that we must meet again abroad. If that's how you define work, we part company. Out! I'm no longer working for you. Enough is enough. I'm leaving on the first flight.'

"Beresnev: 'I am not going anywhere. You must obey my orders!'

"Socrates: 'All right, pay me $250,000 a year, then I'll obey your orders.'

"They've been talking this way for about an hour and a half," the Tatiana girl wound up her brief story.

I had never heard anything like this. It sounded like a lunatic asylum.

"What shall I do?" I asked a colleague of mine with whom I shared the office after I told him about Tatiana's call.

"Nothing," he replied, writhing with laughter. "You've been told to keep your distance, haven't you? So keep your distance! Let the KGB sergeants disentangle themselves."

I called the secretary: "When can we expect Tatiana's report?"

"Beresnev ordered that it be passed on to him personally," she replied.

"All right," I agreed. "So you'll pass it on a bit later. I need to file it."

"This time he is planning to destroy the report," the secretary confided, and I saw the well-known harbingers of imminent danger.

The reports of the eavesdropping service were supposed to be included in the subjects' files. Beresnev's intention to destroy the records strengthened my suspicion that my communist leaders had botched the job and were trying to cover their tracks.

But their problem was that for once a failure could not be successfully covered up. Socrates was the only special source on the U.S. the KGB political intelligence had at its disposal. Scores of his reports had gone to the very top of the Soviet leadership and formed the basis of vital decisions of state. He was known to practically the entire external intelligence brass "shown up" by Bychkov in the case of Papandreou's message.

And now the very same Bychkov in company with Beresnev with their own hands and owing entirely to their own stupidity and pig-headedness had made a complete mess of things. How could they expect to get away with murder? Particularly now that General Shebarshin, a genuine expert, was chief of intelligence. After the triumphant fanfare and drumroll, the spectre of dishonorable discharge loomed large for my immediate superiors.

My initial impulse was to say: to hell with you all, and tender my resignation. I was sick and tired of all that mess, of the need to fight for survival day in, day out. Why should I go on, for Pete's sake? I had joined the intelligence service to serve my country. But what use did I have for the Androsovs, the Bychkovs, the Beresnevs, and other bureaucrats of their ilk? If they called the shots here, I was done with intelligence. It was time to return to the normal world.

But then I recalled my father, who fought his way from the Dnieper River to Budapest in World War II. Telling me of those distant times, my dad used to say: "In war, it's not the young soldier, but the old veteran who dies most often. The young have an acute nose for danger, fear of dying keeps them on their toes all the time. The 'old-timers' are tired of incessantly bowing to the bullets, they often lose the sense of danger. That's why they die more often and generally as a result of stupid accidents."

I realized that I couldn't just resign and forget the whole sordid business. I had no intention of shouldering the responsibility for somebody else's idiocy, thereby saving the bureaucrats. As Ecclesiastes said, ". . . and the wind returneth again according to his circuits." Life again became a fight for survival.

I have to mobilize all my faculties—for the last time, I told myself. I'm not going to make excuses. I'll resign, but only as a winner.

"Honey, could you put the destruction of that report on hold for a little while? Please." I pleaded with the secretary. "My future depends on it."

"All right, I'll do it," the kind girl agreed. She understood everything.

On Monday, Beresnev looked like a beaten dog.

"You failed to provide for a smooth transition of the agent to my purview," he told me with malice that was scary in its intensity. I realized that my worst fears were about to come true.

Beresnev ran away to report to his boss, Bychkov. A short time later, Bychkov summoned me.

"You and Beresnev will go to the airport to see Socrates off," Bychkov told me dourly.

"Why do you want me there?"

"To keep the agent from gouging out Beresnev's eyes."

"To the best of my knowledge, Socrates demands to see you," I observed.

"I'm not going to see him or anybody else," Bychkov blew up. "Tomorrow we'll discuss why you failed to provide for a transition of the agent to Beresnev's control," Bychkov threatened me as a parting shot.

"How was I supposed to do it? Send Beresnev back to the intelligence school for retraining?" I asked.

"Don't you understand that your career depends on your relationship with your superiors, not successes in the field?" Bychkov snarled.

"That's why I am no longer interested in career advancement," I replied.

"You are asking for trouble," he said ominously. "Just you wait till Socrates goes away."

The flight to Athens was delayed. Beresnev was anxiously glancing at his watch, and when another two-hour delay was announced, his patience ran out:

"I've got to go. I have important business to attend to. You'll have to see Socrates off yourself."

And with that he was gone. I knew what kind of "important business" Beresnev had to attend to. He was in a hurry to get to the Armand Hammer International Trade Center. A few months back, he had got a cover job there for one of his trusted aides. That sleuth was not required either to procure intelligence or to recruit agents; his sole responsibility was to sneak Beresnev to the parties thrown almost every night by foreign and Soviet firms. Usually they waited for about half an hour until after the first round of drinks, and then unobtrusively joined the festivities. The next morning, Beresnev would fight his hangover with strong tea—to crash another party. That night, a gala banquet was scheduled at the trade center, and Beresnev just couldn't miss it.

"I am afraid of working with Beresnev," Socrates said. "He is a recipe for inevitable disaster."

"Why do you think so?" I asked.

"He constantly pressures me for meetings in other countries. And each meeting like that is another blow to my nervous system. Nothing went right in Damascus right off the bat. I arrived at the agreed place on time—but he was nowhere to be seen. Five minutes passed, ten minutes, twenty minutes—still no Beresnev. Suspicious types are loitering around, it's raining, I am swearing like hell. To fly across the ocean—only to be stood up, waste half an hour at the Sham Palace Hotel, and leave empty-handed? Thirty minutes later, he turns up. What do you know? The bastard had been inspecting Persian rugs at the local bazaar. Okay, we went to a restaurant to talk. The place is jam-packed, bare-bellied whores plop in your lap—and he is yapping his 'instructions.' Later he told me himself that four counter-intelligence services operate in Damascus. What kind of idiot sets a rendezvous in such a place?"

"Why did you miss the last meeting on Cyprus?"

"I fell ill," Socrates responded. "So what should I do? I find the telephone number of the bar where I was to meet Beresnev, go out, call Cyprus, ask the bartender to call 'Leo the Australian'—my name for Beresnev—to the telephone. I describe Beresnev's appearance. The bartender replies that there are only two customers in the bar, and neither answers the description I gave him. When I came to Moscow, I found out that at the time Beresnev had been at a different bar. In other words, even had I come to Cyprus, we wouldn't have met anyway. It doesn't take a genius to predict what will happen in the future. No, I've had enough. I told him everything I thought about him back at the hotel. He behaves as if he's trying to get me burned. I know that there were people in the Carter administration who wanted to get rid of me; there are people like that in the Greek government. Maybe I've stepped on some toes in your organization, too, and Beresnev is just trying to sabotage our cooperation? What put me on my guard was that in Moscow he always tried to get me out of the hotel. As if I didn't know that the room was bugged. He was just afraid that his chicanery would become known. But I purposely gave him a mouthful right there in the hotel room. Let his superiors think what to do from here on out. But I've had enough. I don't want to go to jail."

"You think you are in danger?" I asked.

"What's there to think about?" Socrates shouted indignantly. "I'm telling you, I am on the verge of a downfall. I can't sleep without nightmares. After I was last summoned to your embassy in Washington, I've literally felt the FBI breathing down my neck. Recently, the IRS has conducted a full-scale audit of my finances, counting my income down to the last cent. Do you think it was a coincidence? Then some strange people asked my next-door neighbors about me. I'm telling you, the FBI is on my tail. Where can I hide? In desperation, I even hired a private detective agency to sweep my house for bugs. They told me that sure, they could do it, but there was no guarantee that new bugs would not be installed the very next day. I feel the noose tightening around my neck. I asked Beresnev, 'Let's meet in Moscow. It's safer here.' But no, he wants to go abroad. Well, it wouldn't be that bad if he worked normally, but no, I have to walk the tightrope all the time. I told you, I've had it. No more meetings. I'm leaving for good."

"You told him all that in the hotel room?" I asked.

"Yes," replied Socrates.

At that moment, they invited passengers to board the Athens flight.

The next day, I wrote a memo describing my conversation with Socrates at the airport. The report ended with a clincher: "According to Socrates, he voiced all his complaints in a talk with Beresnev in his hotel room." Of course, I knew that Bychkov and Beresnev had no intention of sabotaging Socrates. On the contrary, they wanted everything to be nice and cozy. But that was the way of communist leaders—Midas touch in reverse: anything they touched turned to rot.

I entered Beresnev's office, without a word put my memo on his desk, and proceeded to wait. As he read it, his face turned green. I am sure any FBI or CIA officer would have given his arm to be in my place at that instant. The poor guy could be taken with bare hands. He was so scared he would have agreed to any proposition. If Chief of Intelligence Shebarshin got hold of that memo, it would be curtains for Beresnev.

"Can we work out an understanding?" he mumbled pathetically.

"No way," I said firmly.

I went into the locker room at halftime with the score in my favor. I had to hold on to my lead. As I saw it, the denouement was at hand. With my airport conversation with Socrates recorded in a memo, Bychkov and Beresnev would not be able to destroy Tatiana's report the tape recording of Socrates' conversation with Beresnev in the hotel room. To destroy the tape now would be tantamount to official misconduct. So they would have to lie low, but not for long. Pretty soon, they would have to make an accounting of their work with the agent. And then . . .

10

ANY Western news correspondent upon arrival in Moscow is automatically slated for development by the Second Chief Directorate of the KGB (counterintelligence). This fate also befell Angus Rocksburgh, the correspondent for the British *Sunday Times*, who was singled out by the KGB counterintelligence for particularly nasty treatment.

Angus had a flawless command of Russian and he knew the Soviet Union too well. Before long, he developed extensive connections with Soviet citizens, which naturally included a liberal sprinkling of KGB informants. They diligently supplied reports on the British journalist, whose KGB file was swelling at an unprecedented rate.

The file contained absolutely no dirt on Angus, but that didn't matter. The RT Directorate of the KGB intelligence service also had a file on Angus Rocksburgh started a few years back when he had come to the Soviet Union for the first time as an exchange student. Now he reappeared as a Moscow correspondent of the *Sunday Times*, and Deputy

Chief of Directorate Bychkov had ordered me to establish contact with him.

Once I thoroughly perused Angus's case and made his acquaintance, I came to an unambiguous conclusion that for him Sovietology was a passion as well as a career choice. He was sincerely fond of Russia, much more so, in fact, than most of my past and present superiors. They needed a totalitarian Russia as the only environment where they could realistically hope for success. Angus yearned to see my country a democracy and was passionately pulling for perestroika. In short, I had much more in common with the British journalist than with my bosses, and I was too far gone in the reappraisal of values to devote myself whole-heartedly to his development. On the contrary, I had to save him from the talons of the Second Chief Directorate of the KGB. I began pressuring him to use my services in establishing contacts in Moscow, trying to be as obvious and aggressive as I could. I told him that I was a Tass correspondent. But what Soviet correspondent could dare behave so brazenly in those days unless he was affiliated with the KGB? Besides, I had not worked in the news agency since my return from the U.S., and Angus had no problem in establishing the truth. I hoped he would get the message, and he did.

Angus Rocksburgh did become more cautious. That might have been the end of the story, had the British authorities not expelled another batch of KGB operatives. The Second Chief Directorate, its spirits bolstered by London's decision, declared that a group of British nationals would be expelled from Moscow as a retaliatory measure. Angus's name was on the list of the undesirables.

Angus was desperate. For him expulsion meant the loss of a job he loved. It was like barring a surgeon from the operating table or forbidding an artist to touch the brushes.

"Can you do anything to help?" he asked me.

"I'll try," I said, and that same day wrote a memo to the chief of intelligence.

In a nutshell, I argued that the official charges against Angus were bogus, and if we were indeed concerned about improving our image abroad, expulsion of a totally innocent journalist would be tantamount to shooting ourselves in the foot. After all, we had to have friends, didn't we?

General Shebarshin saw merit in my position and sent my report to KGB Chairman Kryuchkov, who relayed it to the Second Chief Directorate. The counterintelligence service admitted a mistake but pointed its finger at the Kremlin, arguing that it had been under pressure to kick out somebody, anybody, to square accounts with England. While the memos were flying back and forth, Angus Rocksburgh left for London and I became anathema to the Second Chief Directorate.

A few months later, Angus unexpectedly turned up in Moscow with a BBC TV team to shoot a documentary film about perestroika. He called me at home and suggested a meeting. The Second Chief Directorate flew into a rage, and Bychkov demanded that I find out how Angus had managed to get a Soviet visa.

I set out for a rendezvous with Rocksburgh at the Hotel Sovetskaya. Under the existing rules, the day before, I had called counterintelligence and told them the time and venue of the meeting. I had no doubt that tails would be breathing down our necks and the hotel room would be jam-packed with microphones—but that was exactly what I wanted.

"Has the KGB changed? Why was I allowed to come back?" Angus asked.

"Nothing has changed. The KGB still hate you," I replied. "I think it's just another bureaucratic blunder; looks like the KGB never saw your visa application."

"You mean that next time I won't get a visa?"

"You certainly won't," I assured him.

"What shall I do?" Angus asked in anguish. "I've written a script for a perestroika movie. Does it mean I won't be able to shoot it?"

"Who are you planning to interview for your movie?" I asked.

"Just about all Soviet leaders, from Gorbachev down."

"And who is the first in line?"

"Alexander Yakovlev. I have an appointment with him the day after tomorrow."

Boy, am I lucky! Looks like my plan is doomed to success, I thought in glee. Yakovlev is about the only Soviet leader who will not only sympathize with Angus's plight but will dare take on the KGB. He will never refuse to help a man planning to shoot a film about perestroika. I have to take the plunge. It's now or never.

"Listen, Angus, I have a great idea," I said. "When you interview Yakovlev, tell him your story and explain that you will need to come to the Soviet Union on a regular basis to shoot your movie. I think he will help."

Angus perked up.

"Hey, thanks for the advice," he said. "I think that's exactly what I'll do."

So the die is cast, I thought. If there is anything the KGB will never let me get away with, this is it.

The next day, the secretary of the department entered my office. She was white with fear.

"Bychkov is calling you," she whispered with trembling lips. "This morning, he and Beresnev have sent a terrible report to the internal counterintelligence department."

"What does it say?" I asked, knowing that my fate hung in the balance.

"Treachery," she said with difficulty and looked at me like I was already a corpse.

"Treachery!" Bychkov roared, sputtering. "You have betrayed the interests of the KGB! How could you give such advice!"

He was terrifying in his rage. On his desk I saw the record of my conversation with Angus Rocksburgh, which the Second Chief Directorate had sent down accompanied by its own indignant commentary.

Next to Bychkov sat Beresnev, menacing and haughty. To my surprise, I felt quite at ease. I was ready to take decisive action. It was too late to backtrack.

"Who authorized you to give Rocksburgh the idea about Yakovlev?" Bychkov bellowed.

"Who authorized me not to give him that idea?" I asked.

"Don't play the fool!" Bychkov snapped. "You have betrayed the KGB! Now you cannot be trusted to have access to other contacts of ours, including Socrates. You are liable to divulge some secret to him, too! Or maybe you already have? Why would the agent all of a sudden refuse to cooperate with us any longer?"

Not bad. So that's how he planned to build a bridge between Angus Rocksburgh and Socrates! Not bad at all. My Yakovlev advice would be used to take me off the Socrates case, officially and with a lot of noise, whereupon they would make me take the fall for their failure with the agent.

"You think Socrates is untrustworthy?" I asked with interest.

"He sure is," Bychkov replied indignantly.

"Why?" I asked with a flippant smile that apparently took him aback.

"Because we have always suspected that Socrates is a plant foisted on us by the American special services," Bychkov snarled. "If you fail to see it, you are an imbecile."

Over the years in the intelligence service, I had arrived at a very valuable conclusion: the superiors should never be resisted or interfered with. Let them dig a grave for themselves, let them fall into it and pull the dirt down on themselves. The important thing is not to miss the opportunity when it presents itself.

"Wait a second," I said with a naive air. "Do you mean to say that you have suspected Socrates of cooperating with the FBI or the CIA all along?"

"Of course," Bychkov said. He was sincerely surprised.

But Beresnev finally figured it out. Arrogant and terrible like a cliff just a minute ago, he was now shrunken and crestfallen.

"Where were you with your suspicions, I wonder, when Socrates was put on the agent rolls?" The ocean of rage that had been building up inside me over the years broke through and cascaded in a mighty flow on the heads of my Red commanders. At that instant, there was no stopping me. "Don't you know that a person suspected of cooperation with the enemy special services cannot be our agent?" I was revving up, watching Bychkov's eyes pop out in astonishment. "Where were you when we sent the intelligence supplied by Socrates to Gorbachev? Why did you keep your suspicions to yourself? In all my special reports to the Kremlin, I explicitly indicated that the source of intelligence was one hundred percent reliable. And you signed those cables! Therefore, you consciously and deliberately kept your doubts about the agent from the country's leadership. In light of your suspicions, Socrates' stuff takes on an entirely different hue. Do you remember the decree of the Central Committee of the Communist Party on the USSR policy in Europe based on the agent's intelligence? Its principles were subsequently shown to be wrong. What does it mean?" Bychkov was looking at me like a prisoner in the dock. "It means that the American special services might have slipped strategic disinformation to Gorbachev—with your connivance! As a matter of fact, you had a chance to figure out Socrates yourself. He asked to see you in person. You refused. Why, I wonder? Having kept your suspicions to yourself, you've committed a dereliction of duty!" I wound up defiantly and took a theatrical pause.

Bychkov fell into his chair and tried to loosen his tie with unsteady fingers.

"What are you going to do?" he asked, panting.

"I'm going to go to my office and write a report on how you have sabotaged Socrates," I replied.

My commanders looked like dying swans. As a matter of fact, they were of little interest to me as personalities. But looking at them, I saw the Soviet bureaucrat incarnate, stupid, lazy, but still all-powerful. He was torturing the country at will, turning it into a lunatic asylum. Of course, I could not change anything on the scale of the whole country, but at the place of my employment, I could teach that bureaucrat a lesson.

I turned around and without a word started walking. The huge, armored, black-leather-upholstered door—the symbol of power and impunity—was in my way. Never in my life had I opened any door with my foot. But this time I put all my strength into a kick. The door opened obediently. After the stuffy atmosphere of Bychkov's office, the air in the corridor felt like that in the Alps.

Three days later, I completed an analysis of the Socrates case and together with my report put it on the desk of the head of the directorate.

"I demand an internal investigation," I said. "If I am not satisfied with its outcome, I'll write another report to the chief of intelligence. In the event it also fails, I'm going to complain to the KGB chairman. And so on . . . all the way to Gorbachev himself. He should know the way things are at his intelligence service."

The combat general, an Afghan war veteran who had faced death intrepidly on many occasions, read my document closely and ordered an investigation to be conducted under the supervision of . . . Bychkov. The bureaucratic system broke even those who had gone through thick and thin and come out unscathed.

From that day on, practically all operations on U.S. citizens carried out by the RT Directorate were virtually put on hold. Every day, Bychkov and Beresnev would lock themselves in Bychkov's office and conduct an "investigation" from early morning till late at night. But for all their diligence, they had no chance. Each word in my report was supported by precise references to documentary evidence from the Socrates file.

Meanwhile, the American Section officers gladly went about their own business. Many of them were intimately familiar with my campaign against the communist leaders and openly expressed their support for me. Only now did I see how deep ran the contempt of the rank-and-file intelligence officers for most of their superiors.

Soon thereafter, with perestroika in full swing, came an unprecedented occurrence in the history of the KGB—the first multi-candidate party elections at the intelligence service. Only the chief of intelligence, General Shebarshin, received a vote of confidence. All Kryuchkov's cronies went down to ignominious defeat. It meant in effect that the rank and file did not trust their commanding officers and refused to follow them into battle.

Desperately trying to improve the morale in the intelligence service, Kryuchkov went to extraordinary lengths. Among other things, he introduced a KGB intelligence officer just back from the U.S. His name remained secret, but according to fragmentary rumors, that youngish man of fortysomething had posed for many years as an American citizen and managed to penetrate none other than the Pentagon itself. He was awarded the gold star of Hero of the Soviet Union for outstanding success in accomplishing the motherland's assignment.

But even that heavy artillery failed to advance Kryuchkov's cause. Pretty soon, skeptics ferreted out the truth— and the truth was that the hero spy for a long time had relied on his own devices and maintained no contact with Moscow, which was the reason he had avoided failure. It was the spring of 1990, perestroika seemed irreversible, and only extreme naïfs or hopeless idiots still believed in the infinite wisdom of the brass.

★   ★   ★

Five months passed, but the end of the "investigation" into the case of Socrates being conducted by Bychkov and Beresnev was nowhere in sight. It was clear that it would be dragged out indefinitely. Under the KGB bylaws, the investigators were supposed to keep me informed about the results of their labors. But what results could they come up with? Obviously, they could not refute, much less agree with, my assertions. There was no point waiting any longer, particularly in view of the momentous events unfolding beyond the walls of the intelligence service.

Democracy was in full swing, and it seemed that nothing would be able to check its advance. The KGB brass watched the developments in horror and secretly made preparations for a coup. I was aware that security agents were infiltrated into the topmost echelon of the democratic movement. The intelligence service was dragooned into internal political spying, and finally, sidearms were issued to all officers.

It was explained to us that "hordes of democrats" would soon try to storm the intelligence building and we would have to defend our filing cabinets with our lives. I realized that the KGB stupidity was now becoming criminal. I had long known what I believed. It was time to declare my allegiance openly. The very idea that I would have to shoot at my compatriots seemed the height of folly.

When I handed my resignation application to Beresnev, he beamed with immense, almost superhuman joy. How little one sometimes needs to be happy. Soon afterward, I was summoned to Colonel Bychkov's office.

"I hope you are leaving us in good spirits?" he asked with a smooth smile.

"Couldn't be better," I replied. "But I wish I did it a couple of years ago."

"What's the reason for your resignation?" Bychkov's face bore the expression of naive simplicity.

"Disagreement with the policies of the KGB leadership and resolve to have nothing to do with their implementation."

Bychkov never heard such strong stuff in his office. He had destroyed scores of operative careers and earned the nickname "Cannibal," but now he looked pathetic. Not long ago, he could have made mincemeat of me, but now he had to listen, in impotent rage, to incredible political pronouncements.

"Our fathers shed their blood for that?" Out of habit Bychkov raised his voice. "I'll man the barricades if I have to to defend our socialist gains."

"I'll be on the other side," I vowed, and Bychkov realized that the customary methods were no longer effective.

"What are you planning to do for a living?" he asked with a scowl.

"Journalism."

"What genre of journalism?"

"The idiocy genre," I said, "because I have spent the last few years of my life in that genre."

For the last time I emerged from the checkpoint of the intelligence service and closed my eyes tight to shut out the brilliant rays of the warm autumnal sun. Free at last! The calendar said September 12, 1990.

In August 1991 came the coup attempt against Gorbachev. Once I found out that the plotters were led by Kryuchkov, I told my wife: "They'll be lucky to last a week."

They lasted merely three days. At one of the post-coup press conferences, Gorbachev said that he had appointed Kryuchkov head of the KGB because he believed that the latter was a politician, not a professional spy. "Experts can be extremely dangerous," explained the general secretary. He still had no clue that the country had been run into the ground not by experts, but by dilettantes with political ambitions.

Before long the Soviet Union ceased to exist. That day, people still went to work and patiently waited in endless lines in grocery stores—in short, led a normal life seemingly oblivious to the historic event. A giant lie factory fell to pieces, but the people were already dead tired of its products.

For the first time, I felt the crazy joy of life, and words can't describe the beauty of that incomparable feeling. But it didn't last long. A very short time later, symptoms of yet another giant-scale folly began cropping up. The mass media vigorously debated the various concepts of reform—but I saw an entirely different reality rearing its ugly head.

All talk of the many models of Russian reform seemed to be little more than a smokescreen hiding from view what was really going on: another redistribution of property; the emergence of a new class of the haves; ruthless fighting for the privilege of being rich. Each interest group selected the concept of "reform" that legitimized its preferred method of acquisition of the property left behind by the dead state.

In vain did a handful of young, brilliantly educated economists call upon the Russians to see reason and consciously embark upon the path already traversed by civilized countries of the world. Theirs was a cry in the wilderness. The common people did not understand their calls, while the politicians and the bureaucratic hordes were too busy lining their pockets. The country was gradually sinking into the chaos of the initial accumulation phase. It seemed that Russia was under a curse, that it was destined to show the world, time and again, how not to live.

Was that the Russia of my dreams?

Once I listened to the latest news about a debate in the Russian Parliament on my car radio. At a closed-door session, the legislators resolved to privatize their apartments assigned them by the government.

I bit my lip in disgust. Was there no limit to cynicism? A ruined and downtrodden country is writhing in agony; almost two thirds of its people live below the poverty line;

women refuse to bear children; the fires of civil war are blazing at the periphery, threatening at any moment to engulf the very heart of the country; the people have lost all capacity to believe that a change for the better is possible—and meanwhile the "people's representatives" set aside this important business to make a grab for the state property, in secret, at bargain-basement prices, and with unprecedented unanimity!

It was the straw that broke the camel's back. This dry news item shocked me. With sudden horrified clarity, I realized that Russia had not left its awful past behind and was not going to become a normal country in ten to fifteen years, not even while my generation was alive. Not because the system was inadequate or a good reform plan was lacking. My motherland was cursed because the idiots filling the bureaucratic structure from top to bottom remained in power, and were destined to rule for a long time to come.

Of course, there are honest and talented individuals in the ranks of the political and bureaucratic class, but the shots are invariably called by the incompetents. It is only natural. Decent political elites are out of place in a poverty-stricken country where power is the surest path to personal enrichment. In such a country, political fighting is centered on a nice dacha, a well-appointed apartment, a government-assigned car—and the country be damned!

As long as the idiots remain in power, the future is hopeless.

Who is to blame? Who else but I and millions of Russian citizens just like me. The best and the brightest rise to the top only in normal countries. In the "country of fools," as Russian citizens have come to openly call their country, the fools fill all the top niches.

Thus I lost all hope that someday I would see the triumph of common sense in my country. I yearned to shake free from the leaden embrace of my "beloved government" and take my fate in my own hands.

Once I unexpectedly received a telephone call from

Socrates, and we met at a Moscow restaurant. He had come as a journalist and as a consultant on Russia's economy for a Western government.

"What brings you here?" I asked without trying to hide my surprise.

"I have nowhere else to go," Socrates replied. "The CIA is busy looking for me. Russia is my last refuge. I've come to stay."

I wondered if it was because of the information on the CIA secretary that he passed on to me.

"What about Phyllis?" I asked.

"Her parents look after her."

"Do you see Beresnev?"

"How can I avoid him?" He spread his arms in a gesture of helplessness.

As Russian custom dictates, most of our conversation was a political polemic. Socrates turned out to be a fervent supporter of Russian nationalists, with particular fondness for the group headed by a former KGB general. For the democratic leaders he had nothing but contempt bordering on hatred.

"Why do you dislike them so much?" I asked in surprise.

"They have sold out to the Americans," he replied.

Isn't life incredible? The search for meaning led my agent to Russia, where I had been unable to find it.

EPILOGUE

No sooner did I deliver my manuscript to my publisher than events began to happen at breathtaking speed.

On April 9, 1994, the *New York Times* published a front-page story about *Washington Station*. The Russian Intelligence Service, successor to the KGB, reacted swiftly. In a Russian publication, *Moscow News*, a spokesman for the Russian Intelligence Service commented on my recruitment of Socrates, which was referred to in the *New York Times* story. "[E]ven if such a person exists," the spokesman said, "Shvets will not give his name because he risks his life both there [in the United States] and here [Russia]. He has no right to such speculations, and has no right to discuss this theme." What he meant, of course, was that I had better not reveal Socrates' name if I knew what was good for me.

On April 22, the office of my literary agent, John Brockman, was broken into. Nothing was stolen, but files were ransacked. The identity of whoever did this is unknown, as is the identity of whoever broke into the office of the International Center for Policy Development in 1986.

Then I received a letter from the Immigration and Naturalization Service, to which I had applied for political asylum. Dated April 21, the letter denied my request. Despite calling my story "believable, consistent and sufficiently detailed" and calling me "credible," the INS said: "By divulging classified information on the KGB . . . it appears that you have violated laws of your country with regard to state secrets known to you as a former KGB agent."

Astonishingly, the U.S. government was denying me asylum apparently because I had broken the laws of the USSR, revealing secrets about its spying operations. The U.S. government had, of course, spent a fortune trying to learn these same secrets for forty years and had lost the lives of several people in the process. A greater irony would be hard to imagine.

I hired an attorney to file an appeal on my behalf, but even before the appeal was filed, I received a second letter from the INS, dated May 16, informing me that "it has been determined you have established a well-founded fear of persecution were you to return to Russia." There was no reference to the April 21 letter. I was granted political asylum and could remain with my family in the United States.

After I completed my manuscript, I tried to get a response from Socrates, who has been living abroad since 1992. But he refused to comment unless he could read my entire manuscript, which my publisher and I both declined to permit, following standard practice. We did agree to discuss the allegations in the book with him, and we sent Socrates three pages of specific questions related to his activities with me. This proved to be a frustrating and fruitless endeavor. Typical was Socrates' response to the question whether he had ever been compensated by either Tass or the KGB: "As you will readily appreciate, there is a huge gap here. One claim is consistent with honorable conduct.

The other charges one of the most serious crimes a citizen can commit." I suspect that Socrates did not respond to the questions because he maintains that he did not know whether I was acting on behalf of Tass or the KGB, although practically everyone in official Washington knew that Tass was a widely used cover for KGB officers.

Unable to get Socrates' reaction to my book, my publisher and I decided to use a fictional name for him and his wife, and I changed certain personal characteristics.

I have told my story to the FBI, and as far as I know, there is an ongoing investigation. I do not know whether Socrates violated any U.S. law, and I have only recounted what I know from first-hand experience.

As I mentioned in the book, Socrates was registered as a KGB agent by order of Colonel Victor Cherkashin, my former boss, the man who had recruited Aldrich Ames. Cherkashin was among the best officers in the KGB, a man who detested the fake achievements that came to characterize the KGB in the 1980s. Although Cherkashin was awarded the Order of Lenin for recruiting Ames, he was ostracized by jealous superiors and eventually was pensioned off. He was just another victim of the bureaucracy and paranoia of the spy system, like the innocent officers of the CIA who were driven out by the paranoia of Angleton. The KGB and the CIA had more in common than either of them would admit.

Both intelligence agencies were happy to be hated by each other; they were flattered when they heard that the other agency feared them. What they did not want was to be thought of as fools or incompetents, which, despite their occasional achievements, such as the KGB's recruiting of Ames, they both were. Did the CIA predict the tearing down of the Berlin Wall or the collapse of the Soviet Union? For that matter, did the KGB? In the late 1980s, the KGB opposed the democracy movement in the Soviet Union and, in fact, precipitated the collapse of the country. The leader of the August 1991 coup against Gorbachev was none other than General Kryuchkov! (When we heard this in Russia, we knew the coup was doomed to failure.)

The problem of moles within intelligence services is easy to solve. It is time to say it out loud: shut down the so-called human intelligence.

Is this unthinkable? Russia is struggling economically right now. Without an intelligence service the country would be better able to feed itself. In the United States, bastion of democracy, the intelligence services still manage to keep their budgets secret from the public (they even manage to keep some parts of their budgets secret from Congress). For the first time in history, influential members of Congress are saying that we don't need intelligence services. Certainly in this age of technological sophistication, it is difficult to justify human intelligence or spies.

Look at how long the CIA covered up for Ames. It happened because secrecy and efficiency are inherently incompatible, and sooner or later intelligence services turn themselves into something different. They call it "fraternity" in the CIA. In the KGB we called ourselves the "Mafia." There is not much difference, because in both cases the well-being of the bureaucracy is more important than anything else. In his statement in court Aldrich Ames said that "the espionage business, as carried out by the CIA and a few other American agencies, was and is a self-serving sham, carried out by careerist bureaucrats who have managed to deceive several generations of American policymakers and the public about both the necessity and the value of their work." I could have used those exact words to characterize the KGB.